GW01605360

Published by Slater Books in December 1988

Re-printed January 1989

Front Cover photographs: Molineux in 1972 and players before the Sherpa Van Trophy Final at Wembley versus Burnley in 1988.

Rear Cover photographs: During and after the Sherpa Van Trophy Final at Wembley versus Burnley in 1988.

The views expressed in this book are solely those of the author and do not represent Wolverhampton Wanderers.

ISBN 0 9513991 0 1

Printed in Great Britain by
G & A Printers & Stationers
Stone Cross, Penkridge, Stafford.

MOLINEUX MEMORIES

by the

NORTH BANKER

MOLINEUX — Home of Wolverhampton Wanderers
for a Century by the Summer of 1989

110 Years of the Wolves 1877 - 1987

& 1988 Update

CONTENTS

Foreword

by

John Richards

Former Wolves Player (1969-1983) and Club Captain

I will never forget the first time I stood in the main reception area of the Waterloo Road Stand, Molineux. I was surrounded by display cabinets crammed with the visible history of Wolverhampton Wanderers. Cups, plaques, photographs, international caps, a football from the 1893 F.A. Cup Final — an Aladdin's cave of trophies. Peering through the glass, straining to read the fading print and engraving, I tried to visualise those moments which had resulted in a triumph for the Wolves, and imagine how proud the players and everyone connected with the team must have felt.

That entrance into Molineux was, and is, very significant. Instantly, one is aware of the achievements and importance of the club, a founder member of the Football League, and one of the first English teams to journey abroad to compete with the world's best.

Present day Wolves followers will have no difficulty in reeling off such names as Cullis, Buckley, Wright, Mullen and Hancocks who are embedded in the history of Wolves illustrious past. However, they themselves were only the continuation of an institution which had been set up in 1877 at a school in Blakenhall. It is people such as Brodie and Mason who we have to thank for, quite literally, setting the ball rolling.

We all like to reminisce, to relive memorable matches, and to compare teams from different eras. It is an enjoyable pastime. However, opinions can, and do, differ quite widely, and often quite loudly, with no satisfactory solution at hand. To support the fading memory and to bolster the weakening argument it is useful to have the exact facts and figures. Detail is very important.

Michael Slater's book contains a wealth of information, enough to satisfy the most discerning of Wolves followers. Wolverhampton Wanderers have a long and proud history. Enjoy reading about it.

John Richards

THE AUTHOR

When Wolves won at Wembley in 1974 I decided to write a book about the history of the club, which has since become a story in itself. I began to compile information and wrote to several of football's governing bodies though I seldom received a full answer to my queries, in fact even a S.A.E. could not guarantee a reply. I made some visits to Molineux to wade through old programmes but soon realised I was wasting my time, eminent local historian Percy Young having been commissioned to produce a book to celebrate Wolves Centenary in 1977. There was little point in trying to compete with that but I continued to keep records until the 1980 Wembley win re-kindled my interest. I noticed that in the build up to the big day supporters were prepared to buy more or less anything connected with the club!

I was wary of my book being similar to Mr. Young's masterpiece so in contrast to him I concentrated more on the post-war era, virtually ignoring the earliest years that he had recorded in fascinating detail. I unearthed facts about Wolves that had not been mentioned in his or any other book and though I had to include all the milestones I presented them in a different manner. Mine was to be more of a statistical and pictorial history but a lot of research was still necessary. I often spent hours in the attic of the town's library looking at old newspapers, only to finish with something that could be read in a few seconds. I found the more ancient Sporting Stars at the offices of the Express & Star and sent letters to all the various soccer organisations again, only for the response to be equally poor. I even visited the libraries of the Football League in Lytham St. Anne's and the Football Association in London yet still could not find everything I required.

Despite the setbacks the book was eventually taking shape with my goal being that it would be ready for the 1982-83 season which would be the 100th since my story began-in seeking to contrive an anniversary for the club I had observed that 1883-84 was a significant campaign. The book was split into four chapters: 1883-84 to 1918-19; 1919-20 to 1945-46; 1946-47 to 1980-81 and 1981-82. I hoped that the latter would develop into an annual handbook which I felt many supporters wanted. The chapters were further divided into six sections to reduce the repetition of certain phrases and because much of it could not be neatly fitted into a particular season. Wolves Results were a complete list of matches played and League tables; Wolves Careers showed the appearances and goals of every first team player; Wolves Internationals accounted for honours awarded to any of the staff; Wolves Miscellaneous covered non-first team competitions; Wolves Quiz consisted of information I wished to include that did not come under any of the other categories and last but by no means least came Wolves Photographs.

Even if the book was good enough the process of actually becoming an author was a bit of a mystery to me despite letters asking for help to Wolves, the Citizens Advice Bureau, a writing school and a local publishing firm. Then I heard of a firm in the West Country famed for assisting would-be authors but my informant did not know their address, another friend pointing out that the Writers Yearbook would contain it. I duly contacted the publishers who replied that my best bet would be to purchase a certain item - the Writers Yearbook!

I desperately needed Wolves to be successful in 1981-82, to reach the F.A. Cup Final would be ideal, but by the time they were knocked out in January the season was already a complete disaster which prompted me to merge it into the third chapter to divert attention from it. I had chosen my pen name from the part of Molineux I normally occupied and considered it wise to become known before I released my book on an unsuspecting public. Compiling a Wolves Quiz or doing well in one would help so I wrote to the club, the E & S and Beacon Radio suggesting the idea but there were no developments. I then did an article about John Richards for his testimonial brochure and three statistical pieces for the match-day programme, but I did not get anything printed. The book was duly completed as Wolves were relegated with attendances 6,000 lower than in any season for 50 years, leaving me to wait for a better moment for such a publication.

The Receiver was called into Molineux that summer and the closure of the club could well have ensured my book would get into the shops, though I was obviously still very relieved when the crisis was averted. The new regime stated they were keen to improve public relations and make fans feel part of the set-up and I wrote to Commercial Manager Eric Woodward, a skilled journalist who agreed to evaluate the book. I left it at the ground for him and because he had said he was too busy to make a response in the near future I revised my target date to the start of 1983-84, when I hoped interest would be high as Wolves returned to Division One.

In December I read in a football magazine that there was £100 prize for the best soccer book of 1983 by a non-professional author and I eagerly requested details. In January I made some amendments to my book and took them to Molineux, adding an article about my own experiences at Wolves matches which I hoped other supporters could relate to. In February I finally heard from the magazine, only for the editor to say he knew nothing of the competition despite the publication naming him as one of the judges. He asked me when I had read it and his next letter revealed the address of the organiser. He in turn sent those details as well as the chance to win £50 in a football-forecasting contest, which I might have won except that the closing date for entrants had just passed. The organiser was from the Association of Football Statisticians, a superb club based in Essex who could have saved me scores of hours if I had known about them previously. In the event I wrote back and paid for photostat copies to fill some of the gaps in my records.

When Wolves clinched promotion in May I added a review of 1982-83 so there were again four chapters, also editing the bit about myself. I took all this to the club and it was only then that I knew my book had safely reached Mr Woodward who I had been unable to contact, though I was assured he would get in touch with me when he had time. The Wolves programme of 1982-83 was voted the best in the country, with statistician Tony Matthews making the sort of contributions that caught my eye and made me feel it would be nice to be involved in such a success. I suggested that in the 1983-84 programmes I would do a serialisation of Wolves history up until World War II, as a prelude to a post-war only book that would be ready for the 1984-85 kick-off. There was still no word from Mr Woodward and I presumed my work was not up to standard and gave up on the project, especially when the latter months of 1983 indicated Wolves were heading back for Division Two.

March saw the long-overdue forming of an official Wolves Supporters Club, ironically at a time when crowds were diminishing faster than ever at Molineux. Mr Woodward announced he was departing that month though I only read about it on his last day, so I went to the ground to pick up my book the next week and happened to bump into him as he collected some belongings. We had a long talk and it transpired that apart from the vast amount of work he had undertaken he had also been plagued with health problems, though he offered to take the book home to study properly. By April he had returned to his desk and told me that it was unlikely the book would be printed in it's present form, giving me some useful guidance in another long discussion. I also reverted back to the idea of three chapters when I updated it, as 1983-84 produced Wolves worst playing record in 85 seasons in the League.

During the summer I finally believed all the people who had constantly told me that I would never get it into print as a book, deciding to do the entire history as a serialisation. I maintained the 1883-84 link by starting '1984 has been an unhappy year so far but it was a different story a century ago' and duly sent the first few pages to Mr Woodward as an example.

On the opening day of 1984-85 I had heard nothing, before being overjoyed at seeing the first instalment of Wolves history in the programme. Closer inspection revealed it was not my account though, Mr Matthews writing a version of the club's fortunes in the Football League. I left it until October before going to the ground to collect my excerpts, only to be informed nobody knew where they were. I was asked to return prior to a match when I was also given a note from Mr Woodward saying that the same faults existed to a lesser extent, with too much detail and insufficient narrative. I also received a complimentary ticket, though I could not help wondering if any of the other fans present worked so hard for their free admissions.

By November I had abandoned all hope when the WSC handbook came out, featuring many of the sort of items I specialised in. I regretted not being involved in it and became a member and visited the home of two of the main organisers, Muriel and Albert Bates, to see if they had any use for my data. I left the book with them and went back in February only to find that Mr Bates had been so busy with WSC issues he had not read it, and with Wolves struggling even in the Second Division I had lost heart again and concluded there was little point in getting it ready for 1985-86. Instead I decided to produce two booklets that would be only slightly larger than the WSC newsletter, leading up to a post-war book. I had reduced my pre-war summaries because I did not wish it to clash too much with the programme's serialisation that would attract many of the same readers. I dropped the seasonal results and tables altogether, and with Mr Matthews listing the appearances and scorers each term I edited the careers section to cover just the main 25 of around 400 pre-war players. I also concentrated more on the F.A. Cup but there were no records available of some of Wolves ties in the 1880's.

I soon realised the cost of setting it up made it wiser to merge the booklets into one and I hoped to complete the task for 1985-86, with the main book to follow at Christmas when perhaps Wolves fortunes had changed. I rushed to finish the former and took it to Molineux on a rare day in the sense that Mr Bates was not at the WSC shop, so I left it to be passed on to him. A month elapsed without me hearing from him, the reason being that he had not received it though he eventually tracked it down. I had also left a small piece for the second handbook which now appeared unlikely to ever get printed as Wolves were relegated again, ending 55 years as a top club. Only 4,000 were at the last home match and only around 50 went to the A.G.M. of the WSC, on a night that saw Mr Bates elected as chairman.

The summer saw Wolves future in jeopardy once more while I went back to my original plan of a complete book of their history. I added 1984-85 to the third chapter, fitted in the statistical articles and Richards piece I had done back in 1981-82 and omitted the miscellaneous section. Finally I realised I did not have enough material left to warrant the two pre-war chapters so I put it all together, leaving five straightforward sections beginning with the re-named Wolves Record followed by careers, internationals, quiz and photographs.

In September Mr Bates confirmed that he would try to help me with the book but Wolves slumped to the bottom of Division Three that day, losing 5-1. This prompted me to change the title from 'Molineux's Golden Wanderers' and the closure of the North Bank cast doubts about my pen name. The research continued and I rang the E & S to solve one of the many conflicting reports but they did not return the call as they lost my number. They did prove helpful though and it was a shame their library was no longer open to the public. The old papers at the town's library were on tape now which made it easier to find the relevant details-after a few tangles.

This umpteenth version of the book was completed in November but on the day I handed it to Mr Bates relations between Wolves and the WSC deteriorated, with the latter having to vacate their shop at the rear of the North Bank immediately. The WSC had protested outside the London offices of the club's owners, then held a march prior to a home fixture and also staged a meeting that attracted some eminent speakers in a campaign aimed at bringing an end to the current regime. The WSC devoted time and money to this and naturally projects such as mine were pushed into the background. May saw further relegation and the WSC tabled a 14-point charge of bringing the game into disrepute against the club's owners, in fact after the A.G.M. some members set off for Newcastle at three am to lobby a League meeting.

Meanwhile, I had written the book again with yet more alterations as well as the addition of 1985-86 which was the 40th post-war season and with that in mind I decided it would be fitting to have the book ready for 1986-87, despite the fact Wolves would be spending it in Division Four. I spoke to Mr Bates about getting it costed and possible financial backing from the WSC, but first he passed it on to his friend Richard Binns who seemed the ideal person to help me. He was a former journalist and now successful travel writer with his own small publishing company in Buckinghamshire, also being a keen Wolves fan. I then endured a tense summer with my book in the hands of Mr Binns and Wolves in the hands of the Receiver again.

1986-87 was well under way when I got it back from the home of Mr Bates, who passed on the comments of Mr Binns regarding what further work I had to do. The former also spoke of a Wolves Quiz the WSC were organising and I suggested he might use some of my questions. There were 60 altogether but about half were unsuitable in that context and I revised them, also adding 40 new ones to bring up the 100. I was then left with the tricky task of putting the information from most of those questions back into the book along with the other necessary changes. The careers section had not been well-received by some as it was statistics only so that was omitted as well, leaving the international section somewhat out on a limb so I incorporated that into the main text. The book now had a lot more continuity and would be easier to print as a serialisation if that was the only option. I was aiming for the 1987-88 kick-off and informed Mr Binns of my plans and he wrote back early in 1987 expressing confidence the book would eventually be published-words I had long-awaited.

Ironically, not many of the questions were used in the quiz though I was still not allowed to enter, while the research went on and after placing an advert requesting certain information in the AFS newspaper most of the letters that ensued were from Wolves fans around the country asking me for details! At the end of the prolonged season Mr Binns was forwarded the latest book and I was still nervously waiting for his response on the day of the WSC A.G.M. in July. Mr Bates told me that he had not heard from him since dropping the book off at his place yet on arriving home I found a letter from Mr Binns saying he had been in touch with the WSC Chairman about it, prompting me to contact them both again. Mr Binns had not got sufficient time to take the project on himself and felt it would obviously be easier for a West Midlands group to make a success of it, while Mr Bates could not take the issue up with the WSC committee until he had a better idea of the money involved. I rang a local printing company and was shocked to learn that just the type-setting and making of plates would be £1,500 before any copies were run off, then there were other expenses such as the jacket, binding and photographs. Both gentlemen encouraged me to seek local sponsorship but first I had to get the book back and I spoke to the Post Office about a quick, safe delivery, though as it turned out Mr Bates would soon be able to retrieve it for me, Mr Binns being reluctant to send it through the post in the normal way as he fully appreciated the time and effort that had gone into it.

I received it at the end of August and had faint hopes that it would be ready by Christmas but Mr Bates felt it required a little bit of editing and approached E & S writer David Instone, who reports on most Wolves matches, and I passed it on to him. An advert in a national newspaper then caught my eye as the firm wished to help would-be authors, but their reply revealed they expected the author to pay for half of the costs while they put up the rest and did all the work. Unfortunately they also added the average price of a book was somewhere in the region of £9,000.

After more weeks of tension I met Mr Instone in October and although he had not been under the impression he was to do some editing I was quite relieved that he had not done, having left a lot out myself. He was extremely helpful and gave some phone numbers, including that of Mr Matthews who had produced a detailed statistical history of West Bromwich Albion. I also had the number of the publishers he had used but my plans were shattered when he revealed that he was teaming up with them again to do a similar account on Wolves. At least he was aiming for a slightly different market to me but I feared that other Wolves books coming out might reduce my chances of getting into print, ex-player Ted Farmer being about to produce his autobiography. I spotted it in the shops in November and was relieved that it did not clash with mine hardly at all. Meanwhile, I had decided to try the Wolves Football Club themselves and met Commercial Manager Joe Witherington to see if he could suggest anything. He advised me on several aspects while I tried to persuade him that it would be good publicity for Wolves. Mr Witherington finally agreed to consult Ted Farmer and generally investigate the possibilities for my material when he returned from a well-earned holiday in December, though as with all the other people mentioned in this saga he was a very busy man.

Introduction

The first general meeting of the Goldthorn Football Club at St. Luke's School in Blakenhall led to the formation of Wolverhampton Wanderers in 1877. They were not known by that name until 1879-80 when St. Luke's amalgamated with the Wanderers Cricket Club, though it was 1883-84 before they made a real impact. Wolves turned professional in 1888 and continued to do well for the rest of the century, finally being relegated in 1906 and remaining outside the First Division until 1932.

From 1936-37 to 1962-63 Wolves had a Football League record superior to that of any other club, a wonderful era that also contained F.A. Cup successes and victories in friendlies against some of the best teams in the world. Wolves then began to struggle and went down but returned to the top flight in 1967, losing their place just once up to 1982. Wolves were amongst the best 10 sides in the country during those 15 years yet suffered unfavourable comparisons with their past teams, since which this period has in turn become the "Good old days" for my generation.

Wolves immediately gained promotion but in January, 1984, their Division One status was again being threatened. By January, 1987, they were 16th in Division Four and six clubs could overtake them by winning games in hand, which would have left Wolves 90th in the League after the most dramatic slump in English football. This was easily the lowest point of their 110-year history yet they recovered to such an extent that only a ludicrous change in the rules denied them promotion. After three relegations it was the fourth consecutive season to end in misery but at the end of 1987 there were indications that providing the long-term future of the club is secured there will be a new chapter of success to report, making it an appropriate time to recall some Molineux memories.

Chapter 1

1883 - 84 to 1935 - 36

1883 - 84

Wolves proved themselves the premier team in Wolverhampton by defeating chief rivals Stafford Road 5-1, also collecting their first trophy in the shape of the Wrekin Cup. In what was the 13th year of the Football Association Challenge Cup Wolves made a good debut, crushing Long Eaton Rangers 4-1 before an estimated attendance of 3,000 only to go down 4-2 to Wednesbury Old Athletic. According to some sources England goalkeeper Billy Rose had already began his Wolves career, and though this was not the case it is the earliest instance of anyone who has ever played for the club being an international.

1884 - 85

It was the turn of Derby St. Luke's to beat Wolves 4-2 in the Cup after a goalless draw in Wolverhampton. Having spent their first seven years at Goldthorn Hill the club must have had itchy feet, moving approximately a mile to a new ground at Dudley Road.

1885 - 86

Spectacular revenge was gained over Derby in the first of three home home Cup-ties. The result was 7-0, followed by victories against Stafford Road (4-2) and Walsall (2-1). Wolves then lost 3-1 at West Bromwich Albion, who went on to reach the final.

1886 - 87

A 6-0 Cup drubbing of Matlock was merely a prelude to Wolves all-time record score. They absolutely slaughtered Croswell's Brewery, who must have felt punch drunk after conceding 14 goals. An epic confrontation with Aston Villa proved to be a complete contrast. Wolves shared four goals at Villa before playing them twice at home, which made little difference as the results were 1-1 and 3-3. Villa got through by a 2-0 margin in Birmingham, the fact that they won the Cup underlining Wolves status as one of the leading teams in the country. They did capture the Birmingham Charity Cup though, as well has having Wolverhampton-born Charlie Mason selected for England.

1887 - 88

The 2-1 defeat of Walsall was the first away success for Wolves in the F.A. Cup competition. They also trimmed Aston Shakespeare 3-0 before losing 2-0 to Albion, who kept the trophy in the area. Wolves had the consolation of the Staffordshire Senior Cup and more international honours. Harry Allen played in all three games as England won the Home Championship, while Mason made his second appearance for them.

1888 - 89

LEAGUE: Wolverhampton Wanderers were a worthy choice as one of the original 12 members of the Football League. Their 22 fixtures commenced on September 8th when the visit of Aston Villa ended in a 1-1 draw, Wolves receiving unexpected help as George Cox scored the League's first own goal. The month was completed by the first defeat (v. Preston), the first victory (v. Burnley) and a draw with Blackburn. Curiously, all four September games were at home while in October they had to travel four times yet had an identical record. Wolves steadily improved to finish third, though Preston North End had long wrapped up the title. The table below shows the points totals of each team, with Wolves results against them in brackets.

1 Preston 40 (0-4, 2-5)	7 Accrington 20 (4-0, 4-4)
2 Villa 29 (1-1, 1-2)	8 Everton 20 (4-0, 2-1)
3 WOLVES 28	9 Burnley 17 (4-1, 4-0)
4 Blackburn 26 (2-2, 2-2)	10 Derby 16 (4-1, 0-3)
5 Bolton 22 (3-2, 1-2)	11 Notts County 12 (2-1, 0-3)
6 Albion 22 (2-1, 3-1)	12 Stoke 12 (4-1, 1-0)

CUP: Just two wins were sufficient to give Wolves an unprecedented place in the Quarter-Finals, Old Carthusians being pipped 4-3 and Walsall trounced 6-1. Wolves tamed Sheffield Wednesday 3-0 to set up a Semi-Final against Blackburn Rovers. It was interesting to note that the interval scores from Wolves view-point were 0-2, 1-1 and 0-0, so there were no alarm bells ringing when Blackburn had secured the only goal of the first half. It was a 1-1 (Wykes) stalemate but Wolves then triumphed 3-1 (Hunter, Allen, Wood) to reach their first F.A. Cup Final, both meetings with Blackburn being held at Crewe, while in the other tie Preston scored once to eliminate Albion.

FINAL: In those days it was staged in March and the venue was Kennington Oval, London. A record final attendance of 22,000 waited patiently to see the last of the 149 Cup entrants, the kick-off being delayed by the Boat Race which created much congestion in the city. The fans did not have to wait long for goals though unfortunately it was the Lancastrians who went ahead through DEWHURST, the lead shortly being increased by ROSS. Wolves battled hard under the captaincy of John Brodie but there was no doubting Preston's supremacy, THOMSON making it 3-0 in the 70th minute. The Wolves team was as follows: Baynton,

Baugh, Mason, Allen, Fletcher, Lowder, Hunter, Wykes, Brodie, Wood & Knight.

TOTAL RECORD: PLD 28 W 16 D 5 L 7 F 67 A 46 (Home - W11 D 2 L 1 & Away or neutral grounds - W 5 D 3 L 6).

SCORERS: Wood 17, Brodie 12, Knight 12, Cooper 7, Hunter 6, Wykes 5, White 3, Allen 1, Fletcher 1, Lowder 1, Mason 1 & Own Goal 1.

INTERNATIONALS: Brodie became Wolves first goalscorer in this standard of football, while there were England debuts for Albert Fletcher and Arthur Lowder, all three players coming from Wolverhampton. Appearances: Allen (E1), Brodie (E2), Fletcher (E1) & Lowder (E1).

1889-90

LEAGUE: Wolves were fourth with 25 points, not quite keeping up with Preston (33), Everton (31) and Blackburn (27). They produced a couple of sensations, a 2-0 victory at Preston and a 9-1 hammering of Burnley after being level at half-time at their new Molineux home.

CUP: Old Carthusians again went back empty-handed as Wolves ran out 2-0 winners in front of around 13,000 fans. Birmingham were beaten 2-1 to pave the way for some sharpshooting against Stoke. It was 4-0 to Wolves yet that was not the end of the matter as Stoke lodged a protest about the condition of the pitch. Brodie made them regret the subsequent re-match, notching five as Wolves whipped them 8-0, only to bow out to a single Blackburn goal in the SF at Derby.

RECORD: PLD 27 W 14 D 5 L 8 F 67 A 40 (10-3-2 & 4-2-6).

SCORERS: Wood 18, Wykes 15, Brodie 14, Worrall 11, Perry 3, Allen 2, Booth 2, Fletcher 1 & OG 1.

INTERNATIONALS: Wolves provided five England men including David Baugh, a local hero who had already gained a cap whilst with Stafford Road, and Harry Wood who scored a goal. Apps: Allen (E1), Baugh (E1), Fletcher (E1), Mason (E1) & Wood (E2).

1890-91

LEAGUE: 4th (26). The term "if only" was starting to crop up in football because if only Wolves had collected two points from their fixtures with Everton the championship would have been theirs. As it was they were even denied third spot on goal-average, trailing behind Everton (29), Preston (27) and Notts County (26). Perhaps that was all they deserved in view of a 9-0 disaster at lowly Derby. Wolves also had problems off the field and were fined a hefty £50, punishment for making an illegal approach to Preston's Sam Thomson.

CUP: The luck of the draw deserted Wolves as they had to make three trips. They knocked out Long Eaton (2-1) and Accrington (3-2) but lost the QF 2-0 to Blackburn who were to retain the Cup, thus for five consecutive years Wolves had only succumbed to the tournament winners.

RECORD: PLD 25 W 14 D 2 L 9 F 44 A 55 (8-1-2 & 6-1-7).
SCORERS: Wood 13, Thomson 10, Wykes 6, Booth 5, Brodie 3, Bowdler 2, Topham 2, Worrall 2 & Allen 1.

INTERNATIONALS: Jack Bowdler netted twice for Wales but could not prevent Scotland from winning 4-3. International football came to Molineux, where 15,000 watched England slam Ireland 6-1 with the assistance of Brodie and Rose. Apps: Bowdler (W1), Brodie (E1) & Rose (E1).

1891 - 92

LEAGUE: 6th (26). There were now 14 teams involved and Wolves could only average a point-per-game. It was their lowest position yet their achievement in coming in the top six every season was equalled only by Preston. In a match with Accrington one Wolves player got his name in the record books, Bill Heath converting the first penalty to be awarded in the League. 1891-92 also saw Wolves adopt their renowned gold and black colours, having previously worn white along with red, blue and black respectively.

CUP: Much to their annoyance Wolves were held 2-2 by Crewe, though they made amends in Cheshire 4-1. Next opponents were Sheffield United, who Wolves accounted for by 3-1 only to lose by the same score to Villa in the QF. This was their only reverse in 20 Wolverhampton Cup-ties and was witnessed by 21,000 people. Villa went down to Albion in the final, the Baggies having twice drawn 1-1 with Nottingham Forest at Molineux before settling their SF elsewhere.

RECORD: PLD 30 W 13 D 5 L 12 F 69 A 53 (9-3-4 & 4-2-8).
SCORERS: Devey 19, Wykes 11, Baker 9, Booth 6, Wood 6, Topham 5, Heath 4, Allen 3, Johnston 3, Bowdler 1 & OG 2. Wolves excelled themselves in other competitions, grabbing both the BCC and the Birmingham Senior Cup.

INTERNATIONALS: Joe Davies and George Kinsey added to the list of Wolves men who had been picked for their country. Apps: Bowdler (W1), Davies (W1) & Kinsey (E1).

1892 - 93

LEAGUE: 11th (28). The Football League was now extended to two divisions with 16 clubs in the top flight. A poor campaign was summed up when an experimental Wolves X1 crashed 10-1 to wooden-spoonists Manchester United, which remains their worst-ever result. On a brighter note Champions Sunderland failed 2-0 at Molineux and Joe Butcher scored all five against Accrington.

CUP: Wolves 10th F.A. Cup venture began quietly with a 1-1 draw at Bolton, the replay being won 2-1. Non-League Middlesbrough were also thwarted 2-1 then Wolves cut loose against D2 Darwen 5-0. They continued to make a mockery of their League form in the SF at Nottingham, disposing of old rivals Blackburn 2-1 (Butcher, Topham). Everton, third in the League, needed three attempts to oust Preston by the same score.

FINAL: Manchester's Fallowfield hosted the showpiece of English football, a record 45,000 paying £2,559 to see the best of the record 183 Cup participants. As half-time loomed without a goal Everton began to lose their composure, the underdogs slowly gaining the initiative. On the hour a long, high shot by skipper ALLEN broke the deadlock to the delight of the Midlands contingent. Wolves hung on to their slender lead to give the town national glory, the heroes including Amateur International Dick Topham and Butcher, who at 18 was the youngest person to gain a Cup-winners medal. Team: Rose, Baugh, Swift, Malpass, Allen, Kinsey, Topham, Wykes, Butcher, Wood & Griffin.

RECORD: PLD 36 W 17 D 5 L 14 F 60 A 72 (14-2-2 & 3-3-12).
SCORERS: Butcher 17, Wood 14, Wykes 11, Devey 5, Topham 4, Johnston 3, Allen 2, Kinsey 2, Griffin 1 & Swift 1. Wolves Reserves were Birmingham League Champions and a hatrick of honours was completed with the BSC.

INTERNATIONALS: Topham made his full England debut and Wood scored in one of the earliest matches for the Football League XI, which was virtually as strong as the full team. Apps: Davies (W 1), Kinsey (E 1), Topham (E 1) & Wood (FL 1).

1893 - 94

LEAGUE: 9th (31). Goalkeeper Rose wrote to all the D1 captains to propose the formation of a players union though Wolves defence must have been on strike as they suffered their biggest-ever mauling at Molineux, with Albion of all teams responsible for the 8-0 scoreline. After a home match with Sheff Utd spectators attacked the referee, who it seemed everyone loved to hate even then. Wolves received a 7-1 pounding at Forest but it was not all gloom, Champions Villa sliding to a 3-0 defeat in Wolverhampton.

CUP: There was no Cup joy at the expense of Villa, Wolves losing 4-2 to have the unique indignity of not surviving their opening tie. It was also the only season in six they had not aspired to the QF stage.

RECORD: PLD 31 W 14 D 3 L 14 F 54 A 67 (11-1-3 & 3-2-11).
SCORERS: Butcher 16, Wood 12, Edge 8, Wykes 7, Black 3, Griffin 3, Haynes 1, Kinsey 1, Malpass 1, Owen 1 & Woodhall 1.

INTERNATIONALS: It was the turn of David Wykes to find the net on behalf of the FLXI. Apps: Wood (FL 1) & Wykes (FL 1).

1894 - 95

LEAGUE: 11th (25). Wanderers finished just three points off the bottom after the new experience of a battle against relegation. It was a torrid time mainly because the 43 goals scored was the lowest D1 total.

CUP: Wolves drew 0-0 at D2 Darwen before ousting both them and Stoke out by 2-0 margins. This restored their recent tradition of reaching the last eight, where the only goal conceded in four ties was enough to help Black Country neighbours Albion towards the final.

RECORD: PLD 34 W 11 D 8 L 15 F 47 A 64 (9-4-4 & 2-4-11).
SCORERS: Griffin 12, Wood 10, Wykes 7, Fleming 5, Reynolds 5, Butcher 2, Haynes 2, Black 1, Edge 1 & OG 2.

1895 - 96

LEAGUE: 14th (21). Only two points separated Wolves from the foot of the table yet they still went on a 7-2 rampage against Birmingham. The 15 away journeys yielded a solitary point, while the visit of Everton led to trouble in the form of a brief ground closure as an unruly element again took out their frustrations on the man in black.

CUP: The trail began at Molineux against D2 Notts County where Wolves drew 2-2, coming out 4-3 on top of an exciting return. Wolves fended off the challenges of D2 Liverpool 2-0 and Stoke 3-0 to push their League worries into the background. A tremendous 2-1 (Malpass, Tonks) SF victory over high-riding Derby at Villa Park made Wolves finalists for the third time in eight seasons. Sheff Wed, seventh in the League, qualified by beating Bolton 3-1 in a replay.

FINAL: Again there were records for the Cup entrants (210) and final attendance (48,836). The receipts were £1,824 with the event back in London, at Crystal Palace. Barely 100 seconds had gone when SPIKSLEY put Wednesday in front before Wolves hopes of another upset soared as BLACK hooked in the equaliser. Sadly, the Northerners restored their advantage when a SPIKSLEY effort went in off the post. The second half was something of an anti-climax with Wolves unable to level matters again. Team: Tennant, Baugh, Dunn, Griffiths, Malpass, Owen, Tonks, Henderson, Beats, Wood & Black.

RECORD: PLD 36 W 14 D 2 L 20 F 75 A 73 (13-0-5 & 1-2-15).
SCORERS: Beats 17, Wood 14, Henderson 11, Black 9, Tonks 7, Malpass 6, Wykes 4, Owen 3, Griffin 2, Topham 1 & OG 1.

INTERNATIONALS: Wood returned to the England side to prevent another season without representative honours for the club. Apps: Wood (E 1).

1896 - 97

LEAGUE: 10th (28). In contrast to 1895-96 Wolves away form kept them out of difficulties, while at Molineux they had easily their most inconsistent term to date.

CUP: NL Millwall provided the initial barrier in London as Wolves sought to maintain their splendid Cup reputation. Wolves made it by 2-1 but lost by that score at Blackburn.

RECORD: PLD 32 W 12 D 6 L 14 F 48 A 44 (6-4-5 & 6-2-9).
SCORERS: Beats 11, Smith 6, McMain 5, Miller 5, Tonks 5, Wood 4, Lyden 3, Nicholls 2, Owen 2, Black 1, Eccles 1, Edge 1 & OG 2. Wolves Cup success this season was restricted to the SSC.

INTERNATIONALS: Billy Beats scored and Billy Malpass made his debut as a trio of Wolves staff were selected for an Inter-League match. Apps: Beats (FL 1), Malpass (FL 1) & Wood (FL 1).

1897 - 98

LEAGUE: 3rd (35). Wolves rounded off the opening decade of the League with a revival in fortunes. Only Sheff Utd (42) and Sunderland (37) accumulated more points and an extra goal at the latter's ground would have made Wolves runners-up. Wood departed having been the first Wolves player to score 100 League goals, netting 106 in 234 appearances.

CUP: Wolves were 1-0 winners at Notts County but 1-0 losers to Derby, spoiling a run of eight Cup victories at Molineux. Finalists Derby also won their SF with Everton 3-1 at that venue.

RECORD: PLD 32 W 15 D 7 L 10 F 58 A 42 (10-4-2 & 5-3-8).
SCORERS: Beats 12, Wood 11, Smith 9, Tonks 7, Miller 6, McMain 4, Harper 2, Blackett 1, Chadburn 1, Fleming 1, Griffiths 1, Owen 1 & OG 2. The second team also did well, heading the Birmingham League.

INTERNATIONALS: Beats was in good shooting form for the FLXI, hitting the net three times in all. Apps: Beats (FL 2) & Wood (FL 1).

1898 - 99

LEAGUE: 8th (35). There were now 18 teams in D1 which was topped by Aston Villa. As in 1893-94 this did not guarantee them a happy visit to Molineux, where they were tanned 4-0.

CUP: Despite being held 0-0 by Bolton, Wolves got the vital goal in Lancashire to earn a trip to Derby. The Rams succeeded 2-1, history further repeating itself as they won 3-1 at Molineux in the penultimate round (v. Stoke) only to lose the final.

RECORD: PLD 37 W 15 D 8 L 14 F 56 A 50 (9-6-3 & 6-2-11).
SCORERS: Miller 11, Beats 10, Blackett 10, McMain 7, Worton 5,

Tonks 4, Smith 3, Davies 2, Annis 1, Fleming 1, Harper 1 & Nurse 1. Wolves showed they had plenty in reserve, retaining their Birmingham League title.

1899 - 1900

LEAGUE: 4th (39). Wolves lagged behind Villa (50), Sheff Utd (48) and Sunderland (41) but for the fifth time in 12 seasons could claim to be one of England's best four clubs. In nine of their travels to the other 10 leading sides they managed to avoid defeat.

CUP: A 1-1 draw at NL Queens Park Rangers made the return an apparent formality, yet Wolves followers had to put up with a 1-0 shock.

RECORD: PLD 36 W 15 D 10 L 11 F 49 A 39 (8-4-6 & 7-6-5).

SCORERS: Harper 11, Beats 9, Bowen 6, Miller 5, Worton 5, Owen 4, Pheasant 3, Bryan 2, Tonks 2 & OG 2. Wolves only trophy in 1900 was the BSC.

INTERNATIONALS: Wolves were once more prominent at FLXI level, newcomers being Hill Griffiths and John Miller. Apps: Beats (FL 1), Griffiths (FL 1) & Miller (FL 1).

1900 - 01

LEAGUE: 13th (31). The Wolverhampton public witnessed several close encounters of the footballing kind, Wolves drawing 10 home games and winning five by the odd goal including the 2-1 demise of Champions Liverpool. Not so evenly-balanced was the 7-2 pasting handed out to them at Sunderland. At one point all 25 of Wolves professionals were local men, 21 hailing from Staffordshire and the others from Shropshire.

CUP: Having mustered five goals in eight ties it was a relief to see Wolves topple NL New Brighton Tower 5-1, followed by a 3-2 success at Notts County. In the QF Wolves crashed 4-0 to Sheff Utd before a stunned Molineux audience.

RECORD: PLD 37 W 11 D 13 L 13 F 47 A 62 (7-10-2 & 4-3-11).

SCORERS: Bowen 10, Wooldridge 10, Harper 7, Beats 5, Miller 4, Pheasant 4, Poppitt 3, Annis 1, Colley 1, Fleming 1 & Worton 1. The stiffs won the Birmingham League and the SSC also came to the town again.

INTERNATIONALS: Beats made a well-deserved breakthrough into the full England team. Apps: Beats (E 1).

1901 - 02

LEAGUE: 14th (32). All five top clubs returned pointless from Molineux which made Wolves mediocre League position all the more surprising. The form that saw off title-winners Sunderland 4-2 was seldom produced at other venues.

CUP: Visiting this particular South Staffs pitch in the Cup had become a far easier proposition, as Bolton emphasised 2-0. Molineux hosted a SF replay which Derby and Sheff Utd were still unable to settle, notching a goal apiece.

RECORD: PLD 35 W 13 D 6 L 16 F 46 A 59 (12-3-3 & 1-3-13).

SCORERS: Wooldridge 14, Beats 8, Pheasant 6, Haywood 5, Miller 4, Fellows 3, Gueilliam 1, Jones 1, Pope 1, Preston 1, Robotham 1 & OG 1. Wolves won the BSC for the fourth time outright.

INTERNATIONALS: Beats played at both levels while Billy Wooldridge must have felt confused after his hatrick had helped blast the Irish League 9-0, as he was not chosen for the FLXI again! Apps: Beats (E 1 + FL 1) & Wooldridge (FL 1).

1902 - 03

LEAGUE: 11th (33). Latest champions to be victims at Molineux were Sheff Wed, who lost 2-1. Generally it was an uneventful campaign, stressed by the novel statistic of Wolves never scoring or conceding five goals.

CUP: There was no disgrace in the quick 1-0 exit at Bury as they were to lift the coveted trophy a few months later.

RECORD: PLD 35 W 14 D 5 L 16 F 48 A 58 (12-2-3 & 2-3-13).

SCORERS: Haywood 11, Smith 9, Wooldridge 8, Fellows 6, Miller 5, Beats 4, Walker 2, Bowen 1, Jones 1 & Pheasant 1. Wolves were winners of the BCC this season.

INTERNATIONALS: Tom Baddeley had a fine season in goal, the highlight coming at Molineux where 24,000 saw England drub Ireland 4-0. Apps: Baddeley (E 2 + FL 2).

1903 - 04

LEAGUE: 8th (36). Wolves had contrasting fortunes against the Sheffield duo, repeating the 2-1 scoreline over Champions Wednesday yet losing 7-2 to United. This contributed to them having the worst defence in D1 as they let in 66 goals.

CUP: A convincing 4-1 win at NL Stockton and a draw at Derby offered much promise. However, the replay went the same way with Derby scraping home 1-0 in a third meeting at Villa Park. Derby lost in the SF at Molineux as Bolton got the only goal of the afternoon.

RECORD: PLD 38 W 15 D 10 L 13 F 52 A 72 (10-7-1 & 5-3-12).

SCORERS: Wooldridge 18, Miller 7, Haywood 6, Smith 6, Baynham 3, Bevan 2, Pheasant 2, Whitehouse 2, Jones 1, Pilsbury 1, Preston 1, Walker 1 & OG 2.

INTERNATIONALS: Baddeley continued to fly the flag for Wolves at both levels. Apps: Baddeley (E 3 + FL 1).

1904 - 05

LEAGUE: 14th (26). The rearguard continued to be the weak link of the Wolves team, the 73 goals that went past it being the highest number in D1.

CUP: Wolves did very well to draw 1-1 at Sunderland and beat them 1-0 in the replay, only to flop 3-2 to NL Southampton in a simpler-looking task at Molineux.

RECORD: PLD 37 W 12 D 5 L 20 F 51 A 77 (11-2-6 & 1-3-14).

SCORERS: Smith 16, Wooldridge 14, Bevan 7, Haywood 4, Hopkins 3, Baynham 2, Vesey 2, Betterley 1, Jones 1 & Miller 1.

INTERNATIONALS: Defender Jack Jones was the only person to gain recognition this term. Apps: Jones (FL 1).

1905 - 06

LEAGUE: 20th (23). Even the presence of two additional teams could not save Wolves from the bitter experience of relegation. The 99 goals conceded was not just the biggest D1 total, it also remains an unwanted club record. The North-East was a particularly bleak area for Wolves as they were thumped 8-0 at Newcastle and 7-2 at Sunderland. Wolves finished eight points adrift at the bottom, despite conjuring up a remarkable 7-0 eclipse of Derby in the last fixture.

CUP: There was no respite here after the 3-0 win at NL Bishop's Auckland, Wolves suffering a 5-0 nightmare at D2 Bradford City.

RECORD: PLD 40 W 9 D 7 L 24 F 61 A 104 (7-5-7 & 2-2-17).

SCORERS: Wooldridge 13, Pedley 11, Smith 11, Hopkins 5, Jones, 4, Corfield 3, Layton 3, Pope 3, Breakwell 2, Gorman 2, Baynham 1, Boon 1, Lloyd 1 & Williams 1.

1906 - 07

LEAGUE D2: 6th (41). Although there was no real promotion challenge Wolves beat Champions Forest 2-0, as well as recording some healthy scores over teams who were strangers to the ground. The fans did not need football to warm them up when Hull came to town, temperatures topping 90 degrees fahrenheit in the shade. Baddeley was the first Wolves player to make 300 League appearances, leaving after reaching that exact number, while Jones was an ever-present for the fifth season out of six.

CUP: Wolves fought boldly at D1 Sheff Wed, losing by the odd goal in in five. The Owls carried on to be the eighth side to hold the Cup having knocked out Wanderers.

RECORD: PLD 39 W 17 D 7 L 15 F 68 A 56 (13-4-2 & 4-3-13).

SCORERS: Roberts 15, Hedley 11, Hawkins 9, Pedley 6, Wooldridge 6, Hopkins 4, Jones 4, Bishop 3, Williams 3, Gorman 2, Breakwell 1, Corfield 1, Raybould 1, Ward 1 & OG 1.

1907 - 08

LEAGUE D2: 9th (37). There was even less likelihood of Wolves going up this time round, the team above them being nine points better off.

CUP: The quest for Cup fame began nicely with a 1-1 draw at Bradford City and 1-0 replay win. Wolves progressed further at the expense of D1 Bury 2-0 and NL Swindon 2-0 to bring Cup fever back to Wolverhampton. They had the bit firmly between their teeth now and managed a 1-0 QF victory at Stoke. On to Stamford Bridge where NL Southampton were cast aside 2-0 (Radford, Hedley) to give Wolves a surprise place in the final. Newcastle, fourth in D1, rammed Fulham 6-0 and most experts branded Wolves as no-hopers.

FINAL: Newcastle were so confident they wanted to be photographed with the Cup even before the kick-off, a request that was sadly refused. An audience of 74,967 paid £5,998 to see the remaining two of the 348 Cup entrants meet at Crystal Palace. In the opening 40 minutes Wolves did little to suggest they could become only the second team to win this prize whilst in D2 though Amateur International Kenneth Hunt had other ideas. In 1908 he helped Great Britain beat Denmark 2-0 in the final of the Olympic Games while in the F.A. Cup goals by HUNT and HEDLEY transformed the match to put a demoralised Newcastle 2-0 in arrears at half-time. The Geordies pulled one back through HOWIE but with seven minutes to go the issue was placed beyond doubt by HARRISON, thus the only four players on the field with surnames beginning with H had shared the goals. This superb 3-1 triumph probably even surpassed the 1893 feat and the town celebrated accordingly. Team: Lunn, Jones, Collins, Hunt, Wooldridge, Bishop, Harrison, Shelton, Hedley, Radford & Pedley.

RECORD: PLD 45 W 21 D 8 L 16 F 62 A 47 (14-4-4 & 7-4-12).

SCORERS: Hedley 16, Radford 13, Shelton 10, Harrison 6, Pedley 4, Wooldridge 4, Corbett 2, Lloyd 2, Bould 1, Hunt 1, Jones 1, Mason 1 & Wake 1.

1908 - 09

LEAGUE D2: 7th (39). Hopes that Wolves Cup exploits would be a launching pad for the club to return to the premier division were not fulfilled in a dull season.

CUP: A typical anti-climax saw Wolves draw 2-2 with NL Crystal Palace and then slump 4-2 in London.

RECORD: PLD 40 W 14 D 12 L 14 F 60 A 54 (10-7-3 & 4-5-11).

SCORERS: Radford 24, Hedley 12, Blunt 9, Harrison 4, Pedley 3, Shelton 3, Jones 2, Harris 1, Hoskins 1 & Hunt 1.

INTERNATIONALS: Hunt added to his astonishing variety of honours. Apps: Hunt (FL 1).

1909 - 10

LEAGUE D2: 8th (40). Mixed fortunes were epitomised by the

results against Grimsby (won 8-1) and Barnsley (lost 7-1). Wolves habit of beating the best in the division continued, Manchester City slipping 3-2.

CUP: The differing standards of NL clubs was illustrated as a 5-0 joyride at Reading preceded a sound 5-1 dismissal from West Ham at home, proving nothing could be taken for granted in this sport.

RECORD: PLD 40 W 18 D 6 L 16 F 70 A 68 (14-3-3 & 4-3-13).
SCORERS: Blunt 27, Radford 11, Hedley 10, Harrison 7, Pedley 3, Shelton 3, Jones 2, Wooldridge 2, Bishop 1, Needham 1, Payne 1, Shinton 1 & OG 1.

1910 - 11

LEAGUE D2: 9th (38). Wolves were well and truly in a D2 rut, having not been involved in either a promotion or relegation struggle during their five-year stay. Wooldridge ended his stay after scoring 82 goals in 329 games for them.

CUP: NL Accrington, D1 Man City and Chelsea all came to Molineux, the latter attracting 33,000 spectators. The outcomes from Wolves angle were 2-0, 1-0 and 0-2.

RECORD: PLD 41 W 17 D 8 L 16 F 54 A 54 (12-5-5 & 5-3-11).
SCORERS: J. Needham 15, Hedley 12, Harrison 9, Blunt 6, A. Needham 6, Walker 3, Bishop 1, Deakin 1 & Wooldridge 1.

1911 - 12

LEAGUE D2: 5th (42). Wolves attained their highest position to date in this section without being serious candidates to say goodbye to it. The 8-0 massacre of Hull is the Humbersiders record defeat.

CUP: The goalless draw at NL Watford gave little indication of what was in store. Wolves 10, Watford 0 remained an F.A. Cup replay record score for several years and is still the worst result the men from Vicarage Road have had. NL Lincoln must have approached Molineux with some trepidation about their second round tie, though they did restrict Wolves to a modest 2-1. A tricky journey to D1 Blackburn saw Wolves edged out 3-2.

RECORD: PLD 42 W 18 D 11 L 13 F 71 A 37 (14-3-4 & 4-8-9).
SCORERS: Halligan 24, Hedley 9, Needham 9, Harrison 8, Young 6, Yule 6, Parsonage 4, Brooks 3, Garratly 1 & Groves 1.

INTERNATIONALS: Willie Halligan was rewarded for his scoring achievements by being the club's first Irish International. Apps: Halligan (I 1).

1912 - 13

LEAGUE D2: 10th (38). The almost customary scalp of the champions (Preston 2-0) was consolation for Wolves lowest-ever League position.

This was despite the debut of Bill Jordan, who like colleague Hunt was a parson.

CUP: Wolves eliminated NL London Caledonians 3-1 before bowing out to Bradford Park Avenue 3-0.

RECORD: PLD 40 W 15 D 10 L 15 F 59 A 58 (11-6-3 & 4-4-12).
SCORERS: Halligan 17, Needham 10, Brooks 7, Groves 6, Parsonage 4, Harrison 3, Hedley 3, Young 3, Garratly 1, Jones 1, Jordan 1, Mulholland 1, Yule 1 & OG 1.

1913 - 14

LEAGUE D2: 9th (41). Wolves sequence of shock results over title-winners was lengthened by the 4-1 routing of Notts County. On the other side of the coin, Hull belatedly got their own back on Wolves to the tune of 7-1.

CUP: NL Southampton were comprehensively beaten 3-0 but D1 Sheff Wed proved a different kettle of fish. Wolves squandered their main opportunity when they could only draw 1-1 at home, a single goal in the replay being enough to end their Cup dreams.

RECORD: PLD 41 W 19 D 6 L 16 F 55 A 54 (15-2-4 & 4-4-12).
SCORERS: Brooks 11, Hughes 10, Needham 8, Harrison 6, Groves 4, Francis 3, Richards 3, Griffiths 2, Howell 2, Lockett 2, Young 2, Garratly 1 & Lloyd 1.

INTERNATIONALS: Ted Peers became the last line of defence for Wales to continue the Wolves tradition of finding good goalkeepers. Apps: Peers (W 3).

1914 - 15

LEAGUE D2: 4th (45). Wolves collected 18 points out of 20 including eight wins in a row at the end of the season, Leicester being demolished 7-0 in this spell. They were top D2 scorers with 77 and were obviously emerging from the soccer wilderness. What a pity war reared it's ugly head to interrupt the League after 27 campaigns.

CUP: Wolves won 1-0 at NL Reading only to fall by the wayside at Hillsborough again, where they failed to respond to D1 Wednesday's two goals.

RECORD: PLD 40 W 20 D 7 L 13 F 78 A 54 (12-4-3 & 8-3-10).
SCORERS: Curtis 25, Brooks 18, Needham 15, Howell 4, Dunn 3, Garratly 3, Langford 3, Richards 3, Harrison 2, Bishop 1 & Groves 1.

INTERNATIONALS: Sammy Brooks completed a fine season with an international honour that he had thoroughly earned. Apps: Brooks (FL 1).

1919 - 20

LEAGUE D2: 19th (30). Wolves had restricted themselves to

friendlies during the four-year break, which had clearly been detrimental to them as they only retained their D2 status by virtue of the fact that it was now comprised of 22 clubs. Officials of Wolves had to save the referee from the crowd after a match in which he awarded Bury a dubious penalty, scenes which led to Molineux being closed down and Wolves twice using The Hawthorns as their home ground. They conceded double-figures at Hull, losing 10-3, a humiliation that has not been repeated since. There was a debut for Dick Baugh, whose father lined-up in Wolves 1896 F.A. Cup Final team, while Albert Bishop sought pastures new after 357 appearances and six goals.

CUP: Wolves began smartly, drawing 2-2 at D1 Blackburn and getting the vital strike in the return. NL Cardiff gave Wolves a taste of their own medicine when they arrived in the Midlands, going through 2-1.

RECORD: PLD 45 W 11 D 11 L 23 F 59 A 84 (9-4-10 & 2-7-13).

SCORERS: Richards 12, Brooks 6, Bate 5, Needham 5, Sambrook 5, Cutler 4, Groves 4, Harrison 4, Wright 4, Lea 3, Howell 2, Green 1, Hodnett 1, Smart 1, Woodward 1 & OG 1.

INTERNATIONALS: Brooks played in a Victory International and Peers played in two, the Welshman also being involved in two official fixtures. Dick Richards joined him in the latter pair, scoring once. Apps: Brooks (E 1), Peers (W 4) & Richards (W 2).

1920 - 21

LEAGUE D2: 15th (38). Results improved slightly though Wolves were one of many teams in the danger zone. Their cause was hindered in the goalless draw with Bristol City, when it was discovered after the final whistle that a shot from George Edmonds had literally gone through the net. Perhaps the expression "We wuz robbed" originated from this incident. A couple of very loyal servants finished their Wolves careers, Jones having made 355 League appearances (19 goals) and Billy Harrison 317 (43).

CUP: Wolves shaded Stoke 3-2 before gaining a 1-1 draw at D1 Derby, completing the job 1-0. It was also 1-0 at Fulham in the third round and even the tough trip to D1 Everton could not halt the 1-0 series. Wolves met their now-divisional rivals Cardiff in the Anfield SF and neither defence wilted. A marvellous Cup run reached a peak at Old Trafford as Wolves made it by 3-1 (Richards, Edmonds, Brooks) in the replay while Tottenham, sixth in D1, defeated Preston 2-1 in the other tie.

FINAL: The venue was Stamford Bridge and the cost to the 72,805 crowd was £13,414, while the number of teams taking part in the Cup had risen to a record 674. It was only the seventh time a D2 outfit had been in the final and of course Wolves were twice on that list. A cloudburst reduced the pitch to a quagmire resulting in some untidy first half play. Spurs at last justified their billing as favourites in the 55th minute, DIMMOCK taking advantage of a mistake by Wanderers captain Val Gregory. Brooks almost equalised in the dying seconds, the ball being kicked off the line to end Wolves hopes of another giant-killing act. Team: George, Woodward, Marshall, Gregory, Hodnett, Riley, Lea, Burrill, Edmonds, Potts & Brooks.

RECORD: PLD 50 W 21 D 8 L 21 F 59 A 71 (13-4-6 & 8-4-15).
SCORERS: Edmonds 15, Burrill 10, Potts 10, Brooks 7, Richards 4, Hodnett 3, Gregory 2, Sambrook 2, Hales 1, Harrison 1, Jones 1, Price 1, Riley 1 & OG 1.

INTERNATIONALS: Peers remained part of the Welsh XI and despite the loss of four war seasons he became the first Wolves player to reach double-figures of appearances for his nation, making exactly 10 (eight full). Apps: Peers (W 3) & Richards (W 1).

1921 - 22

LEAGUE D2: 17th (37). This was virtually an action-replay of the two previous terms as Wolves floundered in the D2 basement. A considerable boost was derived from a 2-0 win over Champions Forest.

CUP: There were no thrills this year, Wolves losing 3-0 to D1 Preston who were the eventual finalists.

RECORD: PLD 43 W 13 D 11 L 19 F 44 A 52 (8-7-6 & 5-4-13).
SCORERS: Edmonds 13, Bissett 9, Hargreaves 5, Burrill 4, Richards 4, Baugh 3, Brooks 2, Caddick 1, Lea 1, Marshall 1 & Smart 1. Wolves took the SSC and the reserves joined the Central League.

INTERNATIONALS: Richards maintained the Wolves link with Wales. Apps: Richards (W 2).

1922 - 23

LEAGUE D2: 22nd (27). Inevitably Wolves went down, the gap between them and the 21st side being eight points. They did not register an away success and their goalkeeper was left helpless 77 times, making Wolves defence the worst in D2. Somehow they managed to pip Champions Notts County 1-0 but defeats at Leicester (7-0) and Coventry (7-1) were a more accurate reflection of the season. Things went badly off the field with the death of Jack Addenbrooke who had been secretary for 37 years and was in charge of team affairs, George Jobey being appointed as manager-coach.

CUP: Wolves embarked on what was now the road to Wembley at D3 (South) Merthyr. A 1-0 win meant that D1 Liverpool, on course for the title, would be their next opponents. Somewhere in the region of 40,000 fans assembled at Molineux hoping to witness an upset, but the Merseysiders beat the Midlanders 2-0.

RECORD: PLD 44 W 10 D 9 L 25 F 43 A 79 (9-4-9 & 1-5-16).

SCORERS: Edmonds 14, Fazackerley 13, Burrill 3, Hargreaves 3, White 3, Baugh 1, Bissett 1, Caddick 1, Hodnett 1, McCall 1, McMillan 1 & Rhodes 1.

1923 - 24

LEAGUE D3 NORTH: 1st (63). A limited company was formed and they purchased the Molineux site from the brewery that owned it, while on the pitch the shame of descending to this level was soon forgotten as Wolves stormed to the title. Sporting a new strip of gold shirts with a black V instead of stripes they were unbeaten at home and went a record 20 League games without a reverse. They lost only three times, a total that was never to be bettered in D3N, finishing a point ahead of Rochdale and nine clear of third-placed Chesterfield. Wolves were the most prolific D3N scorers with 76, which included a 7-1 runaway at Ashington.

CUP: Wolves disposed of Darlington 3-1 and, after a goalless draw in the capital, D3S Charlton 1-0. A fine 1-1 draw at D1 Albion was ruined when they failed 2-0 at Molineux.

RECORD: PLD 47 W 26 D 17 L 4 F 81 A 31 (20-3-1 & 6-14-3).

SCORERS: Lees 22, Fazackerley 17, Phillipson 12, Edwards 7, Martin 6, McMillan 4, Harrington 3, Legge 3, Marson 2, Bowen 1, Davidson 1, Getwood 1, Kay 1 & OG 1. Wolves also re-captured the BSC.

1924 - 25

LEAGUE D2: 6th (46). Under the new management of Fred Scotchbrook revitalised Wolves chased another promotion for the majority of 1924-25, only to fade in the later stages. They extended their unbeaten run at Molineux to 27 but then struggled before their home fans. The ground itself had problems when the stand on the Waterloo Road side was moved to the Molineux Street side to make way for a new development, which did not turn out to be a very secure switch as it was blown down by a gale.

CUP: Optimism after a 1-1 result at Hull proved unfounded, Wolves spoiling the good work again in a 1-0 setback.

RECORD: PLD 44 W 20 D 7 L 17 F 56 A 53 (14-1-7 & 6-6-10).

SCORERS: Phillipson 15, Lees 14, Bowen 8, Edwards 6, Fazackerley 3, Harris 2, Marson 2, Mitton 2, O'Connor 2, Gummery 1 & Harrington 1.

1925 - 26

LEAGUE D2: 4th (49). The position was somewhat deceptive as Wolves were eight points short of the runners-up. However, it was a satisfying effort enhanced by the 7-1 hiding of Barnsley and the 36 goals in 31 appearances of Geordie Tom Phillipson. The visit of Portsmouth saw the opening of that new stand, the first major one to be built at Molineux.

CUP: The format of the Cup was altered to the present-day method, clubs from the higher two divisions entering at the third round stage. Wolves shared a couple of goals with D1 Arsenal then lost 1-0 at Highbury.

RECORD: PLD 44 W 21 D 8 L 15 F 85 A 62 (15-5-2 & 6-3-13).
SCORERS: Phillipson 37, Price 8, Bowen 7, Keetley 5, Kerr 5, Lees 5, Scott 5, Caddick 2, Hann 2, Harrington 2, Mitton 2, Homer 1, Meek 1 & OG 3.

1926 - 27

LEAGUE D2: 15th (35). Not such a good term, though Barnsley would still not be relishing trips to Wolverhampton after a 9-1 slaughter. Their Yorkshire neighbours Bradford City fared little better, crashing 7-2 on Christmas Day as Phillipson got five out of his total of 31 in 32 games.

CUP: A 2-0 win at NL Carlisle was followed by two home ties. Wolves overcame Forest (2-0) and Hull (1-0) to march into the QF where they faced D1 Arsenal. Playing at Highbury was again an insurmountable hurdle for Wolves, though at 2-1 it was a close thing. Cardiff were to beat Arsenal in the final to take the Cup to Wales for the only time, having seen off Reading 3-0 in a Molineux SF.

RECORD: PLD 46 W 17 D 7 L 22 F 79 A 77 (12-4-7 & 5-3-15).
SCORERS: Phillipson 33, Chadwick 12, Weaver 10, Boswell 5, Lees 4, Bowen 3, Harrington 2, Kerr 2, Legge 2, Watson 2, Higham 1, McDougall 1, Mitton 1 & Scott 1.

1927 - 28

LEAGUE D2: 16th (36). Major Frank Buckley was recruited from Blackpool but in his opening season as manager results were very similar, his worst moment probably being when Wolves were pounded 7-0 by lowly Fulham. Phillipson was released after scoring 104 in 144 matches, returning to the town as mayor during the war.

CUP: The 2-1 win over Chelsea provided a little bit of Cup cheer before Wolves fell 3-1 to D1 Sheff Utd.

RECORD: PLD 44 W 14 D 10 L 20 F 66 A 95 (12-5-5 & 2-5-15).
SCORERS: Chadwick 19, Phillipson 12, R. Weaver 11, Bowen 5, Baxter 4, Marshall 3, W. Weaver 3, Watson 2, Charnley 1, Cock 1, Green 1, Harrington 1, Higham 1, Richards 1 & Rotton 1.

1928 - 29

LEAGUE D2: 17th (37). Wolves continued to look more likely

to go down than up, the gap they had to bridge being illustrated by an 8-3 drubbing at Champions Middlesbrough.

CUP: To the horror of their supporters Wolves were shown up 1-0 by Midland League Mansfield. As there were now far more members of the Football League this was a bigger disgrace than any previous exits to NL clubs.

RECORD: PLD 43 W 15 D 7 L 21 F 77 A 82 (9-6-7 & 6-1-14).
SCORERS: Weaver 18, Green 16, Chadwick 13, Baxter 10, Ferguson 4, Featherby 3, Marshall 3, Pritchard 3, Hartill 2, Johnson 2, Coundon 1, Richards 1 & OG 1.

1929 - 30

LEAGUE D2: 9th (41). Although they received a 7-3 trouncing at West Brom at least Wolves were back in the right half of the table. Billy Hartill had proved a great local discovery, netting 34 goals in 36 outings including all five versus Notts County.

CUP: Wolves ambitions of treading the hallowed turf of Wembley were a long way from being fulfilled, one goal from Oldham preventing them from even reaching the fourth round.

RECORD: PLD 43 W 16 D 9 L 18 F 77 A 80 (14-3-4 & 2-6-14).
SCORERS: Hartill 34, Deacon 9, Hetherington 7, Marshall 7, Rhodes 5, Featherby 3, Forshaw 3, Lowton 2, White 2, Barraclough 1, Crook 1, Richards 1 & OG 2.

1930 - 31

LEAGUE D2: 4th (47). The influence of Buckley was finally beginning to tell, victories over Bury (7-0) and Champions Everton (3-1) indicating that Wolves had turned the corner.

CUP: Poor D3N Wrexham were subjected to a 9-1 drilling but there were no goals at Bradford City in the next round. Wolves won the replay 4-2, then performed well at Barnsley (3-1) and Albion (1-1). Having seemingly done the hard bit Wolves lost the QF replay 2-1, Albion taking full advantage of the reprieve to lift the Cup at Wembley.

RECORD: PLD 48 W 24 D 7 L 17 F 102 A 74 (17-2-5 & 7-5-12).
SCORERS: Hartill 31, Bottrill 16, J. Deacon 16, Phillips 11, Martin 8, Lowton 7, Hetherington 4, Hollingworth 3, Barraclough 2, R. Deacon 1, Lax 1 & OG 2.

INTERNATIONALS: As if to underline that Wolves were on their way back both Charlie Phillips and Dai Richards made their debuts for Wales with the former scoring. Apps: Phillips (W 1) & Richards (W 1).

1931 - 32

LEAGUE D2: 1st (56). Champions Wolves fought their way back

into the big League after an absence of 26 years, pipping Leeds by two points and having four to spare over third-placed Stoke. Success was mainly due to an attack who were easily top D2 scorers with a club record 115, Hartill getting 30 in his 37 appearances. Wolves won 7-1 at Port Vale while Molineux fans enjoyed the visits of Man Utd (7-0) and Oldham (7-1), along with three other victories by the margin of 6-0.

CUP: Having won 2-1 at D3S Luton in the third round, Wolves Cup interest ended 2-0 at Preston.

RECORD: PLD 44 W 25 D 8 L 11 F 117 A 52 (17-3-1 & 8-5-10).

SCORERS: Hartill 30, Bottrill 21, Phillips 19, Deacon 13, Lowton 10, Barraclough 7, Buttery 6, Hollingworth 4, Crook 2, Martin 1, Redfern 1, Richards 1, Smalley 1 & OG 1. The reserves completed a memorable double by taking the Central League title with 61 points and 128 goals, an incredible average of more than three-per-game.

INTERNATIONALS: Arthur Lumberg joined the growing band of Wolves and Wales players. Apps: Lumberg (W 1) & Phillips (W 1).

1932 - 33

LEAGUE: 20th (35). It was nearly a case of straight back down but Wolves were saved by a shock result against Everton, who had just won the Cup. 1932-33 was also notable for eye-catching results against Champions Arsenal, as Wolves pulled off a 2-1 sensation in London yet were pulverised 7-1 at home. Ever-present Hartill silenced critics who claimed he would not produce the goods in D1 with a fine tally of 33 goals. The Molineux Street Stand with it's distinctive multi-span roof was opened for this campaign, holding 3,400 seats while the standing enclosure in front of it could accommodate 4,500.

CUP: Derby showed how fragile Wolves defence were on their own soil by whacking them 6-3. Local football followers had to be content with a neutral role in the SF as Everton beat West Ham 2-1.

RECORD: PLD 43 W 13 D 9 L 21 F 83 A 102 (10-4-8 & 3-5-13).

SCORERS: Hartill 33, Deacon 15, Crook 10, Bottrill 7, Hetherington 6, Barraclough 4, Lowton 2, Phillips 2, Nelson 1, Rhodes 1, Richards 1 & OG 1.

INTERNATIONALS: Richards and Phillips extended their careers for Wales this term. Apps: Phillips (W 1) & Richards (W 3).

1933 - 34

LEAGUE: 15th (40). Points-wise Wolves were nearer to the fourth team than any relegation victims in a season of consolidation. Outstanding feats were the 8-0 lashing of Man City and four goals in seven minutes against Huddersfield, while at the other end of the scale they were thrashed 7-1 at Blackburn.

CUP: Wolves only required a goal to seal Newcastle's fate but they were still no test for Derby, going down 3-0 at The Baseball Ground.

RECORD: PLD 44 W 15 D 12 L 17 F 75 A 89 (14-4-4 & 1-8-13).
SCORERS: Phillips 14, Hartill 13, Goddard 12, Jones 10, Beattie 7, Lowton 6, Barraclough 5, Hetherington 4, Nelson 2, Richards 1 & OG 1.

INTERNATIONALS: Wales were Home Champions with a Wolves duo boosting them in each fixture. Apps: Phillips (W 3) & Richards (W 3).

1934 - 35

LEAGUE: 17th (38). Wolves had the worst D1 defence conceding 94, including seven at Arsenal. With the exception of the Gunners the Wolves forward-line compared with any in England which made it an entertaining period for their fans. Hartill scored all five past Aston Villa and departed with a Wolves record of 164 League goals under his belt, after making just 221 appearances.

CUP: D2 Notts County presented no difficulties, Wolves taming them 4-0. Sheff Wed were in no mood for such surrender though, scraping by 2-1 at Molineux en route to a Wembley triumph.

RECORD: PLD 44 W 16 D 8 L 20 F 93 A 96 (14-3-6 & 2-5-14).
SCORERS: Hartill 29, Phillips 12, Martin 8, Jones 7, Wrigglesworth 7, Beattie 6, Iverson 4, Clayton 3, Crook 3, Hetherington 3, Shaw 2, Brown 1, Deacon 1, Galley 1, Hollingworth 1, Nelson 1, Rhodes 1, Richards 1 & OG 2. Wolves other teams did well, collecting the SSC and adding the Birmingham Combination to their roll of honours.

INTERNATIONALS: Wolves boasted five selections at full level, though none of them were English. The Northern Ireland pair of Jackie Brown and Dave Martin were the first from the club to be called upon by an Irish XI since it had became two nations in 1921. Bryn Jones was one of three Wolves men in the line-up when he made his debut for Wales while Phillips had a good season, scoring twice. Apps: Brown (NI 2), Jones (W 1), Martin (NI 1), Phillips (W 3) & Richards (W 3).

1935 - 36

LEAGUE: 15th (40). Wolves smashed Blackburn 8-1 and despite languishing in the lower part of the table only eight points separated them from the second-placed team. An oddity concerning Bournemouth arose over this and the 1934-35 term, the South Coast outfit having 15 ex-Wolves players on their books.

CUP: Leeds made it another brief Cup flirtation for Wolves, winning 3-1 after a 1-1 draw in Wolverhampton. The Wanderers ground was the venue for the SF that resulted Sheff Utd 2, Fulham 1.

RECORD: PLD 44 W 15 D 11 L 18 F 79 A 80 (13-8-1 & 2-3-17).

SCORERS: Wrigglesworth 13, Martin 10, Smalley 10, Jones 9, Phillips 7, Shaw 6, Thompson 6, Ashall 3, Brown 3, Clayton 2, Gardiner 2, Greene 2, Iverson 2, Henson 1, Morris 1 & OG 2. Wolves retained the SSC trophy.

INTERNATIONALS: All five capped in 1934-35 were in action again with the Welsh trio together once more in a match, Phillips scoring. They also played at Molineux before a 22,000 gathering though only Jones was still with the club, and he netted in a 2-1 win for Wales, while Brown was also on target for Northern Ireland. Richards total appearances for his country whilst with Wolves reached 11 and Phillips got to 10, some as captain. Apps: Brown (NI 1), Jones (W 3), Martin (NI 1), Phillips (W 1) & Richards (W 1).

Chapter 2

1936 - 37 to 1962 - 63

1936 - 37

LEAGUE: 5th (47). A top position was occupied for the first time since 1900 as Wolves recovered brilliantly from a poor start. In the early months the departures of quality players prompted one disgruntled supporter to daub "Stop me and buy one" on the team-bus. Crowd disorder of a more serious nature occurred in November after the visit of Chelsea, the goalpost being uprooted as Wolves tumbled to 20th. They then dramatically soared up the League chart, highlights being v. Champions Man City (2-1) and Everton (7-2). Cecil Shaw created a pre-war record of 163 successive appearances for Wolves, while an oddity this season was that everyone on the playing staff was single.

CUP: Middlesbrough were slammed 6-1 as Wolves endeavoured to put five lean Cup years behind them. They stuttered to the fifth round, pipping D2 Sheff Utd 2-1 away after a 2-2 draw. A record Grimsby attendance of 31,657 then watched their team hold Wolves to 1-1, though nearer 57,000 saw Wolves take the replay 6-2. In the QF Sunderland attracted almost 58,000 to Molineux where it ended 1-1. At Roker Park the four goals were equally shared but eventual Cup-winners Sunderland settled it 4-0 at Hillsborough, bringing down the curtain on an exciting run.

RECORD: PLD 50 W 24 D 9 L 17 F 104 A 81 (18-4-3 & 6-5-14).
SCORERS: Clayton 29, Galley 16, Ashall 15, Jones 14, Thompson 8, Westcott 6, Brown 3, Waring 3, Wharton 2, Wrigglesworth 2, Iverson 1, Morris 1, Smalley 1 & OG 3. Wolves made it a hatrick of successes in the SSC.

INTERNATIONALS: Tom Galley and Tom Smalley put Wolves back on the map as far as England were concerned, the former scoring for them. Shaw also restored Molineux interest in the FLXI, Jones netted again for Wales and the Republic of Ireland used Dave Jordan. Apps: Galley (E 2), Jones (W 3), Jordan (ROI 2), Shaw (FL 1) & Smalley (E 1).

1937 - 38

LEAGUE: 2nd (51). Wolves highest spot to date underlined they were now a force to be reckoned with. Champions Arsenal finished a mere point ahead, losing 3-1 on their visit to Molineux. Wolves recorded their greatest League victory when caning Leicester 10-1 while perhaps the greatest oddity occurred at Huddersfield. In the 86th minute Stan Cullis conceded a penalty for hands from which Hayes beat Alex Scott, the remarkable thing being that in 1936-37 the same incident happened in the same fixture at the same ground in the same minute involving the same three men!

CUP: Wolves signalled their intentions with a 4-0 romp at D2 Swansea to make the tie of the fourth round a reality. Wolves tackled Arsenal and the modern Molineux stadium with two fine stands and coverings over both North and South Bank terraces was bursting at the seams with 61,267 people inside. However, it was a frustrating afternoon for most of them as the Londoners ran out 2-1 winners.

RECORD: PLD 44 W 21 D 11 L 12 F 77 A 51 (11-8-3 & 10-3-9).
SCORERS: Westcott 22, Jones 17, Galley 11, Dorsett 6, Clayton 5, Maguire 5, Langley 3, Thompson 3, Kirkham 2, Ashall 1, Smalley 1 & OG 1. Wolves made history in the SSC, picking it up for a record fourth consecutive year.

INTERNATIONALS: Jones snatched another goal for Wales and had worn the red shirt 10 times in all by the end of 1937-38. Cullis made his mark on the England team as well as being one of a trio from Wolverhampton who played in an Inter-League fixture, George Ashall gaining his solitary honour. Apps: Ashall (FL 1), Cullis (E 5 + FL 1), Galley (FL 1) & Jones (W 3).

1938 - 39

LEAGUE: 2nd (55). It was a case of so near and yet so far as Wolves bulldozered Champions Everton 7-0 but lost to a single goal at Goodison Park, where two points would have given them the title on goal-average. Before the season began Wolves transferred Jones to Arsenal for a pre-war world record £14,000, though a new hero emerged in Dennis Westcott who struck 32 times in 37 games. Wanderers had the best defence in D1 letting in 39, the lowest total since changes to the offside law in 1925. Major Buckley had created controversy with his monkey-gland treatment which was similar to the anti-cold injections that ensued, as well as his watering of the pitch as the muddy conditions were said to favour Wolves. Nevertheless, he had patiently built a brilliant young team and 1938-39 saw the unique selection of two 16-year-old wingers for a D1 match, Alan Steen and Jimmy Mullen lining up v. Man Utd. Over the three pre-war seasons Wolves had gained the most D1 points and it was a shame this talented side, who equalled Wolves record of 27 unbeaten home games, were not allowed to realise their full potential.

CUP: Wolves confidently brushed aside D2 Bradford Park Avenue 3-1 and then routed Leicester 5-1. Molineux's record attendance of 61,315 were treated to a 4-1 dismissal of Liverpool and almost 60,000 watched Everton sunk 2-0 as Wolves completed a Merseyside double. Old Trafford's biggest-ever gate of 76,962 saw a one-sided SF with an injury to the Grimsby goalkeeper being partly responsible for Wolves 5-0 (Westcott 4, Galley) jaunt. The other tie produced a more characteristic 2-1 scoreline as Portsmouth, 17th in D1, got the better of Huddersfield.

FINAL: With 554 teams knocked out Wolves were strongly tipped to add Pompey to that list, a stark contrast to their other F.A. Cup Final outings. Receipts totalled £29,116 as 99,370 gathered to see Wolves debut at the mecca of English football-Wembley Stadium. On the half-hour BARLOW opened the scoring for Portsmouth, ANDERSON lobbing in another prior to the interval. Inexperience cost Wolves dear as PARKER piled on the agony though DORSETT did give them a little hope. Westcott was unable to add to his 11 Cup goals and in the 72nd minute PARKER struck again with a header to make it an embarrassing 4-1. Stan Burton was to have the unprecedented distinction of playing in the Cup Final then making his debut for a new team the same season, so it was a sad climax to his spell at Molineux. Team: Scott, Morris, Taylor, Galley, Cullis, Gardiner, Burton, McIntosh, Westcott, Dorsett & Maguire.

RECORD: PLD 48 W 27 D 11 L 10 F 108 A 46 (18-6-1 & 9-5-9).

SCORERS: Westcott 43, Dorsett 29, Galley 12, McIntosh 9, Burton 4, Maguire 4, Kirkham 3, Barlow 1, McAloon 1, Steen 1 & Wright 1.

INTERNATIONALS: Cullis became the youngest-ever England captain at 22, Bill Morris joining him in the defence. The FLXI defeated the Scottish League 3-1 at Molineux, with Joe Gardiner keeping Cullis company on this occasion. Apps: Cullis (E 7 + FL 2), Gardiner (FL 1) & Morris (E 3).

1939 - 40

The Football League was abandoned after just three fixtures though there was a national Cup competition and several regional championships. Wolves won the Midlands League with their best result coming against Northampton (7-2), while the goalscoring was still dominated by Westcott (24) and Dorsett (16). Wolves gained 41 points from their 28 matches, winning 13/14 at home and hitting a total of 76 goals.

INTERNATIONALS: Cyril Sidlow and Westcott were used by their countries during the opening season of wartime games, all of which were classed as unofficial. Apps: Cullis (E 3), Sidlow (W 2) & Westcott (E 1).

1940 - 41

Because 1939-40 had been something of a financial disaster, Wolves withdrew from soccer this term, their promising teenagers Billy Wright and Mullen temporarily going to Leicester and being amongst their three leading scorers.

INTERNATIONALS: Cullis and Sidlow remained on Wolves books to continue the club's international links. Apps: Cullis (E 4) & Sidlow (W 2).

1941 - 42

Wolves won the Football League (War) Cup which was held for the third and final time. They progressed to the final with these aggregate scores: Chester 4-1, Man Utd 6-5, Man City 2-1 and Albion 7-0. Wolves then travelled to Sunderland for the first leg and drew 2-2 (Westcott 2) with this team: Sidlow, Dowen (loaned from Hull), Robinson, Thornhill, Galley, Dorsett, Broome (loaned from Villa), McIntosh, Westcott, Stevenson & Mullen. For the return Wolves brought in Frank Taylor and Jack Rowley (loaned from Man Utd) in place of Stevenson and Thornhill and over 43,000 saw them win 4-1 (Rowley 2, Broome, Westcott) to make it 6-3 on aggregate. During the first half of 1941-42 Wolves played in a Southern League and in the latter half were fifth in the war's only national championship, Rowley collecting five as Everton were battered 11-1.

INTERNATIONALS: Cullis was still a vital member of the England XI. Apps: Cullis (E 3).

1942 - 43

Although Wolves were involved in two Northern Leagues as well as the League Cup (North) they were not close to any honours. They did create a stir by fielding the youngest person to play in an English first-class match, 14-year-old Cameron Buchanan. Wulfrunian Arthur Rowley made several appearances and after the war went on to become the most prolific scorer in League history with 434, yet brother Jack was an even better footballer and in his solitary Wolves outing in 1942-43 he netted all eight as Wolves crushed Derby 8-1.

INTERNATIONALS: Back in 1920-21 Wales had beaten England 2-0 in the only Amateur International staged in the town and having then won a full match they now made it a hatrick at Molineux, recording a 2-1 success to the despair of the 25,000 crowd who cheered on their heroes Cullis and Mullen. Westcott may have made a difference as his five goals this term included three in a 5-3 win over the Welsh. Apps: Cullis (E 5), Mullen (E 1), Sidlow (W 1) & Westcott (E 3).

1943 - 44

Wolves participated in three tournaments again but the main talking point did not concern what happened in the football arena. After approximately 17 years in charge Buckley resigned for reasons that were never made public, taking over at Notts County while Welshman Ted Vizard was given the hot seat at Wolverhampton.

INTERNATIONALS: Taylor was drafted into the England side and Cullis took his wartime appearance tally to 20, many as skipper, the maestro donning the white shirt 32 times altogether. Apps: Cullis (E 5),

Sidlow (W 2) & Taylor (E 1).

1944 - 45

There were again two Northern League campaigns and a League Cup (N) bid for Wolves, who lost 4-3 on aggregate to Bolton in the SF. The tie with Birmingham had been ordered to carry on until there was a goal with Morris breaking the deadlock in the 153rd minute, which was better than the modern idea of deciding matches on penalties.

INTERNATIONALS: John Harris became the first Wolves man to wear the blue colours of Scotland. Apps: Harris (S 1), Mullen (E 1) & Sidlow (W 2).

1945 - 46

Wolves found themselves back in the Southern League which lasted throughout 1945-46, their position being sixth. The F.A. Cup resumed briefly under a two-leg system, Wolves blasting NL Lovell's Athletic 4-2 (away) and 8-1 (home) before being on the receiving end of a 5-2 scoreline at Charlton in the next round. They could not wipe out the deficit at Molineux where it was 1-1, Charlton going on to reach the final.

INTERNATIONALS: Victory Internationals were the welcome theme of 1945-46, a season which heralded the arrival on the scene of that gentleman William Ambrose Wright. Bert Williams kept goal for England and Sidlow for Wales in the same match, the latter bringing his wartime appearances up to 11. Apps: Mullen (E 1), Sidlow (W 2), Williams (E 2) & Wright (E 4).

1946 - 47

DEBUTANTS: Jim Alderton, Ray Chatham, Billy Crook, Jimmy Dunn, Ted Elliot (Carlisle), Willie Forbes (Dunfermline), Johnny Hancocks (Walsall), Bob King (Northampton), Angus McLean, Dave Miller (Middlesbrough), Roy Pritchard, Jesse Pye (Notts County), Fred Ramscar (Stockport), Peter Ratcliffe (Notts County), Bert Williams (Walsall) & Billy Wright. Most of the men had played for Wolves in wartime matches while their previous clubs are in brackets, providing they are members of the Football League, Scottish League or Irish Leagues. The following made their debuts before the war: Bill Morris (1933-34), Stan Cullis (1934-35), Tom Galley (1934-35), Dennis Westcott (1936-37), Dick Dorsett (1937-38), Alex McIntosh (1937-38) & Jimmy Mullen (1938-39). There were 18 Englishmen amongst Wolves 23 players of 1946-47 while Dunn, Forbes and McIntosh were born in Scotland, McLean in Wales and Ratcliffe in Eire.

SUMMARY: Weather proved to be a major factor in the title race, Wolves looking well set to win it until the big freeze-up disrupted the fixture list. In their purple patch Wolves had won 17/20, the only setback coming at Molineux where the aggregate attendance was just 5,000 short of a million. Individually, Westcott took the honours by repeating his goal-per-game average of 1938-39 to make it 81 in two campaigns, underlining his ill-fortune in losing the seven seasons in between. Wolves Reserves also had a frustrating outcome to their bid for Central League joy, being runners-up.

LEAGUE: 3rd (56). Williams, Morris, McLean, Galley, Cullis, Crook, Hancocks, Pye, Westcott, Ramscar & Mullen. That was the opening day line-up as D1 football returned to Molineux, though at half-time neither they or visitors Arsenal had got on the scoresheet. Pye helped show Wolves supporters what they had been missing as the Londoners were buried under a six-goal avalanche yet it was soon Wolves turn to feel demoralised. They were involved in a goalless draw 48 hours later as tough inside-forward Dorsett made his farewell, then promptly lost four in a row.

Wolves produced championship form with seven straight victories including one at Everton when Wright scored within 20 seconds, no opponent having touched the ball. Middlesbrough then won at Molineux and Wolves trailed at Charlton with not long remaining, only to blast in four quick goals to prove they had not gone off the boil. There was a significant win over Man Utd thanks to two more late goals and some fine saves by Williams, with another top-of-the-table meeting immediately to follow. Wolves went on a 5-1 rampage at Liverpool, who had Sidlow between the posts, to replace the Scousers at the head of D1. Westcott scored four in both that match and the next, but traffic problems prevented him getting to Chelsea where Wolves won anyway. A Christmas double over Sunderland and other good results pushed Wolves towards 34/38 points before they finally crashed at Brentford, though they recovered to beat Leeds and Stoke with 55,592 seeing the latter.

Things were going so well for Wolves that they could give teams like Preston a goal start and yet beat them with ease, the ball-playing Ramscar netting in that game. After 32 matches Wolves led with 46 points, followed by Blackpool (36-44) and Liverpool (32-41). There was a considerable backlog of fixtures and a couple of defeats raised question marks, only for Wolves to slaughter Derby and then see off Bolton and Chelsea to ensure they kept their four-point advantage into the month of May.

Wolves drew at Portsmouth, lost at home to Everton then watched a 2-0 lead over Blackburn turned into 3-2 deficit. In the closing moments Galley equalised though both he and Westcott received knocks that afternoon that ended their contributions to the season. A spirited win at Huddersfield indicated Wolves could pull it off after all, victory over Liverpool on May 31st would make certain but they were also strong contenders. Wolves were frustrated beyond measure as they trailed 2-0 despite having the lions share of the play, and although Dunn reduced the arrears in the 65th minute fate seemed to be against them. As it transpired a draw would have been sufficient, Stoke failing to get the points they needed to leap-frog over Liverpool on June 14th.

It was a sad note for Stan Cullis to retire on at the age of 31, a decision that surprised many people in the town. He came from a Wolverhampton family though he was actually born in Ellesmere Port and he gained a reputation as a masterful centre-half with that rare breed of toughness and skill. He had remarkable balance, a most underestimated asset for a footballer, and fans can still vividly recall how he used it so well to wriggle out of awkward situations in his own penalty-area. Westcott also deserved more from a season in which he scored a club record 37 League goals in 35 outings, making him top D1 marksman by eight clear goals with a total that has only been surpassed on two occasions. Wolves were leading D1 scorers with 98 but their haul of 12 points from their last 12 matches was not good enough, the top four being: Liverpool 57, Man Utd 56, Wolves 56 and Stoke 55.

CUP: Wolves eased past D3N Rotherham only for another Yorkshire side, Sheff Utd, to knock them out in the fourth round as their goal-touch suddenly deserted them. To add to the misery the first tie with Sheffield was the final appearance for Morris, a man famed for running backwards at speed. He had hurt himself at Everton and aggravated matters by playing on, the Cup heralding his comeback but he was forced to hang his boots up.

RESULTS: (Opponents in block letters denotes Wolves at home) ARSENAL 6-1 (Pye 3, Westcott 2, Mullen); Grimsby 0-0; Blackpool 0-2; VILLA 1-2 (Pye); BRENTFORD 1-2 (Westcott); Villa 0-3; Blackburn 2-1 (Westcott 2); GRIMSBY 2-0 (Pye 2); PORTSMOUTH 3-1 (Westcott, Galley, King); Everton 2-0 (Wright, Westcott); HUDDERSFIELD 6-1 (Pye 2, Westcott, Hancocks, Crook, Galley); LEEDS 1-0 (Hancocks); Stoke 3-0 (Pye 2, Mullen); MIDDLESBROUGH 2-4 (Mullen, Pye); Charlton 4-1 (Westcott 2, Mullen 2); SHEFF UTD 3-1 (Westcott 2, Pye); Preston 2-2 (Forbes 2); MAN UTD 3-2 (Westcott 2, Hancocks); Liverpool 5-1 (Westcott 4, Mullen); BOLTON 5-0 (Westcott 4, Pye); Chelsea 2-1 (Forbes, Mullen); Sunderland 1-0 (Hancocks); SUNDERLAND 2-1 (Galley, King); Arsenal 1-1 (King); BLACKPOOL 3-1 (Pye, Forbes, Mullen); FAC ROTHERHAM 3-0 (Pye, Hancocks, Westcott); Brentford 1-4 (Westcott); FAC SHEFF UTD 0-0; FAC Sheff Utd 0-2; Leeds 1-0 (Westcott); STOKE 3-0 (Westcott, Mullen, Forbes); Middlesbrough 1-1 (Westcott); CHARLTON 2-0 (Mullen, Westcott); Sheff Utd 0-2; PRESTON 4-1 (Westcott, Pye, Ramscar, Hancocks); Man Utd 1-3 (Westcott); Derby 1-2 (Westcott); DERBY 7-2 (Pye 3, Westcott 2, Forbes, Hancocks); Bolton 3-0 (Hancocks, Pye, Mullen); CHELSEA 6-4 (Hancocks 2, Forbes 2, Westcott 2); Portsmouth 1-1 (Westcott); EVERTON 2-3 (Mullen, Westcott); BLACKBURN 3-3 (Westcott, Pye, Galley); Huddersfield 1-0 (Hancocks) & LIVERPOOL 1-2 (Dunn).

RECORD: PLD 45 W 26 D 7 L 12 F 101 A 58 (16-2-5 & 10-5-7).

SCORERS: Westcott 38, Pye 21, Mullen 12, Hancocks 11, Forbes 8, Galley 4, King 3, Crook 1, Dunn 1, Ramscar 1 & Wright 1.

INTERNATIONALS: Wright established himself by participating in every England match and Mullen also made his full debut, Westcott having to be content with a goal for the FLXI. Apps: Mullen (E 1), Westcott (FL 1) & Wright (E 8 + FL 1).

FAREWELLS: Alderton 11-0 (Coventry), Cullis 40-0, Dorsett 1-0 (Villa), King 9-3 (Northampton), McIntosh 3-0 (Birmingham), Miller 2-0 (Derby), Morris 11-0, Ramscar 17-1 (QPR) & Ratcliffe 2-0 (Plymouth). The numbers are the appearances and goals of the player in post-war competitive games for Wolves and the club in brackets are the ones they moved on to. These men all made their last appearance in the first team in 1946-47 and did not necessarily leave Wolves this season.

1947 - 48

DEBUTANTS: Gordon Brice (Luton), Laurie Kelly, Les Mynard, Bill Shorthouse, Alex Simpson, Leslie Smith, Sammy Smyth (Linfield), Terry Springthorpe & Ernie Stevenson. Simpson was born in Scotland and Smyth in Ireland.

SUMMARY: Wolves performed well under the leadership of Wright without quite attaining the high standards of 1946-47. Cullis served an apprenticeship as assistant manager to Vizard who resigned in June, 1948, leaving the way clear for Cullis to take over his role.

LEAGUE: 5th (47). Wolves derived nothing from a seven-goal thriller at Man City, where that versatile man by the name of Galley scored his last goal for the team he had served so skilfully. Prospects were bleak as Wolves fell behind in the first minute against Grimsby — they replied eight times though! All five forwards found a route past Blackburn's defence before Forbes was brought in at Grimsby to show he could do it too as Wolves made it 20 goals in their opening four games. Wolves drew at the popular seaside resort of Blackpool only for Middlesbrough to inflict another painful Molineux blow. A single goal in each of the next three matches was sufficient and a draw at Everton left Wolves well placed for an assault on the title, having gained 14/20 points.

Hopes were dashed by the next quartet of results, beginning with the 5-1 reverse at Charlton that was partly due to an injury to Williams, Smyth taking over in goal. Wolves then scored once for the seventh time in succession to draw with in-form Arsenal at Molineux, a clash that attracted 55,998 while the average at the ground was more than 50,000 at this stage. Another point was dropped at Bramall Lane before Wolves limitations were cruelly exposed by Man Utd.

Inconsistency was the theme for the next few months, though Wolves did complete a fine seasonal double over Villa with 65,000 at Birmingham and many locked outside. In the latter stages of 1947-48 Wolves managed four wins running only to lose the 42nd fixture 2-1 to Liverpool again, not that the circumstances were so dramatic this year. Although Arsenal were clear champions this lively finish did enable Wolves to be in the top five for the fifth consecutive season. They were top D1 scorers on 83 despite the transfer of Westcott, no less than seven of their staff notching eight or more goals.

CUP: Wolves began at D3S Bournemouth, duly coming off best on their first trip to Boscombe. Their full title then was in fact Bournemouth and Boscombe Athletic, though with 22 letters the biggest name in the Football League is now of course Wolverhampton Wanderers. In the fourth round Wolves had to settle for a draw as Hancocks had a penalty brilliantly saved by the Everton goalkeeper, the replay bringing more disappointment. Leading 2-1 with a minute left Wolves conceded the equaliser, with injuries to Mullen and McLean proving to great a burden to carry in extra time.

RESULTS: Man City 3-4 (Hancocks, Galley, Westcott); GRIMSBY 8-1 (Pye 3, Smyth 2, Westcott 2, Hancocks); BLACKBURN 5-1 (Smyth, Westcott, Hancocks, Pye, Mullen); Grimsby 4-0 (Forbes 2, Hancocks, Pye); Blackpool 2-2 (Forbes, Hancocks); MIDDLESBROUGH 1-3 (Mullen); DERBY 1-0 (Pye); Huddersfield 1-0 (Pye); CHELSEA 1-0 (Forbes); Everton 1-1 (Hancocks); Charlton 1-5 (Mullen); ARSENAL 1-1 (Pye); Sheff Utd 2-2 (Wright, Smyth); MAN UTD 2-6 (Dunn, Hancocks); Burnley 1-1 (Mullen); PORTSMOUTH 3-1 (Forbes 2, Mullen); Preston 3-1 (Forbes, Pye, McLean); STOKE 1-2 (Pye); Bolton 2-3 (Smyth, Mullen); LIVERPOOL 1-2 (Forbes); MAN CITY 1-0 (Westcott); Villa 2-1 (Westcott, Hancocks); VILLA 4-1 (Hancocks 2, Mullen, Westcott); Middlesbrough 4-2 (Westcott 3, Hancocks); Blackburn 0-1; FAC Bournemouth 2-1 (Mullen 2); BLACKPOOL 1-1 (Hancocks); FAC EVERTON 1-1 (Westcott); FAC Everton 2-3 (Westcott 2); HUDDERSFIELD 2-1 (Dunn, Wright); Chelsea 1-1 (Hancocks); EVERTON 2-4 (Dunn, Westcott); CHARLTON 2-0 (Pye, Hancocks); Arsenal 2-5 (Hancocks, Smyth); SHEFF UTD 1-1 (Wright); Man Utd 2-3 (Dunn, Smyth); Sunderland 1-2 (Wright); BURNLEY 1-1 (Dunn); SUNDERLAND 2-1 (Wright, Smyth); Portsmouth 0-2; PRESTON 4-2 (Pye 2, Hancocks, Dunn); Derby 2-1 (Pye, Dunn); Stoke 3-2 (Dunn, Pye, Mullen); BOLTON 1-0 (Dunn) & Liverpool 1-2 (Pye).

RECORD: PLD 45 W 20 D 10 L 15 F 88 A 75 (12-5-5 & 8-5-10).

SCORERS: Hancocks 16, Pye 16, Westcott 14, Mullen 10, Dunn 9, Forbes 8, Smyth 8, Wright 5, Galley 1 & McLean 1.

INTERNATIONALS: Wright remained a regular choice for England, also scoring in their opening 'B' team fixture. Smyth made a memorable debut for Ireland, weighing in with both the goals in the 2-0 win over Scotland while Pye hit the net for the FLXI. Apps: Pye (FL1), Smyth (NI 3) & Wright (E 6 + E 'B' 1).

FAREWELLS: Brice 12-0 (Reading), Elliot 7-0 (Chester), Galley 43-5 (Grimsby), Mynard 3-0 (Derby) & Westcott 63-52 (Blackburn).

1948 - 49

DEBUTANTS: Bill Baxter, Alf Crook, Dennis Parsons, Eddie

Russell, Nigel Sims & Dennis Wilshaw. Baxter was born in Scotland.

SUMMARY: The F. A. Cup returned to Wolverhampton after 41 years to give Wolves a marvellous start under the command of Cullis. Wolves continued to be a fine D1 team but lacked the consistency of champions, though they were attractive enough for crowds to aggregate almost 1,100,000 this season.

LEAGUE: 6th (46). Newly-promoted Birmingham gave Wolves a scare on the opening day, being 2-1 up until Smyth nipped in with a late opportunist goal. Wolves further disenchanted their supporters against Sunderland before starting the away programme with a 5-0 romp at Bolton. The home 'duck' was broken at the fourth attempt after a good recovery against Man Utd on a very wet night. Victory at Blackpool made it 11 goals in three away games and 9/14 points in all.

Wolves emerged from a brief dodgy spell to thrash Huddersfield only to find that Middlesbrough still had a liking for the Molineux atmosphere. Portsmouth were on their way to the title yet slumped in Wolverhampton and by Christmas a situation of normality had gradually developed in that Wolves were actually doing better at home, as illustrated by the Villa results.

In 1949 the happenings in the League often took a back seat though there were some notable matches. An eight-goal spectacular at Middlesbrough was followed by a 3-0 win over Newcastle, Wilshaw celebrating his debut with a second half hatrick. Any thoughts Wolves harboured of completing a double against Portsmouth disappeared when they had to field an under-strength team at Fratton Park, losing 5-0. At least the Easter visit from Sheff Utd saw Wolves in their more customary role of handing out the punishment. With the Cup secured a large crowd greeted visitors Preston though the final three games proved an anti-climax.

CUP: D2 Chesterfield posed no problems, Wolves then leaping into the QF at the expense of Sheff Utd and Liverpool. A rare Cup success over D2 Albion was watched by 55,684 and then 62,250 went to Hillsborough as Wolves tackled holders Man Utd in an outstanding SF. They quickly struck the first blow through Smyth but it did not take long for United to cancel it out. Pritchard was limping on the wing having briefly left the field after an early knock, so Wolves were pleased with the 1-1 interval score. United took control in the second half as Wolves temporarily lost Kelly, carried off with splints placed on his right leg. Like his full-back partner Pritchard he bravely returned to keep United at bay as Wolves hung on in extra-time, Shorthouse playing superbly. In the replay Alf Crook and Springthorpe came in for the injured duo and Smyth got the decider that few of the 72,476 at Goodison Park would begrudge. Meanwhile, Leicester rounded off a sterling run by beating Portsmouth 3-1 despite being 19th in D2.

FINAL: There had been 617 entrants and 98,920 folk paid £39,300 to see the all-Midlands final. Wolves showed no complacency after their previous Wembley flop and took a 13th-minute lead when PYE, who had been preferred to Wilshaw, headed in an inch-perfect Hancocks centre. Heroics by the Leicester goalkeeper kept Wolves out until almost half-time, when PYE collected the ball with his back to goal and turned to slam it home. Leicester brought the game to life in the 55th minute by courtesy of GRIFFITHS, and within minutes believed they were level only for a narrow offside decision to rule it out. A stunning individual goal by SMYTH made it 3-1 to end any worries for Wright's men. Team: Williams, Pritchard, Springthorpe, W. Crook, Shorthouse, Wright, Hancocks, Smyth, Pye, Dunn & Mullen.

RESULTS: BIRMINGHAM 2-2 (Pye, Smyth); SUNDERLAND 0-1; Bolton 5-0 (Hancocks 2, Mullen 2, Pye); Sunderland 3-3 (Hancocks 2, Pye); LIVERPOOL 0-0; MAN UTD 3-2 (Hancocks 2, Smyth); Blackpool 3-1 (Smyth 2, Dunn); Man Utd 0-2; DERBY 2-2 (Hancocks, Mullen); Arsenal 1-3 (Smyth); HUDDERSFIELD 7-1 (Pye 3, Forbes 2, Hancocks 2); MIDDLESBROUGH 0-3; Newcastle 1-3 (Smyth); PORTSMOUTH 3-0 (Wright, Hancocks, Smyth); Man City 3-3 (Pye, OG, Smyth); CHARLTON 2-0 (Wright, Smyth); Stoke 1-2 (Smith); BURNLEY 3-0 (Smyth, Mullen, Pye); Preston 1-1 (Pye); EVERTON 1-0 (Pye); Chelsea 1-4 (Hancocks); Birmingham 1-0 (Pye); VILLA 4-0 (Pye 2, Smyth 2); Villa 1-5 (Dunn); BOLTON 2-0 (Mullen 2); FAC CHESTERFIELD 6-0 (Pye 2, Smyth 2, Hancocks, Mullen); BLACKPOOL 2-1 (Pye, Dunn); FAC Sheff Utd 3-0 (Hancocks 2, Dunn); Derby 2-3 (Smyth 2); FAC LIVERPOOL 3-1 (Dunn, Smyth, Mullen); ARSENAL 1-3 (Pye); FAC ALBION 1-0 (Mullen); Middlesbrough 4-4 (Pye 2, Smyth, Mullen); NEWCASTLE 3-0 (Wilshaw 3); Burnley 0-0; FAC Man Utd 1-1 (Smyth); FAC Man Utd 1-0 (Smyth); Liverpool 0-0; STOKE 3-1 (Wilshaw 2, Dunn); Charlton 3-2 (Wilshaw 2, Smyth); Portsmouth 0-5; Sheff Utd 1-1 (Mullen); SHEFF UTD 6-0 (Mullen 2, Dunn 2, Wilshaw 2); MAN CITY 1-1 (Wilshaw); FAC Leicester 3-1 (Pye 2, Smyth); PRESTON 2-1 (Mullen, Hancocks); Everton 0-1; Huddersfield 0-4 & CHELSEA 1-1 (Mullen).

RECORD: PLD 49 W 23 D 13 L 13 F 97 A 69 (16-5-3 & 7-8-10).

SCORERS: Smyth 22, Pye 21, Hancocks 15, Mullen 15, Wilshaw 10, Dunn 8, Forbes 2, Wright 2, Smith 1 & OG 1.

INTERNATIONALS: Hancocks scored a brace on his debut in the 6-0 crushing of poor Switzerland while other England goal-men were Wright and Mullen. Early in the season Wright had become captain, being informed of the glad tidings by a clippie on the bus who had a newspaper. Williams made his full debut and was amongst a Wolves trio in both that and the 'B' side, for whom Wilshaw scored twice and Mullen once. Apps: Hancocks (E 1), Mullen (E 2 + E 'B' 1), Smyth (NI 2), Williams (E 1 + E 'B' 1), Wilshaw (E 'B' 1) & Wright (E 8 + FL 1).

FAREWELLS: Alf Crook 2-0, Simpson 2-0 (Southampton) & Stevenson 9-0 (Cardiff).

1949 - 50

DEBUTANTS: Ken Rowley, Roy Swinbourne & Johnny Walker. Walker was born in Scotland.

SUMMARY: Wolves were unbeaten in their opening 13 matches, the latter being the F.A. Charity Shield draw with Portsmouth at neutral Highbury which was the 11th game in a row that Wolves conceded a single goal. Sadly, they lost the more important battle with the Southerners when they became only the second team ever to be denied the English Championship on goal-average. Attendances totalled 1,100,000 with nine crowds of more than 50,000 making 17 in two seasons, and as in 1946-47 there were no gates under 30,000. Wolves were second in the Central League too, having to settle for winning the SSC.

LEAGUE: 2nd (53). Mullen's swerver and a 25-yarder from Hancocks put Wolves in the driving seat at Fulham, though they were hanging on grimly by the end of the contest. Wolves kept winning tight games and made it 6/6 by sending Middlesbrough back unhappy, which prompted the locals to believe it was their year at last. The Huddersfield result underlined their confidence and Wolves consolidated their lead when a Williams penalty save ensured the points against Derby. Wolves had 20 compared to the 17 of Liverpool and 14 of Man Utd, which was a large advantage after just 11 matches.

Wolves draw with Albion attracted 56,661 yet this 12th outing without defeat was the first of 12 without victory! This included a quartet of 1-1 scorelines during which Liverpool created a then D1 record of being unbeaten for the first 18 fixtures of a season. Swinbourne stopped the slide against Villa but despite lowering the colours of Portsmouth only eight points were gathered from the next eight games. However, nobody was dominating matters and three wins put Wolves well back in contention. They lost valuable ground around the Easter period with only 4/8 points while their rivals hit form, and with 39 matches gone they had to rely on Portsmouth and company making errors.

A white ball was used for the first time in a D1 meeting at Molineux and the Arsenal keeper was forced to pick it up from the back of the net three times within seven minutes. Wolves maintained their slender hopes at Bolton and were level on points with Pompey who had a vastly superior goal-average. Villa went down 5-1 at Fratton Park on the last day while Wolves raced into a 5-0 lead after 35 minutes despite Hancocks missing a penalty. Even if they had continued that incredible scoring rate Wolves would have still suffered another near miss for the title. Their visits to Portsmouth (50,248) and West Brom (60,945) brought in the biggest League crowds at both grounds but they could not add the championship to their records, the top three being: Portsmouth 53, Wolves 53 and Sunderland 52.

CUP: Wolves needed replays to eliminate D2 sides Plymouth and Sheff Utd, coasting 3-0 ahead in the latter tie before being pegged back to 3-3, a Hancocks penalty ending the Blades resistance. In the fifth round it was Wolves who felt aggrieved, losing another replay to Blackpool whose breakthrough looked suspiciously offside.

RESULTS: Fulham 2-1 (Mullen, Hancocks); Charlton 3-2 (Pye, Wright, Forbes); NEWCASTLE 2-1 (Pye, Forbes); CHARLTON 2-1 (Smyth, Wright); Blackpool 2-1 (Mullen, Smyth); MIDDLESBROUGH 3-1 (Hancocks, Dunn, Smyth); Birmingham 1-1 (OG); Everton 2-1 (Mullen, Pye); HUDDERSFIELD 7-1 (Pye 3, Forbes 2, Mullen, Smyth); Portsmouth 1-1 (Pye); Derby 2-1 (Hancocks, Mullen); ALBION 1-1 (Pye); CS Portsmouth 1-1 (Hancocks); Man Utd 0-3; CHELSEA 2-2 (Smyth 2); Stoke 1-2 (Hancocks); BURNLEY 0-0; Sunderland 1-3 (Forbes); LIVERPOOL 1-1 (Wilshaw); Arsenal 1-1 (Mullen); BOLTON 1-1 (Wilshaw); FULHAM 1-1 (Pye); Newcastle 0-2; VILLA 2-3 (Swinbourne, Smyth); Villa 4-1 (Swinbourne 2, Smyth, Pye); BLACKPOOL 3-0 (Pye, Mullen, Hancocks); FAC Plymouth 1-1 (Smyth); FAC PLYMOUTH 3-0 (Swinbourne, Hancocks, Smyth); Middlesbrough 0-2; EVERTON 1-1 (Wilshaw); FAC SHEFF UTD 0-0; FAC Sheff Utd 4-3 (Hancocks 2, Smyth, Mullen); Huddersfield 0-1; FAC BLACKPOOL 0-0; FAC Blackpool 0-1; PORTSMOUTH 1-0 (McLean); DERBY 4-1 (Walker 2, Pye 2); Albion 1-1 (Hancocks); SUNDERLAND 1-3 (Smyth); Liverpool 2-0 (Hancocks, Swinbourne); STOKE 2-1 (Hancocks, Swinbourne); Burnley 1-0 (Walker); MAN UTD 1-1 (Walker); Man City 1-2 (Walker); MAN CITY 3-0 (Swinbourne, Hancocks, Pye); Chelsea 0-0; ARSENAL 3-0 (Walker 2, Pye); Bolton 4-2 (Hancocks, Wright, Pye, Mullen) & BIRMINGHAM 6-1 (Pye 2, Mullen 2, Walker, Swinbourne).

RECORD: PLD 49 W 22 D 17 L 10 F 85 A 55 (12-10-2 & 10-7-8).

SCORERS: Pye 18, Hancocks 14, Smyth 12, Mullen 11, Swinbourne 8, Walker 8, Forbes 5, Wilshaw 3, Wright 3, Dunn 1, McLean 1 & OG 1.

INTERNATIONALS: Wolves boasted six Full Internationals with Smyth ploughing a lone furrow for Ireland and scoring three times, including both as Scotland battered them 8-2. Wright and Mullen were on target for England, the latter having come on as their first-ever substitute, while Pye made his debut. In the heartbreaking 1950 World Cup Finals both Wright and Williams played in England's three games and Mullen was chosen for two of them. They had been given a good chance of winning the trophy at the first attempt yet amazingly flopped 1-0 to the United States, Mullen having a shot that seemingly crossed the line though not even a draw would have been enough. Wolves also provided a trio for an England 'B' XI and the Inter-League side, but were not represented when the FLXI beat the League of Ireland 7-0 at Molineux. Apps: Hancocks (E 1 + FL 1), Mullen (E 3 + E 'B' 2), Pye (E 1 + E 'B' 3), Smyth (NI 3), Williams (E 9 + FL 1) & Wright (E 10 + FL 1 + E 'B' 1).

FAREWELLS: Forbes 75-23 (Preston), Kelly 69-0 (Huddersfield), Rowley 3-0 (Birmingham) & Springthorpe 38-0 (Coventry).

1950 - 51

DEBUTANTS: Peter Broadbent (Brentford) & John Short.

SUMMARY: It was a reasonable sort of season, highlighted by a 10-match unbeaten spree, up until March 14th. On that date Wolves narrowly missed out on a trip to Wembley and from then on slid down the table alarmingly. This caused them to fall around 8,000 short of having a million clicks at the turnstiles again, though the reserves lasted the pace better to top the Central League.

LEAGUE: 14th (38). A rasping Crook shot and a Swinbourne header removed the first obstacle in the shape of Liverpool.\Wolves won at Derby but defeats from Fulham and Derby in a quick return put them back to square one. Hancocks re-signed after being upset at the terms offered and his belated start to 1950-51 lifted the team against Bolton. Useful results ensued culminating in victory over champions-to-be Tottenham at Molineux. Unfortunately, Wolves then had three bad results which were completed by Middlesbrough's fourth post-war win in Wolverhampton.

During Wolves best part of the campaign Hancocks roasted Albion with a hatrick and in the festive season Wolves twice celebrated by quickly going 2-0 ahead against Huddersfield. With 32 points from 25 games Wolves had to come good at White Hart Lane to remain in the title chase, the majority of the 67,000 present feeling relieved as they were pipped 2-1. Two more setbacks followed before Wolves retaliated with a 4-0 jaunt, leaving them confident of extending their sequence of top six finishes.

A mere 4/26 points were mustered as Wolves lurched to a sorry 14th, salvaging nothing at all from their last five appearances at Molineux. Yet the disappointing 1950-51 could so easily have been a different story as 18 of the 19 defeats were by the odd goal, the exception being only 2-0. Having pulled in 55,364 spectators for the visit of Tottenham and 55,648 against Arsenal the decline was emphasised by the fact under half that number saw the final home fixture with Newcastle.

CUP: Wolves ousted D3S Plymouth at the first attempt this year and there were three big Molineux crowds to watch them march towards the SF in style. They then had to overcome Newcastle at Hillsborough and Swinbourne soon found the net, only for Glaswegian Walker to be deemed offside. There was a similar incident at the other end, while throughout the tie Hancocks was unlucky not to break the deadlock. In the replay at Huddersfield there was a dream start, Walker getting his fifth Cup goal, but late in the first half Newcastle dramatically scored twice in a minute and went on to make a successful journey to Wembley.

RESULTS: LIVERPOOL 2-0 (Crook, Swinbourne); Derby 2-1 (Walker 2); Fulham 1-2 (Swinbourne); DERBY 2-3 (Dunn, Pye); BOLTON 7-1 (Swinbourne 3, Hancocks 2, Dunn, Mullen); SUNDERLAND 2-1 (Hancocks, Pye); Blackpool 1-1 (Swinbourne); SPURS 2-1 (Swinbourne, Hancocks); Charlton 2-3 (Swinbourne, Mullen); MAN UTD 0-0; MIDDLESBROUGH 3-4 (Swinbourne, Hancocks, Dunn); Sheff Wed 2-2 (Hancocks, Mullen); CHELSEA 2-1 (Hancocks, Swinbourne); Portsmouth 4-1 (Walker 2, Hancocks 2); ARSENAL 0-1; Burnley 0-2; EVERTON 4-0

(Swinbourne, Dunn, Hancocks, Mullen); Stoke 1-0 (Dunn); ALBION 3-1 (Hancocks 3); Newcastle 1-1 (Hancocks); Liverpool 4-1 (Walker 2, Wilshaw, Swinbourne); FULHAM 1-1 (Wilshaw); Huddersfield 2-1 (Walker, Swinbourne); HUDDERSFIELD 3-1 (Hancocks, Dunn, Swinbourne); FAC Plymouth 2-1 (Dunn, Walker); BLACKPOOL 1-1 (Walker); Spurs 1-2 (Walker); FAC VILLA 3-1 (Walker, Swinbourne, Mullen); CHARLTON 2-3 (Walker, Mullen); FAC HUDDERSFIELD 2-0 (Dunn 2); Man Utd 1-2 (Wilshaw); FAC Sunderland 1-1 (Walker); FAC SUNDERLAND 3-1 (Dunn, Swinbourne, Walker); SHEFF WED 4-0 (Swinbourne 2, Hancocks 2); FAC Newcastle 0-0; FAC Newcastle 1-2 (Walker); PORTSMOUTH 2-3 (Walker, Swinbourne); Arsenal 1-2 (Wilshaw); VILLA 2-3 (Wilshaw, Hancocks); Villa 0-1; BURNLEY 0-1; Everton 1-1 (Pye); Middlesbrough 2-1 (Swinbourne 2); STOKE 2-3 (Smith, Dunn); Albion 2-3 (Broadbent, Hancocks); Chelsea 1-2 (Swinbourne); Bolton 1-2 (Pye); NEWCASTLE 0-1 & Sunderland 0-0.

RECORD: PLD 49 W 19 D 10 L 20 F 86 A 67 (12-3-9 & 7-7-11).

SCORERS: Swinbourne 22, Hancocks 19, Walker 16, Dunn 11, Mullen 6, Wilshaw 5, Pye 4, Broadbent 1, Crook 1 & Smith 1.

CENTRAL LEAGUE: PLD 42 W 30 D 3 L 9 F 110 A 35 PTS 63.

SCORERS: Whitfield 29, Smyth 17, Wilshaw 14, Smith 12, Walker 12, Rowley 9, Pye 5, Mullen 3, Long 2, Baxter 1, Broadbent 1, Clark 1, Crook 1, McLean 1, Russell 1 & Taylor 1.

INTERNATIONALS: Williams was the only England ever-present as Wright missed two games through injury and was surprisingly omitted from another, though he did have the consolation of scoring once. Apps: Hancocks (E 1 + FL 1), Williams (E 6 + FL 1) & Wright (E 3 + FL2).

FAREWELLS: McLean 156-2 & Russell 35-0 (Middlesbrough). ANGUS McLEAN was the first man to depart from the club having made over 100 post-war appearances, 44 of them being when he topped the chart in 1946-47. He was born in Queensferry though his parents were Scottish, and he joined Wolves during the war. McLean was a sturdy right-back who was as tough as they came, nevertheless cartilage trouble disrupted his 1948-49 campaign and prevented him from playing at Wembley. He finally moved to Aberystwyth Town, where he was given the job of player-manager.

1951 - 52

DEBUTANTS: Brian Birch (Man Utd), Malcolm Clews, Norman Deeley, Len Gibbons, Bill Guttridge, Eddie Stuart & Ken Whitfield. Stuart was born in South Africa.

SUMMARY: Most of the light in 1951-52 was provided by the new flourescent shirts Wolves wore on the darker afternoons. There was an unusual spell of seven away draws in a row before another dreadful finish upset the fans. At least the younger element at the club did well, retaining the Central League and taking the SSC for the 10th time outright with a record final score of 9-0 against Stoke.

LEAGUE: 16th (38). A Maine Road stalemate got proceedings under way and then Derby were responsible for Wolves Molineux misery continuing from 1950-51. The jinx was happily ended when Arsenal visited town and there was revenge at Derby before Blackpool just had the edge in a fine game at Bloomfield Road.

Wolves soon found their rhythm with victories over Liverpool and Portsmouth a prelude to scoring 18 in four games. They were moving in the right direction with15/22 points and had even given Huddersfield a 7-1 coshing for the third time in four seasons - the latest coming at Leeds Road.

It all turned sour with four defeats followed by three 2-2 draws, then there was a welcome trouncing of Middlesbrough and a couple more 2-2 results. Guttridge was introduced for the Villa clashes while another player trying to make a first-team breakthrough, Whitfield, scored a hatrick against Blackpool. These were to be his only League goals for the club. Wolves were involved in three 1-1 draws to make it nine score-draws in 12 matches, then improved very slightly to reach 36 points with nine games remaining and a place in the top half looking a certainty.

Lightning struck twice as Wolves gained a pathetic two points more to crash down to 16th, though their total of 38 was as near to the fourth side as the 21st. The Burnley encounter was watched by 16,737 which was the first Molineux attendance of under 20,000 since the war. Stuart made a good debut at centre-forward against Albion, only for the team itself to perform in a way that typified the closing weeks of 1951-52. England's champions this term were Manchester United.

CUP: Wolves were always in control of their third round replay with Man City that pulled in a large crowd despite being staged on a Wednesday afternoon in days of little unemployment and, officially, not much freedom for the workers to have time off when they wished. Wolves reward was a journey to Anfield where a 61,905 record gate was set up and the hosts emerged as victors.

RESULTS: Man City 0-0; DERBY 1-2 (Hancocks); ARSENAL 2-1 (Hancocks, Swinbourne); Derby 3-1 (Wilshaw 2, Dunn); Blackpool 2-3 (Mullen, Smyth); LIVERPOOL 2-1 (Pye, Wilshaw); Portsmouth 3-2 (Hancocks, Mullen, Dunn); CHELSEA 5-3 (Pye 2, Dunn, Wilshaw, Hancocks); Huddersfield 7-1 (Dunn 3, Mullen 2, Pye, Hancocks); Newcastle 1-3 (Walker); BOLTON 5-1 (Pye 3, Hancocks, Dunn); Stoke 0-1; MAN UTD 0-2; Spurs 2-4 (Pye, Mullen); PRESTON 1-4 (Mullen); Burnley 2-2 (Pye 2); CHARLTON 2-2 (Dunn, Swinbourne); Fulham 2-2 (Pye, Smith); MIDDLESBROUGH 4-0 (Pye 2, Mullen, Swinbourne); MAN CITY 2-2 (Smith 2); Arsenal 2-2 (Walker, Smith); Villa 3-3 (Smith, Wilshaw, Baxter); VILLA 1-2 (Smith); BLACKPOOL 3-0 (Whitfield 3); Sunderland 1-1 (Mullen); Liverpool 1-1 (Smith); FAC Man City 2-2 (Broadbent, Whitfield); FAC MAN CITY 4-1 (Short 2, Mullen 2); PORTSMOUTH 1-1

(Broadbent); Chelsea 1-0 (Hancocks); FAC Liverpool 1-2 (Mullen); HUDDERSFIELD 0-0; NEWCASTLE 3-0 (Hancocks 2, Dunn); SUNDERLAND 0-3; Bolton 2-2 (Mullen, Pye); STOKE 3-0 (Hancocks 2, Mullen); Man Utd 0-2; SPURS 1-1 (Pye); Preston 0-3; BURNLEY 1-2 (Hancocks); Charlton 0-1; Albion 1-2 (Birch); ALBION 1-4 (Stuart); FULHAM 2-2 (Swinbourne, Mullen) & Middlesbrough 0-4.

RECORD: PLD 45 W 13 D 15 L 17 F 80 A 78 (9-6-7 & 4-9-10).

SCORERS: Pye 15, Mullen 14, Hancocks 12, Dunn 9, Smith 7, Wilshaw 5, Swinbourne 4, Whitfield 4, Broadbent 2, Short 2, Walker 2, Baxter 1, Birch 1, Smyth 1 & Stuart 1.

CENTRAL LEAGUE: PLD 42 W 27 D 6 L 9 F 101 A 48 PTS 60.
SCORERS: Smith 17, Walker 16, Whitfield 12, Wilshaw 9, Hancocks 8, Swinbourne 7, Clews 6, Stuart 5, Broadbent 4, Short 4, Stockin 4, Crook 2, Baxter 1, Birch 1, Deeley 1, Long 1, Price 1, Smyth 1 & Taylor 1.

INTERNATIONALS: Wright settled back into the England routine and capped the season with his 43rd appearance — a record for his country. Apps: Williams (E 2) & Wright (E 8 + FL 2).

FAREWELLS: Birch 3-1 (Lincoln), Clews 1-0 (Lincoln), Parsons 27-0 (Villa), Pye 209-95 (Luton), Smyth 119-43 (Stoke) & Walker 44-26 (Southampton). JESSE PYE was from the Rotherham area though he was quickly accepted by the Wolverhampton public after his spectacular League debut. The fuzzy-haired centre-forward could be subtle or aggressive, whatever the situation demanded, and rarely let the side down. Pye continued to score with great regularity until he moved for £5,000 at the age of 30.

SAMMY SMYTH was snapped up from the Irish League having been born in Belfast, and he adapted well to his new surroundings. The tireless inside-forward reached his peak in 1948-49 when he did everything but get a hatrick, being equal top of the appearances chart on 46. He did not get into the first team very often after 1949-50 yet Smyth commanded a £25,000 fee when he left, aged 26.

1952 - 53

DEBUTANTS: Ron Flowers, Bill Slater (Brentford), Ron Stockin (Walsall) & John Taylor (Luton).

SUMMARY: Wolves re-discovered their touch in the League only to narrowly miss out on the big prize for the sixth time. The Castlecroft training ground was opened in 1952 and the improved facilities possibly helped inspire the junior members of the staff, who reached the final of the new Football Association Youth Cup. Their aggregate was 29-0 with the SF results really taking the biscuit, but Wolves took a hammering themselves in the first leg of the final and could only draw the return. England drew 0-0 with Ireland in a Youth International at Molineux, though it was seldom heard of in those days for youngsters from professional clubs to be selected.

Wolves Reserves completed a magnificent hatrick of Central League triumphs.

LEAGUE: 3rd (51). The opening crowd was boosted by a 10,000 Welsh contingent, who sang the praises of newly-promoted Cardiff to no avail. In their eighth game Wolves completed a double over Villa to take their points tally up to 12, their solitary defeat coming at Bolton whose decider came from a harsh free-kick awarded against Chatham.

Liverpool led Wolves on goal-average but Blackpool were rampant at Molineux, despite a goal from Flowers on his debut. Man Utd came to the ground next and were soon 2-0 to the good and another thrashing looked imminent. So it proved, though it was Wolves who won with four goals to spare! A less dramatic meeting with Newcastle saw Wolverhampton sitting proudly at the top of the table when the final whistle blew.

Wolves held on to the position by the skin of their teeth as they dropped points for three matches, and understudy Sims was preferred in goal to Williams for the Man City fixture. In an action-packed game Wolves returned to top gear, Swinbourne blasting in a 20-minute hatrick. Victory at Stoke in the 17th test of the season gave Wolves the breathing space of a two-point lead over their nearest rivals, but the goal supply temporarily dried up until the visit to Sheff Wed, where a severe snowstorm caused a four-minute stoppage. At Cardiff there was little opportunity for Wolves attack to prosper, the acrobatics of Williams earning Wolves a point. In the next quartet of matches it was Wolves defence that got into bad habits, twice conceding five to reduce their championship aspirations.

Suddenly, the magic formula was restored as Wolves collected 13/18 points to go back to the head of D1. It was therefore strange that the visit to Chelsea in this spell attracted only 13,957 to Molineux. In the latter of these games the fast-falling Liverpool were finished off by a typical wing-to-wing move, Mullen providing the ammunition for Hancocks to fire home.

A defeat at Manchester and a draw at Portsmouth left Wolves with it all to do again, as the likes of Arsenal and Preston found some consistency in a term that saw no outstanding club. Though Wolves rallied to produce four good results they had failed once more and when they lost on the last day it was purely academic, top three: Arsenal 54, Preston 54 and Wolves 51.

CUP: Wolves received a tough draw at Preston, though the people who travelled up to Deepdale to support them were entitled to a better display than the one they were given.

RESULTS: CARDIFF 1-0 (Mullen); BOLTON 3-1 (Swinbourne 2, Broadbent); Charlton 2-2 (Hancocks, Swinbourne); Bolton 1-2 (Swinbourne); ARSENAL 1-1 (Swinbourne); VILLA 2-1 (Taylor, Broadbent); Derby 3-2 (Hancocks, Mullen, Swinbourne); Villa 1-0 (Mullen); BLACKPOOL 2-5 (Flowers, Swinbourne); Chelsea 2-1 (Smith, Wilshaw); MAN UTD 6-2 (Swinbourne 3, Wilshaw 2, Mullen); NEWCASTLE 2-0 (Broadbent, OG); Albion 1-1 (Smith); MIDDLESBROUGH 3-3 (Smith,

Wilshaw, Swinbourne); Liverpool 1-2 (Broadbent); MAN CITY 7-3 (Swinbourne 3, Smith 2, Wilshaw, Mullen); Stoke 2-1 (Swinbourne, Mullen); PRESTON 0-2; Burnley 0-0; SPURS 0-0; Sheff Wed 3-2 (Smith, Slater, Swinbourne); Cardiff 0-0; SUNDERLAND 1-1 (Swinbourne); Sunderland 2-5 (Broadbent, Smith); CHARLTON 1-2 (Swinbourne); FAC Preston 2-5 (Wilshaw, Smith); Arsenal 3-5 (Hancocks 2, Mullen); DERBY 3-1 (Hancocks, Wilshaw, Mullen); SHEFF WED 3-1 (Hancocks, Wilshaw, OG); Blackpool 0-2; CHELSEA 2-2 (Stockin, Wilshaw); Man Utd 3-0 (Mullen 2, Wilshaw); Newcastle 1-1 (Wilshaw); ALBION 2-0 (Wilshaw 2); Middlesbrough 1-1 (Wilshaw); LIVERPOOL 3-0 (Wright, Swinbourne, Hancocks); Man City 1-3 (Swinbourne); Portsmouth 2-2 (Swinbourne, Slater); STOKE 3-0 (Stockin 2, Wilshaw); PORTSMOUTH 4-1 (Wilshaw 2, Hancocks, Stockin); Preston 1-1 (Slater); BURNLEY 5-1 (Stockin 2, Wilshaw, Hancocks, Mullen) & Spurs 2-3 (Hancocks, Stockin).

RECORD: PLD 43 W 19 D 13 L 11 F 88 A 68 (13-5-3 & 6-8-8).

SCORERS: Swinbourne 21, Wilshaw 18, Mullen 11, Hancocks 10, Smith 8, Stockin 7, Broadbent 5, Slater 3, Flowers 1, Taylor 1, Wright 1 & OG 2.

CENTRAL LEAGUE: PLD 42 W 23 D 12 L 7 F 77 A 46 PTS 58.

SCORERS: Smith 11, Whitfield 11, Taylor 8, Booth 6, Stockin 6, Abthorpe 5, Clews 4, Dunn 4, Baxter 3, Hancocks 3, Walker 3, Birch 2, Broadbent 2, Stuart 2, Wilshaw 2, Cooper 1, Deeley 1, Slater 1 & OG 2.

YOUTH CUP: Wellington 5-0, ALBION 2-0, Birmingham 5-0, DONCASTER 6-0, HUNTLEY & PALMERS 5-0, Huntley & Palmers 6-0, Man Utd 1-7 (Smith) & MAN UTD 2-2 (Smith 2/ Att- 14,208). Team: Owen, Hodgkiss, Clamp, Timmins, Russell, Bolton, Punter, Walker, Smith, Booth & Cooper. In the second leg Howells replaced Walker.

SCORERS: Smith 13, Cooper 6, Booth 5, Punter 3, Walker 2, Clamp 1, Howells 1 & OG 1.

INTERNATIONALS: Wright moved past the 50 mark for England as well as scoring for the FLXI, though he was not on target when they walloped the Irish League 7-1 at Molineux. Apps: Williams (FL 2) & Wright (E 8 + FL 4).

FAREWELLS: Billy Crook 217-2 (Walsall), Dunn 140-39 (Derby), Taylor 10-1 (Notts County) & Whitfield 10-4 (Man City). BILLY CROOK was a wing-half from Wolverhampton who grabbed a rare goal in 1946-47 to settle a Molineux friendly against Sweden's Norrkoping. During the next four seasons he established himself in the first team, unlike his brother, yet continued his civilian career as a draughtsman. He was a very loyal servant to Wolves, eventually departing for £3,000.

JIMMY DUNN also had a brother amongst his colleagues, but they only lined-up together for the reserves. He was a scheming inside-forward from Edinburgh whose career was hampered by a back injury that caused him to miss the majority of 1949-50. However, he recovered to such an extent that when he did leave Wolverhampton the Molineux kitty was boosted by £20,000.

1953 - 54

DEBUTANT: Eddie Clamp.

SUMMARY: England's Football League Champions Wolverhampton Wanderers shrugged off a determined challenge from Albion to bring a smile to the face of Stan Cullis, who had been so close to the title both as a player and a manager. It was 65 years since the League had been formed, the only mystery being why it had taken Wolves so long to win it. In the first Molineux match under floodlights Wolves defeated a South African national XI 3-1, following it up against Celtic (2-0) and Racing Club of Buenos Aires (3-1). There was more success in the Birmingham League and Wolves scored 41 times in reaching the final of the Youth Cup, Joe Bonson getting five of them against Derby. The first leg with Man Utd was a thriller but in Manchester the Reds just about managed to confirm their superiority at this level.

LEAGUE: 1st (57). As the F.A. Cup Final was to be broadcast in 1954, the May 1st fixtures were switched to August 19th when the scoreline of Burnley 4, Wolves 1 did little to inspire confidence. Wolves did not play at Molineux until their fourth game in which a third defeat was on the cards for most of the afternoon before three late goals defied Cardiff. Those few minutes of excitement proved to be something of a turning point for the Wanderers.

Wolves were unbeaten for 18 matches during which their fans were treated to some happy memories: A rare Hancocks header sealed their second win in 22 visits to Highbury; The 8-1 hiding of Chelsea is the Blues record defeat even today; Wolves gained both points at Newcastle which they had not achieved in their previous 10 tries; They edged by v. Albion 1-0 in a tense Molineux derby watched by 56,590 fans and Wolves swept to the top with their only victory in 13 trips to Tottenham. Their run of 18 unbeaten games in D1 and 14 home League wins in a row were both never to be bettered, though Burnley spoiled it all as they completed a double. Wolves still extended their undefeated away spell to 11 to create another club record but they were struggling at Molineux, the Burnley result sparking off a nine-match hiccup that contained five defeats and handed the initiative back to Albion.

Slater played his first match as a professional as Wolves caned Sheff Utd but Albion still led 45-43 on points, Slater then suffering a knock-out for the club. Wolves had thrown away a 2-0 advantage over Newcastle when he put his head in the way of a bullet-like centre to score a dramatic winner. There was no reward at Man Utd on a day that Clamp was introduced, so it was now 48-45 to Albion. Wilshaw got an important goal at Preston only for Wolves to drop a point to Bolton when a mere 19,617 turned up, then see the Middlesbrough forwards continue their Molineux brilliance.

Albion were showing signs of nerves and when Swinbourne twisted round to slam a 58th-minute goal at The Hawthorns they only headed Wolves on goal-average. A fine display against Charlton eased the tension for Wolves and a draw at Sheffield left them two points to the good, a situation not altered by their Easter meetings with Huddersfield.

Only Tottenham stood in their way yet the ground was by no means full on April 24th. The team was unchanged for the fifth consecutive match and Wolves dominated the early stages, though doubts began to creep in as the near misses included a Slater shot being kicked off the line. Swinbourne made the breakthrough after Hancocks and Mullen had combined well and he added another in the second half to end Wolves years of toil and frustration, with Albion losing anyway. Wolves were the only team to have won all three divisions of the League while in D1 they had both the best attack (96) and best defence (56). Wilshaw was fourth = D1 scorer with 26 in his 39 appearances, with Hancocks and Swinbourne also amongst the countries leading nine marksmen. Only two sides managed to finish within eight points of this fine Wolves outfit, top three: Wolves 57, Albion 53 and Huddersfield 51.

CUP: A surprise exit at the hands of D2 Birmingham enabled Wolves to concentrate on the League, as the saying goes.

RESULTS: Burnley 1-4 (Swinbourne); Man City 4-0 (Swinbourne 2, Wilshaw, Slater); Sunderland 2-3 (Hancocks, Wilshaw); CARDIFF 3-1 (Wilshaw, Mullen, Hancocks); SUNDERLAND 3-1 (Wilshaw, Mullen, Swinbourne); Arsenal 3-2 (Broadbent, Wilshaw, Hancocks); LIVERPOOL 2-1 (Swinbourne, Broadbent); PORTSMOUTH 4-3 (Wilshaw 3, Swinbourne); Liverpool 1-1 (Wilshaw); Blackpool 0-0; CHELSEA 8-1 (Hancocks 3, Swinbourne 2, Broadbent, Wilshaw, Mullen); Sheff Utd 3-3 (Hancocks, Wilshaw, Swinbourne); Newcastle 2-1 (Smith, Swinbourne); MAN UTD 3-1 (Hancocks, Broadbent, Swinbourne); Bolton 1-1 (Hancocks); PRESTON 1-0 (Wilshaw); Middlesbrough 3-3 (Swinbourne, Hancocks, Wilshaw); ALBION 1-0 (Mullen); Charlton 2-0 (Broadbent, Hancocks); SHEFF WED 4-1 (Swinbourne 2, Wilshaw, Hancocks); Spurs 3-2 (Wilshaw, Broadbent, Hancocks); BURNLEY 1-2 (Hancocks); MAN CITY 3-1 (Hancocks 2, Wilshaw); VILLA 1-2 (Wiishaw); Villa 2-1 (Hancocks, Wilshaw); Cardiff 3-1 (Swinbourne, Wilshaw, Hancocks); FAC BIRMINGHAM 1-2 (Wilshaw); ARSENAL 0-2; Portsmouth 0-2; BLACKPOOL 4-1 (Swinbourne 3, Hancocks); Chelsea 2-4 (Swinbourne, Wilshaw); SHEFF UTD 6-1 (Swinbourne 2, Hancocks 2, Broadbent, Wilshaw); NEWCASTLE 3-2 (Broadbent, Wilshaw, Slater); Man Utd 0-1; Preston 1-0 (Wilshaw); BOLTON 1-1 (Broadbent); MIDDLESBROUGH 2-4 (Broadbent 2); Albion 1-0 (Swinbourne); CHARLTON 5-0 (Mullen 2, Hancocks 2, Wilshaw); Sheff Wed 0-0; HUDDERSFIELD 4-0 (Mullen, Hancocks, Broadbent, Wilshaw); Huddersfield 1-2 (Wilshaw) & SPURS 2-0 (Swinbourne 2).

RECORD: PLD 43 W 25 D 7 L 11 F 97 A 58 (16-1-5 & 9-6-6).

SCORERS: Wilshaw 27, Hancocks 24, Swinbourne 24, Broadbent 12, Mullen 7, Slater 2 & Smith 1.

YOUTH CUP: STOKE 7-0, DERBY 8-0, SPALDING 11-1, Forest 1-0, Portsmouth 2-1, WEST HAM 6-1, West Ham 2-1, MAN UTD 4-4 (Bonson, Murray, Mason, Fallon/ 18,246) & Man Utd 0-1. Team: Sidebottom, Griffiths, Harris, Bolton, Timmins, Fallon, Round, Mason, Bonson, Cooper & Murray.

SCORERS: Bonson 14, Cooper 9, Mason 7, Murray 4, Asher 2, Bolton 1, Fallon 1, Round 1, Timmins 1 & OG 1.

INTERNATIONALS: Mullen scored four goals for England and took his appearance total to 15 (12), netting a brace in the 4-4 thriller with the Rest of Europe. Wilshaw struck three times, his brace coming on his debut as Wales were crushed 4-1. This pair shared the goals as England beat hosts Switzerland 2-0 in the 1954 WCF, which saw three appearances for Wright, two for Wilshaw and one for Mullen. Sims kept goal for Young England against England in the first of a series of matches, usually on the eve of the F.A. Cup Final, that went on until the late 1960's. England also began life at Under 23 level, Broadbent being selected for the opener. Apps: Broadbent (E U23-1), Mullen (E 6 + FL 1), Sims (YE v E), Wilshaw (E 3 + E 'B' 1) & Wright (E 10 + FL 3).

FAREWELLS: Baxter 47-1 (Villa), Chatham 84-0 (Notts County), Gibbons 29-0, Short 107-2 (Stoke) & Stockin 21-7 (Cardiff). JOHN SHORT was from Barnsley and a product of Wolves Yorkshire nursery team Wath Wanderers, who were formed by Mark Crook, a man whose first team career at Molineux stretched from 1929 to 1934. Short was very much in and out of the side, often filling gaps caused by absences of the regulars. Although his normal position was right-back he was used as a stand-in centre-forward for a 1952 Cup-tie, getting his only goals during his stay at Wolves which ended in an £8,000 transfer.

1954 - 55

DEBUTANTS: Joe Baillie (Bristol City), Colin Booth, Tom McDonald (Hibernian), Peter Russell, George Showell & Doug Taylor (Walsall). Baillie and McDonald were born in Scotland.

SUMMARY: Molineux hosted the Charity Shield which saw Wolves twice let slip two-goal leads as Ronnie Allen scored a hatrick for Albion. This did at least begin a 10-game unbeaten spree for Wolves, who looked capable of retaining their title only to finish the season weakly. Harry Middleton became the club's first Youth International when chosen by England, also scoring eight in three Youth Cup-ties including five as Walsall were bashed 10-0. The senior team won 10-0 too, Swinbourne notching a hatrick against Tel Aviv (Maccabi) but even that result paled into insignificance compared to two friendlies in 1954-55 that began a quartet of nights that seem to be fondly remembered by everyone in the town above the age of 45.

WOLVES V MOSCOW SPARTAK: The first really outstanding continental visitors to Wolverhampton attracted a 55,184 gate in November. The intense media coverage underlined the importance of the event as there were no European competitions for clubs then. The Soviet aces had slightly the better of a goalless first half, in which Wright and Shorthouse in particular kept Wolves chances alive. The tide gradually turned, leading to a 63rd-minute scramble when WILSHAW broke the deadlock. It was all Wolves from then on though the score remained 1-0 five minutes to go, when HANCOCKS clinched matters. The action was far from finished as Wolves really put on the Molineux magic, SWINBOURNE completing a neat move before HANCOCKS made it an astonishing 4-0 success against one of the world's tightest defences.

WOLVES v HONVED: Television cameras were present again in December for the arrival from Budapest of Honved, who fielded six members of the Hungarian team who had gained that historic 6-3 success at Wembley in 1953-54. They had proved it was no fluke by pasting England 7-1 at home, so national pride badly needed restoring. Building quick, controlled attacks Honved were 2-0 up after 14 minutes, to the despair of a crowd that was just a couple short of being the 10th of 55,000 at Molineux since the war. Wolves finally opened their account with a HANCOCKS penalty just after the break, and from then on the atmosphere was electric. Only 15 minutes remained when SWINBOURNE got his head to a Wilshaw lob to give Wolves a deserved equaliser. Within 100 seconds Shorthouse, Smith and Wilshaw combined beautifully to set up SWINBOURNE, who conjured up a fine hooked shot to put Wolves in front as a cresendo of noise filled the stadium. Even the legendary Puskas could not save Honved with the score staying at 3-2, a result that made front page headlines in at least one national paper as Wolves were proclaimed champions of the world!

LEAGUE: 2nd (48). The domestic campaign started with a neat win over Sheff Wed while a draw at Portsmouth was sandwiched in between the Tottenham games, in which Wolves were grateful to Pat Welton who scored an own goal in each of them.

When 55,374 enjoyed Wolves 4-0 taming of Albion, most of them anyway, it rounded off a run of four successive home fixtures and they were truly looking the best team in the country. With 26 points from 19 matches they had a healthy three-point lead at the top when Chelsea, who were also doing well, stunned Wolves at Molineux with two late strikes to transform the game, though Wolves made amends by winning at Leicester and drawing at Sheffield to remain a point clear.

Everton's double over Wolves marred the festive season, the Molineux affair being the first played there on Christmas Day since 1948. Wolves slowly appeared to be getting back on the right track until they came unstuck at Bolton. Right-back Baillie was selected just once for the first team as Wolves beat Huddersfield in a 10-goal classic that would always be remembered by not only him. Superb results against Man Utd and Leicester put Wolves on top again, having played one less than nearest rivals Sunderland.

Chelsea moved into second place as Wolves faltered at Albion, with further signs of panic showing as they only salvaged a point at home to Newcastle 10 seconds from time. Wolves lost to Burnley and were suddenly three points behind Chelsea, though with two games in hand. Showell made his debut against Preston but with Wright, Williams and Wilshaw on international duty another valuable point slipped away. In the crunch meeting at Stamford Bridge attended by 75,043 a second half penalty confirmed that the pendulum had swung in Chelsea's favour.

Wolves then averaged a point-per-game, making it 8/22 in the last sorry chapter of 1954-55. In the end they were only just runners-up and failed to score seven in a match for the first season since 1934-35. Nevertheless, Wolves were leading D1 goalscorers on 89 with Hancocks third= on the individual front, getting 25 in 32 appearances which was incredible for a winger but not enough to keep the title in the Midlands, top four: Chelsea 52, Wolves 48, Portsmouth 48 and Sunderland 48.

CUP: Despite trailing 2-0 to D3N Grimsby after 70 minutes Wolves won in a canter, McDonald scoring on his debut. Wolves 200th F.A. Cup-tie produced their 100th victory as Swinbourne eliminated Arsenal, before Charlton succumbed to a 22-minute Wilshaw hatrick. A difficult QF at Sunderland saw Shorthouse hospitalised after an early incident, leaving the 10 men with too much to do to maintain Wolves Cup interest.

RESULTS: SHEFF WED 4-2 (Swinbourne 2, Mullen, Wilshaw); Spurs 2-3 (Wright, OG); Portsmouth 0-0; SPURS 4-2 (Swinbourne, Wilshaw, Mullen, OG); BLACKPOOL 1-0 (Slater); SUNDERLAND 2-0 (Wilshaw 2); Charlton 3-1 (Slater, Smith, Swinbourne); Sunderland 0-0; BOLTON 1-2 (Smith); Huddersfield 0-2; CS ALBION 4-4 (Swinbourne 2, Deeley, Hancocks); MAN UTD 4-2 (Hancocks 2, Swinbourne, Broadbent); MAN CITY 2-2 (Mullen, Deeley); CARDIFF 1-1 (Slater); ALBION 4-0 (Swinbourne 2, Hancocks 2); Newcastle 3-2 (Smith, Wilshaw, Swinbourne); BURNLEY 5-0 (Swinbourne 2, Flowers 2, Hancocks); Preston 3-3 (Hancocks, Broadbent, Wilshaw); SHEFF UTD 4-1 (Wilshaw, Smith, Hancocks, Broadbent); Arsenal 1-1 (Hancocks); CHELSEA 3-4 (Broadbent, Swinbourne, Hancocks); Leicester 2-1 (Hancocks 2); Sheff Wed 2-2 (Mullen, Wilshaw); EVERTON 1-3 (Wilshaw); Everton 2-3 (Wilshaw, Broadbent);PORTSMOUTH 2-2 (Mullen, Wilshaw); FAC Grimsby 5-2 (Wilshaw 2, Smith, Swinbourne, McDonald); Blackpool 2-0 (Wilshaw, Swinbourne); CHARLTON 2-1 (Hancocks 2); FAC ARSENAL 1-0 (Swinbourne); Bolton 1-6 (Wilshaw); HUDDERSFIELD 6-4 (Hancocks 3, Wilshaw 2, Slater); FAC CHARLTON 4-1 (Wilshaw 3, Hancocks); Man Utd 4-2 (Flowers, Smith, OG, Wilshaw); LEICESTER 5-0 (Hancocks 2, Wilshaw, Swinbourne, Smith); FAC Sunderland 0-2; Albion 0-1; NEWCASTLE 2-2 (Swinbourne, Hancocks); Burnley 0-1; PRESTON 1-1 (Hancocks); Chelsea 0-1; VILLA 1-0 (Flowers); Villa 2-4 (Wilshaw, Hancocks); ARSENAL 3-1 (Hancocks 3); Man City 0-3; Sheff Utd 2-1

(Wilshaw, Hancocks) & Cardiff 2-3 (Wilshaw, Flowers).

RECORD: PLD 47 W 22 D11 L 14 F 103 A 79 (15-6-3 & 7-5-11).

SCORERS: Hancocks 27, Wilshaw 25, Swinbourne 18, Smith 7, Broadbent 5, Flowers 5, Mullen 5, Slater 4, Deeley 2, McDonald 1, Wright 1 & OG 3.

INTERNATIONALS: Wilshaw became the first Englishman to hit four past Scotland at Wembley in a resounding 7-2 home success. There were full debuts for Slater and Flowers, the latter being introduced in France where he was one of a quartet of Wolves players in the England XI. Swinbourne also began to show his mettle on the international scene, scoring on his debut for the 'B' side. Apps: Flowers (E 1 + E v YE + E U23-2), Slater (E 2), Swinbourne (E 'B' 1), Williams (E 5), Wilshaw (E 4) & Wright (E 7 + FL 2).

FAREWELLS: Baillie 1-0 (Leicester), Guttridge 7-0 (Walsall), Pritchard 223-0 (Villa) & Taylor 3-0 (Walsall). ROY PRITCHARD was born in Dawley and came to the club as a 16-year-old during the war. Although he had once scored 10 for Wrekin Schoolboys Pritchard was to be a steady left-back in his professional career, switching briefly to the right for the 1949 Cup Final. He was also involved in the majority of the 1953-54 championship games and appeared in all nine post-war seasons before departing for £7,000.

1955 - 56

DEBUTANTS: Ron Howells, Gwyn Jones, Bobby Mason, Harry Middleton & Jimmy Murray. Howells and Jones were born in Wales.

SUMMARY: Wolves stretched their unbeaten run at Molineux to 21 games, including 12 wins on the trot, but their main interest in 1955-56 was their quest to be runners-up to Man Utd. Broadbent hit a hatrick in the 5-1 tanning of San Lorenzo though this was not the biggest of the friendly matches this season.

WOLVES v MOSCOW DYNAMO: The third of the never-to-be-forgotten floodlight friendlies was enjoyed by a 55,480 audience in November, who were joined in spirit by millions of English soccer fans in those more patriotic days. Only 14 minutes had passed when SLATER diverted a Mullen centre into the net, the winger then being denied a goal himself by a glorious save from the great Lev Yashin. It was still 1-0 at half-time with the Russians making few threats. Within four minutes of the re-start Murray sent MULLEN away, the Geordie making no mistake with his angled drive. Murray hit the bar but Dynamo came back with some pretty football, having a goal disallowed and another that counted but it was 2-1 to Wolves when the referee signalled time was up on another wonderful night.

LEAGUE: 3rd (49). Wolves drew at Albion before losing at Portsmouth, displaying relief at returning to Molineux by knocking in seven against Man City, Swinbourne leading the rout. Even that effort was surpassed at Cardiff where Wolves equalled the 1908 record away score in D1 of 9-1, a result that has not been seriously challenged since. Wolves then trimmed Huddersfield and had scored 23 in four games, Swinbourne slamming hatricks in three of them.

Leaders Blackpool had played a match more than Wolves who could have dis-lodged them by winning at Bloomfield Road, only to go down by the odd goal in three. Despite some mixed results Wolves were very much in touch when they travelled South to Luton for fixture number 14. A packed crowd saw Mason make his debut but he will hardly recall it with affection, Wolves losing 5-1 with worse news yet to come. Swinbourne, with 17 goals to his credit already, jumped to avoid photographers and caused the damage that spoiled his own footballing future as well as Wolves title hopes for 1955-56.

Funny game, football they say. Wolves were probably not amused as Cardiff of all teams became the first successful Molineux invaders in a year. The season then developed into an anti-climax after the early drama with a home defeat by Man Utd keeping Wolves out of contention. They were strong candidates for second place though, only to see that possibility considerably reduced by two goalless draws with Villa at Easter and a setback at the hands of Everton.

Slater converted two penalties against Spurs, a game that was also notable for the fact that floodlights were used at Molineux for the first time in the League. Wolves final flourish continued against Burnley and Sunderland, which meant that their tussle with Blackpool to determine the runners-up would not be settled until the last day. Wolves had not lost any of their 12 previous meetings with Sheff Utd and Booth notched a hatrick but the Blades also hit back with three and Wolves had to be content with third spot in the table. For the fifth time in 10 post-war campaigns Wolves were top D1 scorers (89) and they had been second twice which made it a pity that goals were not relevant to the points system, top three: Man Utd 60, Blackpool 49 and Wolves 49.

CUP: Slater succeeded where his forwards failed in the tie with Albion, though his strike was not enough to sustain Wolves interest beyond the third round, the event attracting 55,564 fans.

RESULTS: Albion 1-1 (Swinbourne); Portsmouth 1-2 (Hancocks); MAN CITY 7-2 (Swinbourne 4, Hancocks 2, Booth); PORTSMOUTH 3-1 (Broadbent, Swinbourne, Mullen); Cardiff 9-1 (Swinbourne 3, Hancocks 3, Broadbent 2, Mullen); HUDDERSFIELD 4-0 (Swinbourne 3, Slater); Blackpool 1-2 (Hancocks); CHELSEA 2-1 (Swinbourne 2); Bolton 1-2 (Slater); Man Utd 3-4 (Swinbourne 2, Slater); SHEFF UTD 3-2 (Swinbourne, Wilshaw, Hancocks); Newcastle 1-3 (McDonald); BIRMINGHAM 1-0 (Wilshaw); Luton 1-5 (Hancocks); CHARLTON 2-0 (Mullen, Shorthouse); Spurs 1-2 (Broadbent); EVERTON 1-0 (Murray); Preston 0-2; BURNLEY 3-1 (Hancocks 2, Clamp); ALBION 3-2 (Hancocks 2, Murray); Man City 2-2 (Hancocks, Murray); ARSENAL 3-3 (Booth 2, Hancocks);

Arsenal 2-2 (Mullen, Murray); CARDIFF 0-2; Sunderland 1-1 (Flowers); FAC ALBION 1-2 (Slater); Huddersfield 3-1 (Murray 2, Broadbent); BLACKPOOL 2-3 (Hancocks, Murray); Chelsea 3-2 (Broadbent 2, Murray); BOLTON 4-2 (Broadbent 2, Hancocks, OG); MAN UTD 0-2; Birmingham 0-0; LUTON 1-2 (Hancocks); Charlton 2-0 (Wilshaw, Murray); NEWCASTLE 2-1 (Mullen, Murray); VILLA 0-0; Villa 0-0; Everton 1-2 (Mullen); PRESTON 2-1 (Slater, Wilshaw); SPURS 5-1 (Slater 2, Murray, Wilshaw, Broadbent); Burnley 2-1 (Booth, Deeley); SUNDERLAND 3-1 (Mullen, Wilshaw, Slater) & Sheff Utd 3-3 (Booth 3).

RECORD: PLD 43 W 20 D 9 L 14 F 90 A 67 (15-2-5 & 5-7-9).

SCORERS: Hancocks 18, Swinbourne 17, Murray 11, Broadbent 10, Slater 8, Booth 7, Mullen 7, Wilshaw 6, Clamp 1, Deeley 1, Flowers 1, McDonald 1, Shorthouse 1 & OG 1.

INTERNATIONALS: Wilshaw scored two of his three goals in the 3-0 win against Ireland while at the other end Williams took his appearance tally to 26 (24), never conceding more than three in a high-scoring era. Apps: Broadbent (E 'B' 1), Williams (E 1 + FL 1), Wilshaw (E 4) & Wright (E 9 + E v YE + FL 2).

FAREWELLS: Hancocks 378-166, McDonald 6-2 (Leicester), Middleton 1-0 (Scunthorpe), Russell 4-0 (Notts County), Sims 39-0 (Villa), Smith 94-25 (Villa) & Swinbourne 230-114. JOHNNY HANCOCKS cost Wolves £4,000 which made the little outside-right from Oakengates a bargain buy. He was famed for the ferocity of his shooting and once rocketed in a 45-yard free-kick without the goalkeeper moving, also winning a bet by hitting the crossbar from 40 yards to show he had accuracy too. In 1953-54 he was an ever-present in the Wolves team, something that no other player was to achieve in the 16 years after the war. 1954-55 saw him become the first person to score in six successive games for Wolves since the war and in 1955-56 he headed their goal charts yet not selected again. Hancocks got 24 for the reserves in 1956-57 but his age counted against a first team recall, and at 38 he went to Wellington as player-manager in the summer of 1957.

ROY SWINBOURNE was born in Denaby Main, the big centre-forward being a product of Wolves Yorkshire nursery. His career began well and he topped the appearances list in 1950-51 with 48, following up this successful term by scoring 16 times in the first six games of a South African tour. Injury and loss of form restricted his outings to 20 in 1951-52 but he bounced back to be equal top with 42 the next season. Swinbourne's seven hatricks is a post-war Wolves record, the tragedy being that he had just reached his peak when he was badly hurt. A cartilage operation revived hopes of a comeback but he was always fighting a losing battle, managing a few Central League run-outs in 1956-57 before being forced to retire.

1956 - 57

DEBUTANTS: Joe Bonson, Malcolm Finlayson (Millwall), Gerry Harris, Harry Hooper (West Ham), Pat Neil (Portsmouth), Colin Tether &

Bobby Thomson (Airdrie). Finlayson and Thomson were born in Scotland.

SUMMARY: Wolves did quite well but Man Utd continued to dominate the championship race. There was a disaster in the F.A. Cup as Wolves were victims of one of the biggest shocks in the history of the tournament. Consolation came from friendlies as Wolves remained unbeaten against four more teams from abroad watched by a total of 143,000 supporters.

LEAGUE: 6th (48). Murray inspired Wolves to a merry start with four goals while the £20,000 Hooper made a promising debut. A couple of defeats took the shine off that opening result before Molineux staged probably it's finest League match ever. There was a seven pm kick-off for the visit of Luton, the first game under a new League directive that fixtures could begin in daylight and be completed under floodlights if necessary. The first half was a feast of entertainment with eight goals scored and although only one was added after the break there was some classy football, Wolves edging home 5-4 as Harris made his debut.

Highlights during the rest of 1956 were plentiful, Wolves pounding Portsmouth 6-0 then drawing at Chelsea despite being 3-0 behind with 15 minutes to go. Booth stole the glory with four goals against Arsenal but the next visitors to Molineux, Preston, led 3-0 after an hour. Wolves pulled one back and then snatched an amazing win with three goals in the last 15 minutes, Hooper netting a hatrick. It was the turn of Wilshaw to score a hatrick against Blackpool, the fourth Wolves forward to do so in 22 matches but there were no similar presents on Christmas Day as Wolves lost to Charlton at The Valley.

Wolves were not so hot on their travels and suffered a different problem when engine trouble delayed the train taking them to Leeds, proceedings getting under way seven minutes late. There were no goals at Elland Road but Wolverhampton's public continued to have many to enthuse over, Charlton getting three and still being thumped. The draw with Man Utd was a finc spcctaclc though it was the first time in 12 games Wolves had been held on their own ground. Burnley actually won there though Wolves immediately got back to normal by beating Newcastle 2-0, Thomson scoring on his solitary first team appearance. Comfortable victories over neighbours Albion and Villa rounded things off nicely, bringing the home goals total to a fantastic 70.

CUP: To beat D2 Swansea 5-3 was not the most convincing result but how Wolves wished they could have repeated that in the fourth round. Even the goalpost snapped as Stuart and a D3S Bournemouth player crashed into it in the sixth minute. The real sensation was yet to come as Bournemouth forged ahead and try as they did, the talented Wolves XI could not repair the damage. Villa and Albion met in the only post-war Molineux SF, drawing 2-2 in front of a 55,549 attendance.

RESULTS: MAN CITY 5-1 (Murray 4, Hooper); Luton 0-1; Blackpool 2-3 (Murray, Slater); LUTON 5-4 (Murray 2, Slater, Broadbent,

Mullen); EVERTON 2-1 (Booth, Slater); Spurs 1-4 (Hooper); SUNDERLAND 2-2 (Murray, Broadbent); LEEDS 1-2 (Broadbent); Bolton 3-0 (Booth, Wilshaw, Mullen); BIRMINGHAM 3-0 (Hooper, Murray, Wilshaw); Albion 1-1 (Hooper); PORTSMOUTH 6-0 (Wilshaw 2, Flowers, Hooper, Murray, OG); Chelsea 3-3 (Hooper, Flowers, Murray); CARDIFF 3-1 (Booth, Hooper, Mullen); Man Utd 0-3; ARSENAL 5-2 (Booth 4, Murray); Burnley 0-3; PRESTON 4-3 (Hooper 3, Mason); Newcastle 1-2 (Hooper); SHEFF WED 2-1 (Broadbent, Hooper); Man City 3-2 (Murray, Broadbent, Neil); BLACKPOOL 4-1 (Wilshaw 3, Hooper); Charlton 1-2 (Booth); Everton 1-3 (Broadbent); Sunderland 3-2 (Broadbent 2, Flowers); FAC SWANSEA 5-3 (Bonson 2, Flowers, Mullen, Broadbent); SPURS 3-0 (Broadbent 2, Mason); Leeds 0-0; FAC BOURNEMOUTH 0-1; BOLTON 3-2 (Hooper 2, Murray); Birmingham 2-2 (Hooper, Murray); CHARLTON 7-3 (Murray 2, Broadbent 2, Clamp, Hooper, Bonson); Cardiff 2-2 (Bonson 2); CHELSEA 3-1 (Broadbent, Mason, Bonson); Sheff Wed 1-2 (Hooper); MAN UTD 1-1 (Broadbent); Arsenal 0-0; BURNLEY 1-2 (Slater); Preston 0-1; NEWCASTLE 2-0 (Wilshaw, Thomson); ALBION 5-2 (Booth, Broadbent, Deeley, Hooper, Wilshaw); Portsmouth 0-1; Villa 0-4 & VILLA 3-0 (Broadbent 2, Wilshaw).

RECORD: PLD 44 W 21 D 8 L 15 F 99 A 74 (18-2-3 & 3-6-12).

SCORERS: Hooper 19, Broadbent 18, Murray 17, Wilshaw 10, Booth 9, Bonson 6, Flowers 4, Mullen 4, Slater 4, Mason 3, Clamp 1, Deeley 1, Neil 1, Thomson 1 & OG 1.

INTERNATIONALS: Wright led England in a World Cup Qualifier at Molineux, where 54,000 appreciated a 5-2 win over Denmark in one of the last Full Internationals to be staged at a League ground. Wilshaw made his 12th appearance without adding to his tremendous tally of 10 goals, while Hooper scored for the England 'B' team. Apps: Booth (E U23-1), Flowers (FL 1), Hooper (FL 1 + E 'B' 1), Wilshaw (E 1) & Wright (E 8 + FL 3).

FAREWELLS: Bonson 12-6 (Cardiff), Hooper 41-19 (Birmingham), Neil 4-1 (Portsmouth), Shorthouse 373-1, Tether 1-0 (Oxford), Thomson 1-1 (Villa) & Williams 416-0. BILL SHORTHOUSE spent 15 years at the club and was a real stalwart, having been born at nearby Bradley. He was equal top of the 1948-49 appearances chart which was just as well because he was a most reliable defender to have in the line-up. He was centre-half at Wembley and left-back five years later when he completed his set of medals as Wolves won the League. Shorthouse had the rare distinction of never being dropped and only hung up his boots due to the fact a nagging injury showed no signs of clearing up.

BERT WILLIAMS was also from Bradley and Wolves paid £3,500 for his services. He was a magnificent athlete whose sprinting power enabled him to prevent many dangerous situations, in fact he was such a picture of health that people were surprised when a nasty shoulder injury caused him to miss 15 games in 1951-52, Parsons usually deputising. The defence was always heartened to know the safe hands of Williams were there should they slip-up though he retained his soft spot for Walsall, being in the unique situation of president of their supporters club in 1954-55 whilst not only playing for Wolves but topping their appearances with 44. However, it was the Wanderers he served loyally until he hung his gloves up, so to speak, at the age of 35.

1957 - 58

DEBUTANTS: Noel Dwyer, Jackie Henderson (Portsmouth), Allan Jackson & Micky Lill. Dwyer was born in Eire and Henderson in Scotland.

SUMMARY: Wolves latest unbeaten period at Molineux was extended to 24, including 11 wins running, to lay the foundations of their second Football League triumph. The achievements of the club as a whole were miraculous as of the main seven competitions entered only the F.A. Cup was not won! Wolves first four teams all scored more than 100 goals as they respectively headed D1, the Central League, the Birmingham League and the Worcestershire Combination. The fourth team also won the latter's Cup to be the first to do that particular double, this being the only season Wolves won either event. The manner in which the Youth Cup was secured was in some ways the greatest feat of all, Wolves working hard to reach the final especially in the SF against Man Utd who had won it every year. A 5-1 defeat at Chelsea seemed to have ended their dreams but Wolves responded in magnificent fashion to the apparently hopeless task and squeezed home 7-6 an aggregate. No wonder they were so strongly represented in the England Youth team, Les Cocker alone playing 11 times. Wolves also had another very strong continental challenge to deal with at Molineux.

WOLVES v REAL MADRID: The Spaniards had dominated the first two years of the European Champions Cup, duly visiting Wolverhampton in December to complete the quartet of really memorable nights for the locals. Boasting names like Gento and Kopa they were greeted by 55,169 spectators who were in a state of euphoria after eight minutes as WILSHAW converted Mullen's centre. Real equalised shortly and with Wright unavailable Wolves were grateful to his stand-in Showell, who managed to subdue the famed Alfredo di Stefano. A typical hefty clearance by Finlayson was headed on by Murray for BROADBENT to fire Wolves ahead, with MURRAY himself increasing the lead. Real came back to 3-2 with some splendid soccer but Wolves gallantly hung on to bring themselves and their country more sporting glory.

LEAGUE: 1st (64). The initial stumble at Everton seemed unimportant as Wolves banged in 11 goals in their opening two home games. However, a couple of other unsatisfactory away shows left them a modest 12th in the table.

As in 1953-54 Wolves shrugged off an ordinary start to put together 18 matches without a reverse to make them favourites for the title, 32 points being amassed. It all began against Blackpool and for nine games only Leeds gained any joy from meeting the hungry Wolves. Then came three 1-1 draws in four games, in the latter pair Derek Dougan of Portsmouth scored his first League goal and Albion attracted a 55,618 crowd to Molineux, and they had now been visitors on six of the last eight occasions that 55,000 had gone to the ground to see English opponents. Goalkeeper Dwyer was drafted in for his debut at Man City two days prior to his wedding, and he was no doubt relieved Wolves won after trailing 3-1. The next trip was to Preston and saw Lill score on his debut in the opening minute as he gained possession for the first time, while the 18 was completed at the expense of Everton.

Wolves had a six-point lead but dropped five in four outings to give their followers some minor concern. They totalled 40 points, compared to the 35 of Preston and Albion, removing all doubts with an incredible 19/20 spell. The only blot on the copybook came against Man City when Stuart scored an own goal and Deeley wasted a penalty. Arsenal finally dented Wolves pride at Molineux but the only real question was when they would be crowned as champions. They drew at Burnley then met Preston, their main challengers of 1957-58. The Lancashire men had delayed Wolves celebrations so it was appropriate that matters should be settled on this day. In the 38th minute Broadbent weaved a bit of magic to help create a chance for Deeley and a Gordon Milne own goal two minutes from time made it 2-0 to Wolves.

England's finest team lived up to their reputation at Old Trafford and now shared the D1 post-war points record. Victory at troubled Sheff Wed would equal the 66 that was then the all-time best yet they surprisingly went down 2-1. Wolves had to be content with a club record under the old points system and they had the best defence in D1, conceding 47. Murray was fourth top scorer in the League with 29 in 41 starts and Wolves total was 103 which was worthy of their position, top three: Wolves 64, Preston 59 and Spurs 51.

CUP: Wolves scraped past D2 Lincoln and thrashed Portsmouth, despite Clamp's penalty being superbly tipped round the post by Norman Uprichard. Fears of D3N Darlington following in the footsteps of Bournemouth were soon erased to the relief of the 55,778 present, giving Wolves a place in the QF and high hopes of a double. It was 1-1 at Bolton and a replay was beckoning when Finlayson came out to dive at the feet of Nat Lofthouse, a man who had scored six for the FLXI at Molineux a few years previously. Finlayson snatched the ball and was still holding it as he slid out of the area, Bolton winning the tie from the ensuing free-kick to please most of the 69,000 crowd and they went on to lift the Cup itself while Wolves cursed their luck.

RESULTS: Everton 0-1; BOLTON 6-1 (Deeley 2, Murray 2, Booth, Broadbent); SUNDERLAND 5-0 (Murray 2, Mullen, Booth, Deeley); Bolton 1-1 (Deeley); Luton 1-3 (Wilshaw); BLACKPOOL 3-1 (Murray, Broadbent, Mullen); VILLA 2-1 (Murray, Deeley); Leicester 3-2 (Murray 2, Clamp); Villa 3-2 (Murray, Broadbent, Deeley); MAN UTD 3-1 (Deeley 2, Wilshaw); SPURS 4-0 (Broadbent 2, Murray, Flowers); Leeds 1-1 (Deeley); Birmingham 5-1 (Clamp 2, Wilshaw, Murray, Deeley); CHELSEA 2-1

(Deeley, Wilshaw); Newcastle 1-1 (Deeley); FOREST 2-0 (Deeley, Broadbent); Portsmouth 1-1 (Clamp); ALBION 1-1 (Clamp); Man City 4-3 (Murray 2, Mason, Broadbent); BURNLEY 2-1 (Murray, Broadbent); Preston 2-1 (Lill, Murray); SHEFF WED 4-3 (Broadbent, Clamp, Mason, Murray); EVERTON 2-0 (Mullen, Clamp); Spurs 0-1; Sunderland 2-0 (Broadbent, Murray); FAC Lincoln 1-0 (Mullen); LUTON 1-1 (Mason); Blackpool 2-3 (Murray, Deeley); FAC PORTSMOUTH 5-1 (Broadbent 2, Mason, Mullen, OG); LEICESTER 5-1 (Murray 2, Deeley, Broadbent, Mason); FAC DARLINGTON 6-1 (Murray 3, Broadbent 2, Mason); LEEDS 3-2 (Broadbent, Mason, Deeley); BIRMINGHAM 5-1 (Murray 3, Deeley 2); FAC Bolton 1-2 (Mason); NEWCASTLE 3-1 (Broadbent, Deeley, Mason); Chelsea 2-1 (Deeley, Showell); Forest 4-1 (Murray 3, Broadbent); MAN CITY 3-3 (OG, Deeley, Mullen); Albion 3-0 (Murray 2, Mason); PORTSMOUTH 1-0 (Clamp); Arsenal 2-0 (Broadbent, Murray); ARSENAL 1-2 (Broadbent); Burnley 1-1 (Clamp); PRESTON 2-0 (Deeley, OG); Man Utd 4-0 (Flowers, Clamp, Deeley, Broadbent) & Sheff Wed 1-2 (Flowers).

RECORD: PLD 46 W 31 D 8 L 7 F 116 A 51 (19-3-1 & 12-5-6).

SCORERS: Murray 32, Deeley 23, Broadbent 21, Clamp 10, Mason 10, Mullen 6, Wilshaw 4, Flowers 3, Booth 2, Lill 1, Showell 1 & OG 3.

CENTRAL LEAGUE: PLD 42 W 27 D 8 L 7 F 112 A 64 PTS 62.
SCORERS: Middleton 14, Lill 12, Horne 10, Jackson 10, Stobart 10, Booth 9, Hooper 9, Mannion 4, Mason 4, Showell 4, Thomson 4, Wilshaw 4, Bonson 3, Durandt 3, Howells 3, Flowers 2, Henderson 2, Palin 2, Jones 1, Slater 1 & OG 1.

YOUTH CUP: Albion 2-2, ALBION 6-1, Villa 3-0, STOKE 1-1, Stoke 3-2, LEICESTER 9-0, BOLTON 1-1, Bolton 3-1, Man Utd 1-1, MAN UTD 3-1, Chelsea 1-5 (Perry) & CHELSEA 6-1 (Farmer 4, Durandt 2/ 17,704). Team: Cullen, Kelly, Yates, Kirkham, Palin, Cocker, Horne, Hall, Farmer, Durandt & Perry. In the second leg Read replaced Perry.
SCORERS: Perry 9, Farmer 7, Mannion 7, Durandt 5, Hall 3, Cocker 2, Horne 2, Kirkham 2, Berry 1 & Palin 1.

INTERNATIONALS: Wolves made a little piece of history in the 1958 WCF when they provided the entire half-back line for England's three group matches, Clamp joining Wright and Slater in the international arena. He was omitted for the play-off but Broadbent made his full debut to ensure Wolves maintained their treble interest. Wright made his 22nd appearance for the FLXI while Broadbent and Murray were on target for them, the latter also scoring at Under 23 level. Apps: Broadbent (E 1 + FL 1), Clamp (E 4 + FL 1), Flowers (FL 1), Harris (E U23-4), Murray (FL1 + E U23-1), Slater (E 8) & Wright (E 11 + E v YE + FL 1).

FAREWELLS: Dwyer 5-0 (West Ham), Howells 9-0 (Portsmouth) & Wilshaw 219-113 (Stoke). DENNIS WILSHAW certainly took a long time to make the grade, spending 2½ years on loan to Walsall before coming good in 1949. He did consistently well from then on and played a major role in Wolves 1954 success. During the next season he became only the second post-war player to score in six games running for Wolves - by an astonishing coincidence Hancocks had achieved the original feat in the six previous matches. The brainy inside-forward appeared in the four main friendlies but his competitive outings were restricted slightly in his last two full seasons, so he was pleased to link up with his home-city club for £12,000.

1958 - 59

DEBUTANTS: Cliff Durandt, Des Horne, Phil Kelly, Gerry Mannion & Geoff Sidebottom. Durandt and Horne were born in South Africa, Kelly in Eire.

SUMMARY: Wolves comfortably kept their grip on the championship to make it three triumphs in six years, a total bettered by only eight teams in the complete history of the League. Their first venture into European competition was a disappointment, while Bolton again proved a stumbling block as they knocked Wolves out of the F.A. Cup and denied them the Charity Shield at Burnden Park. Wolves Reserves equalled the all-time Central League record of six titles with their fifth in nine seasons, also gaining the highest number of points since it was formed in 1911 while their margin of 15 over the runners-up was another best. A tremendous decade for the football club was completed with a hatrick of honours as the third team topped the Birmingham League.

LEAGUE: 1st (61). Mason prompted Wolves to a fine start against Forest but they did not fare so well in the capital city, losing to West Ham then letting an impertinent young man called Jimmy Greaves put five past them. The Fleet Street writers had never liked Wolves style of play and happily announced that skipper Wright and his men were on the road to oblivion, then Broadbent's equaliser prevented a West Ham double before another large Molineux gathering.

Wolves won four games to silence the critics and jump to second behind Luton, only to falter at Newcastle and then suffer more London sorrow. Chief victim at Tottenham was Slater, who scored then missed from the penalty spot only for both to be re-taken before Clamp ended the saga. It was 1-1 when the ball bounced off Slater's stomach, putting clear a blatantly offside Spurs forward who got the winner to leave Wolves ninth.

A Manchester double was completed as an experimental Saturday night kick-off against United worked well for Wolves, before City were clipped 2-0. Wolves drew at Arsenal and Mullen showed he had not lost his scoring knack in the Birmingham game, but Wolves folded at Albion to make it a disappointing debut for keeper Sidebottom. Jinx team Bolton were the exceptions as Wolves won 4/5 to go fourth as it became very tight at the top with the lead often changing hands. Wolves only defeat in their last 17 meetings with Leicester delayed them from getting in on the act though they did better at another East Midlands venue. A spectacular pair of results against Portsmouth steered Wolves into the number one position, as three players bagged hatricks for them.

Chelsea briefly rocked the boat before Wolves plundered 15 goals in three outings, racing into a 4-0 advantage within 19 minutes of the latter. It took someone of the calibre of Bobby Charlton to halt their progress when he produced a match-winning performance for Man Utd, Wolves quickly recovering at nearby Maine Road. Lowly Spurs gained a point from their visit to Molineux prior to that of North London rivals Arsenal. Both Wolves and the Gunners were locked on 41 points, though Wolves did have a game more to play. A tremendous attacking display ended their 1958-59 capital disasters and the biggest prize in British football looked destined for South Staffordshire again.

Albion's short journey to Wolverhampton was ruined as Lill established himself as Wolves fifth hatrick hero of the season then victories over Preston and Leeds ensured that only Man Utd had a realistic chance of catching Wolves, who had 51 points from their 36 fixtures compared to United's 50 from 38. Burnley forced a draw at Molineux while United won, though Wolves were still above them on goal-average. The Lancashire challenge was virtually killed off as Wolves faced two tricky visits to that same county and negotiated them well.

A fine exhibition of forward play on April 18th saw Wolves declared as champions, when the size of the crowd again failed to do the occasion justice. It was still mathematically possible for Wolves to be overhauled but it would require some astonishing scorelines. Wolves ended such speculation versus Leicester and then beat Everton to equal the post-war D1 record of 11 doubles. This was incredibly their 13th away victory, their highest ever amount in the big League. Wolves were top D1 strikers with 110 of which 71 were in the latter half of the term, and in conceding 49 goals they could also boast the tightest defence so there was no argument about who was the best club in England, top four: Wolves 61, Man Utd 55, Arsenal 50 and Bolton 50.

EUROPEAN CHAMPIONS CUP: Had this been implemented in 1954-55 Wolves might well have been the first winners and their friendlies that season strongly influenced the decision to start the competition a year later. Legends such as Hancocks, Williams, Shorthouse, Wilshaw and Swinbourne had all gone though, and after receiving a first round bye Wolves lost narrowly to Shalke 04 in West Germany. They were confident of rectifying the situation at Molineux but could only draw 2-2.

F.A. CUP: Wolves accounted for D4 Barrow at their tiny Cumbrian ground before tripping up against Bolton in front of 55,621 fans.

RESULTS: FOREST 5-1 (Mason 3, Deeley, Broadbent); West Ham 0-2; Chelsea 2-6 (Mason, Slater); WEST HAM 1-1 (Broadbent); BLACKPOOL 2-0 (Murray, Broadbent); Villa 3-1 (Broadbent, Henderson, Booth); Blackburn 2-1 (Horne, OG); VILLA 4-0 (Henderson 2, Murray 2); Newcastle 1-3 (Broadbent); Spurs 1-2 (Clamp); MAN UTD 4-0 (Murray 2, Mason, Mullen); CS Bolton 1-4 (Durandt); MAN CITY 2-0 (Broadbent,

Deeley); Arsenal 1-1 (Showell); BIRMINGHAM 3-1 (Mullen 2, Showell); Albion 1-2 (Deeley); PRESTON 2-0 (Mason 2); Burnley 2-0 (Jackson, Deeley); ECC Shalke 1-2 (Jackson); ECC SHALKE 2-2 (Broadbent 2); BOLTON 1-2 (Deeley); Luton 1-0 (Mullen); EVERTON 1-0 (Broadbent); Leicester 0-1; Forest 3-1 (Broadbent, Horne, Mason); Portsmouth 5-3 (Broadbent 3, Booth, Deeley); PORTSMOUTH 7-0 (Booth 3, Deeley 3, Horne); CHELSEA 1-2 (Deeley); FAC Barrow 4-2 (Deeley 2, Booth, Lill); FAC BOLTON 1-2 (OG); BLACKBURN 5-0 (Mason 2, Murray, Deeley, Lill); Newcastle 4-3 (Lill 2, Mason, Murray); LEEDS 6-2 (Deeley 2, Murray 2, Broadbent 2); Man Utd 1-2 (Mason); Man City 4-1 (Murray 2, OG, Lill); SPURS 1-1 (Lill); ARSENAL 6-1 (Deeley 2, Broadbent 2, Lill, Murray); Birmingham 3-0 (Murray 2, Broadbent); ALBION 5-2 (Lill 3, Mason, Deeley); Preston 2-1 (Lill 2); Leeds 3-1 (Broadbent, Murray, Clamp); BURNLEY 3-3 (Murray, Broadbent, Harris); Bolton 2-2 (Booth, Murray); Blackpool 1-0 (Murray); LUTON 5-0 (Broadbent 2, Booth, Clamp, Murray); LEICESTER 3-0 (Deeley, Lill, Murray) & Everton 1-0 (Murray).

RECORD: PLD 47 W 29 D 6 L 12 F 119 A 61 (15-4-4 & 14-2-8).

SCORERS: Broadbent 22, Murray 21, Deeley 19, Lill 13, Mason 13, Booth 8, Mullen 4, Clamp 3, Henderson 3, Horne 3, Jackson 2, Showell 2, Durandt 1. Harris 1, Slater 1 & OG 3.

CENTRAL LEAGUE: PLD 42 W 32 D 6 L 4 F 131 A 57 PTS 70.

SCORERS: Stobart 18, Booth 15, Mannion 12, Murray 12, Thomson 10, Durandt 7, Farmer 7, Jackson 7, Lill 7, Horne 6, Howells 6, Showell 4, Palin 3, Clamp 2, Middleton 2, Mullen 2, Cocker 1, Connolly 1, Henderson 1, Kirkham 1, Mason 1, Read 1, Slater 1 & OG 4.

INTERNATIONALS: Wright became the world's first footballer to appear 100 times for his country and had reached 105 when he retired, whilst still a member of the side. The only Englishmen to have passed that total are Charlton (106) and Bobby Moore (108) though more internationals were played during their career-spans, with Wright heading the list if the four wartime games are counted. Other England records for Wright were his 90 matches as captain, 70 in succession and 38 in the Home Championship. He took part in 136 of the main representative fixtures and was one of a Wolves quartet in Brazil, where Deeley made his debut. Flowers finally emerged as a regular choice and scored a brace (v. United States 8-1) as did Broadbent (v. Wales 2-2). Flowers also got a goal against Young England while Murray again netted for the Under 23 XI. Apps: Broadbent (E 5 + E v YE + FL 1), Deeley (E 2), Flowers (E 7 + E v YE + FL 1), Murray (E U23-1), Slater (E 1) & Wright (E 9 + E v YE).

FAREWELLS: Henderson 9-3 (Arsenal), Jackson 6-2 (Bury), Mullen 474-112 & Wright 537-13. JIMMY MULLEN was from Newcastle but settled down well in the Midlands and usually operated on the left-wing, forming a great partnership with Hancocks that could hardly be imagined in modern soccer. He was fast and had a lethal shot as well as being an accurate crosser of the ball. Mullen topped the appearance lists with 47 in

1949-50, 43 in 1951-52 and 42 in 1952-53 when he shared the honour. In 1954-55 he was kept on the sidelines a lot by Smith but eventually regained his place and by 1957-58 he had scored his 13th F.A. Cup goal, a formidable tally for a winger. Mullen was not selected in 1959-60 to agonisingly remain on 99 League strikes and when he retired in the summer he had spent almost 23 of his 37 years at Molineux. His sudden death in 1987 saddened not only sports fans as it seemed nobody had a bad word to say about this wonderful character.

BILLY WRIGHT was told by Buckley he was too small to make the grade, luckily groundstaff persuaded him to give the fair-haired Ironbridge lad another chance. Born in 1924 his career was delayed by the war when he showed a fair amount of ability as a forward, scoring 12 in 1945-46. He first skippered Wolves in 1947-48 when he headed the chart for appearances with 42 and it was success all the way from then on, particularly when he led them at Wembley in 1949. In 1951-52 Wright was the fifth recipient of the 'Footballer of the Year' award and a season later was one of a United Kingdom XI who met Wales. In 1954-55 he switched from wing-half to centre-half and in 1956-57 he was runner-up in a poll to determine the 'European Footballer of the year' as well as topping the appearances for Wolves again with 42. The ambidextrous star could even sign autographs more proficiently than most while on the field he was skilful on the ground and his timing such that he could outjump opponents who were far taller. In 1959 he was honoured with the C.B.E. to indicate what a great ambassador he was for the game, as few sportsmen received such recognition in those days. Wright rarely resorted to fouls, arguing or any other form of gamesmanship and must cringe to be mentioned in the same breath as so-called superstars of today who are guilty of such things, though he would no doubt be too polite to say so. Influenced slightly by the rigours of pre-season training, Wright decided to quit football while still at the very top of the tree. The modest 35-year-old appropriately bowed out in Wolves tradtional Colours v. Whites curtain-raiser to 1959-60, when the first team tackled the reserves in an annual fixture that was soon to die out, though the memory of Wright defending for Wolves will always live on.

1959 - 60

DEBUTANTS: Johnny Kirkham & Barry Stobart.

SUMMARY: Wolves were desperately close to a championship hatrick and the first double since Villa managed it way back in 1897, Wolves themselves having been just a couple of results from it in 1939. They had to be content with the F.A. Cup where they improved their already fine record, in fact only three clubs could better their four wins and eight finals. Over the opening six games of 1959-60 they increased their unbeaten run to a club record 19 including a Charity Shield success, also completing a total of 20 matches at Molineux without a setback. Almost 1,050,000 attended the home fixtures yet plans for a new 70,000-capacity stadium costing £½ m were dashed. Wolves could have financed the project as they had made consistent profits under the long reigns of Buckley and Cullis but were informed it would interfere with the amenities of the town - a town they had put on the map. Meanwhile, the reserves whipped a Rest of Central League XI 6-0.

LEAGUE: 2nd (54). Wolves continued to regard St. Andrews as one of their favourite venues after an opening day win there. The only blemish in the first few weeks came at Fulham, the slate being emphatically wiped clean as Deeley inspired Wolves to a 9-0 slaughter of the Londoners which was their heaviest defeat until they lost 10-0 to Liverpool in a Milk Cup-tie at Anfield in 1985-86.

Back to 1959-60 and by the time Wolves went to Tottenham they were second to their hosts, Bobby Smith plundering four goals to widen the gap. Their next trip to the capital saw West Ham do enough to go top, putting Wolves fifth. Only Man Utd, savagely hit by the Munich air disaster of 1958, were worthy rivals to Wolves had there been an award for the outstanding team of the 1950's. Wolves had probably achieved a shade more, though a double by Bolton at Christmas was a sad epitaph to this period for them.

The Wulfrunian machine was restored to good working order in 1960, producing four goals against Arsenal and Man City and victory at Ewood Park by courtesy of an own goal, which was exactly what happened in the previous term. Blonde bombshell Mannion created both scores on his debut at Man Utd, another new boy Stobart notching the latter. Wolves were finally overcome in mid-March, responding with an onslaught against title-chasers Burnley before cruising at Leeds thanks to Mannion. He was being tipped for a wonderful career though winger Lill had earned similar praise a year earlier and not lived up to expectations. The League table showed Spurs to be in front of Wolves on goal-average with six games left, while third-placed Burnley would join them on 47 points if they did not waste their two extra matches.

Goals continued to flow against West Ham, whose dreams had by now faded and then died. After a stutter at Newcastle, Wolves emerged from their Easter clashes with Forest ahead of the rest. They led Spurs and Burnley by three points but the homely little Turf Moor club still had those two games in hand.

Molineux had 56,283 customers as Spurs gained their only win in their most recent 16 visits, which was tragic timing for Wolves as a draw would have considerably altered the record books. They ended their programme in handsome fashion at Chelsea to at least ensure they would be above Spurs which was some consolation. Burnley had also dropped a couple of points and had to beat Man City to deny Wolves a slice of football history. City hit the woodwork and it was later reported that Burnley's winner was intended to be a centre, such is the thin dividing line between success and failure. Wolves scored 106 times to be leading D1 marksmen as they now had been in half the post-war campaigns. Murray was second= in the charts with 29 in 40 appearances and was amongst a Wolves quartet who shared a massive 70 goals, yet even that figure was not sufficient, top three: Burnley 55, Wolves 54 and Spurs 53.

EUROPEAN CHAMPIONS CUP: Early dominance in East Germany was rewarded by a 16th-minute breakthrough, though after 90 minutes Wolves were relieved to lose only 2-1. There was to be no slip-up this year as Wolves won the return 2-0, then twice rose to the occasion to eliminate the classy Red Star Belgrade of Yugoslavia. There was a rude awakening for them in the QF in Spain, as they suffered a rare mauling from a foreign team. Barcelona then let Wolves come at them in England only to break with devastating effect, seemingly scoring every time they ventured up the field to leave the crowd stunned. The three Molineux attendances were almost identical, being 55,747 then 55,519 and in the QF 55,535.

F.A. CUP: Newcastle made Wolves fight all the way for a fourth round berth, in which they ousted D2 Charlton 2-1. Undaunted by trips to Luton and Leicester, Wolves qualified for a local SF at The Hawthorns against D2 pacemakers Aston Villa. In the 32nd minute Villa keeper Sims could only palm a Murray shot out to his old colleague Deeley, who made no mistake to the differing emotions of the 56,400 assembled. Wolves had the upper hand though another of their ex-players, Thomson, nearly got through with his effort being smothered by Finlayson. In the other tie Blackburn defeated Sheff Wed 2-1.

FINAL: With 460 teams having fallen by the wayside an audience of 98,954 paid receipts of £49,816 to see the Wembley survivors. Surprise choice Stobart sold a dummy to a Rovers defender and centred, McGRATH hooking the ball past his own goalkeeper as Deeley challenged. The event was ruined as a spectacle when Whelan broke his leg to add to the worries of underdogs Blackburn who had finished 17th in D1 and offered little resistance with 10 men. In the 67th minute DEELEY ran the ball in after a good work by Horne, and then Stobart did well again to further justify the omission of Mason when he was involved in a move that finished with DEELEY slamming it into the roof of the net to make it 3-0. Flowers and Murray both had goals disallowed yet Wolves never received due credit for their achievement. Team: Finlayson, Showell, Harris, Clamp, Slater, Flowers, Deeley, Stobart, Murray, Broadbent & Horne.

RESULTS: CS FOREST 3-1 (Broadbent, Lill, Murray); Birmingham 1-0 (Mason); SHEFF WED 3-1 (Murray 2, Clamp); ARSENAL 3-3 (Deeley 2, Lill); Sheff Wed 2-2 (Murray 2); Man City 6-4 (Murray 2, Slater 2, Deeley, Lill); Fulham 1-3 (Deeley); BLACKBURN 3-1 (Mason 2, Deeley); FULHAM 9-0 (Deeley 4, Murray, Mason, Clamp, Broadbent, Flowers); Blackpool 1-3 (Deeley); EVERTON 2-0 (Clamp, Broadbent); ECC Vorwaerts 1-2 (Broadbent); Luton 5-1 (Deeley 2, Murray, Booth, Broadbent); ECC VORWAERTS 2-0 (Broadbent, Mason); Spurs 1-5 (Mason); MAN UTD 3-2 (Murray 2, Broadbent); Preston 3-4 (Horne 2, Murray); NEWCASTLE 2-0 (Murray, Broadbent); Burnley 1-4 (Mason); ECC Red Star 1-1 (Deeley); LEEDS 4-2 (Mason 2, Murray, Horne); West Ham 2-3 (Broadbent, Mason); ECC RED STAR 3-0 (Mason 2, Murray); CHELSEA 3-1 (Flowers 2, Clamp); Albion 1-0 (Murray); LEICESTER 0-3; BIRMINGHAM 2-0 (Mason 2); Bolton 1-2 (Murray); BOLTON 0-1; Arsenal 4-4

(Mason, Clamp, Murray, Horne); FAC Newcastle 2-2 (Flowers, Clamp); FAC NEWCASTLE 4-2 (Murray, Deeley, Flowers, Horne); MAN CITY 4-2 (Broadbent 2, Clamp, Murray); Blackburn 1-0 (OG); FAC CHARLTON 2-1 (Horne, Broadbent); BLACKPOOL 1-1 (Murray); ECC Barcelona 0-4; Everton 2-0 (Murray 2); FAC Luton 4-1 (Mason 2, Murray, Clamp); LUTON 3-2 (Horne, Murray, Broadbent); ALBION 3-1 (Murray, Deeley, Clamp); ECC BARCELONA 2-5 (Mason, Murray); Man Utd 2-0 (Deeley, Stobart); FAC Leicester 2-1 (Broadbent, OG); PRESTON 3-3 (Broadbent 2, Stobart); Leicester 1-2 (Murray); FAC Villa 1-0 (Deeley); BURNLEY 6-1 (Mannion 2, Broadbent, Horne, Mason, Murray); Leeds 3-0 (Mannion 3); WEST HAM 5-0 (Murray 2, Clamp, Horne, Mannion); Newcastle 0-1; FOREST 3-1 (Murray 2, OG); Forest 0-0; SPURS 1-3 (Broadbent); Chelsea 5-1 (Horne 2, Murray, Broadbent, Flowers) & FAC Blackburn 3-0 (Deeley 2, OG).

RECORD: PLD 56 W 33 D 8 L 15 F 136 A 87 (20-3-4 & 13-5-11).

SCORERS: Murray 34, Broadbent 19, Deeley 19, Mason 19, Horne 11, Clamp 10, Flowers 6, Mannion 6, Lill 3, Slater 2, Stobart 2, Booth 1 & OG 4.

INTERNATIONALS: Flowers took over the mantle of ever-present from Wright, and at 25 in one match he was England's youngest-ever oldest player! Slater returned for his 12th appearance in the white shirt and Mannion scored at Under 23 level. Apps: Broadbent (E 1), Flowers (E 7 + FL 1), Mannion (E U23-2) & Slater (E 1).

FAREWELLS: Booth 82-27 (Forest) & Lill 34-17 (Everton).

1960 - 61

DEBUTANTS: Chic Brodie (Aldershot), Les Cocker, Ted Farmer & Alan Hinton. Brodie was born in Scotland.

SUMMARY: Wolves kicked-off the season at Burnley with their fifth Charity Shield involvement in 12 years, while at home the only major post-war ground alteration was the extension of the Molineux Street Stand to cover the enclosure, a far cry from what was planned. The team performed with great distinction in the League again although double-winners Spurs were a cut above the rest. By the end of 1960-61 Wolves had played 31 sides in more than six competitive games since the war and had a superior record against 29 of them, Spurs and Middlesbrough being the exceptions. Friendlies at Molineux were less frequent though Wolves did draw 5-5 with Dynamo Tbilisi watched by over 34,000 fans.

LEAGUE: 3rd (57). With Finlayson injured during the pre-season activities, Sidebottom soon had to fish the ball out of the net against West Ham, though Wolves struck four times before he was beaten again. In the third match memories of 1958-59 were revived as Wolves trailed 3-0 at Chelsea, but on this occasion they fought back well to draw. Wolves gathered 11 points in the first six games yet Spurs were doing even better. Then there were a couple of fruitless trips and only a superb save by

Sidebottom from Blackburn's Chris Crowe prevented more suffering. Black Country boy Farmer made a terrific start to his career at Old Trafford but when Spurs came to Molineux they comfortably made it 11/11 wins. Wolves then wasted two-goal advantages to Cardiff and Newcastle before taming a Sheff Wed defence who had let in just seven prior to that meeting. Wolves pipped Forest 5-3 one Saturday only to lose by the same score to Burnley the next, despite being 3-1 up.

Over the following 10 games Wolves gained 18 points and scored 34 goals in the process, the only setback coming at West Ham where Sidebottom was carried off. The Everton visit on January 21st was remarkable in the sense that Farmer scored his 21st goal in his 21st appearance — all this on his 21st birthday! The goal actually arrived in the eighth minute as Wolves hit four including a Murray brace, the same thing happening when Albion came to town. The good spell finished at Blackburn, though Wolves returned to winning ways as Brodie made his one appearance between the sticks against Man Utd. Despite this splendid form Wolves were eight points adrift of Spurs, making victory at White Hart Lane essential. Unfortunately Slater cracked a rib early on and although he re-joined the action he was virtually a passenger, so Wolves did magnificently to draw.

Farmer's foursome against Birmingham took his tally to an astonishing 28 in his first 25 League appearances, though he struggled to complete the Man City game with damage to the bladder later revealed, bringing his season to a premature end after 27 outings. Wolves created some more soccer history at Arsenal when Mason pierced the home ranks, giving them the distinction of topping 100 goals for the fourth consecutive year. Nobody else has achieved this in any division and no other team have recorded four D1 centuries in all, let alone four in succession. Yet Wolves threw away both the runners-up spot and a sequence of 13 Molineux wins by slumping to Fulham, who had not gained the points in their last 18 trips to the ground.

Even missing 15 games could not stop Farmer being fourth= D1 scorer as Wolves final total reached 103. For the eighth time in nine winters they were in the top three, gaining the highest-ever points for the team in third position, in fact 57 would have been enough to give them the title in 17 of the seasons in which there had been 42 fixtures, top four: Spurs 66, Sheff Wed 58, Wolves 57 and Burnley 51.

EUROPEAN CUP-WINNERS CUP: This new competition attracted just 10 entrants and like most of them Wolves were helped by a first round bye. They took on FK Austria in Vienna and must have spent the journey home wondering how they had lost, having hit the woodwork five times. In a belated second leg Flowers went down with a heavy cold to enable stand-in Kirkham to grab two early goals to set Wolves off on a QF stroll, and they were not unduly concerned that Farmer had three efforts ruled out. A crowd of approximately 80,000 watched the SF in Glasgow, where Murray hit the bar before Scott gave Rangers an interval lead, Brand making it 2-0 in the closing minutes. Local interest in the return leg was not exactly overwhelming, the 45,163 attendance including many from North of the border some of whom invaded the Midlands in rowdy fashion. The Scots were delighted to draw and qualify on a 3-1 aggregate, though they were beaten in the final by Fiorentina.

F.A. CUP: Hinton was given a miserable introduction to first team football as Wolves feebly bowed out to D2 Huddersfield - despite being able to have two bites at the cherry.

RESULTS: CS Burnley 2-2 (Deeley, Murray); WEST HAM 4-2 (Flowers 2, Broadbent, Murray); Bolton 2-0 (Horne, Murray); Chelsea 3-3 (Murray 2, Horne); BOLTON 3-1 (Broadbent, Deeley, Horne); BLACKPOOL 1-0 (Mason); LEICESTER 3-2 (Murray 2, Broadbent); Everton 1-3 (Flowers); Leicester 0-2; BLACKBURN 0-0; Man Utd 3-1 (Farmer 2, Horne); SPURS 0-4; CARDIFF 2-2 (Farmer 2); ECWC FK Austria 0-2; Newcastle 4-4 (Broadbent 2, Farmer, Murray); SHEFF WED 4-1 (Murray 2, Deeley, Broadbent); Birmingham 2-1 (Mason, Murray); FOREST 5-3 (Farmer 2, Deeley, Broadbent, OG); Burnley 3-5 (Farmer 2, Broadbent); PRESTON 3-0 (Mason, Farmer, Broadbent); Fulham 3-1 (Farmer 2, Mason); ECWC FK AUSTRIA 5-0 (Kirkham 2, Broadbent 2, Mason); ARSENAL 5-3 (Farmer 3, Deeley, Durandt); Man City 4-2 (Flowers, Durandt, Mason, Farmer); West Ham 0-5; Villa 2-0 (Durandt, Farmer); VILLA 3-2 (Farmer 2, Murray); CHELSEA 6-1 (Murray 3, Durandt, Farmer, Kirkham); FAC HUDDERSFIELD 1-1 (Murray); FAC Huddersfield 1-2 (Kirkham); EVERTON 4-1 (Murray 2, Deeley, Farmer); ALBION 4-2 (Murray 2, Durandt, Deeley); Blackburn 1-2 (Durandt); MAN UTD 2-1 (Deeley, Flowers); Spurs 1-1 (Farmer); Cardiff 2-3 (Farmer 2); Blackpool 2-5 (Durandt 2); NEWCASTLE 2-1 (Broadbent, Murray); Sheff Wed 0-0; BIRMINGHAM 5-1 (Farmer 4, Murray); Forest 1-1 (Murray); ECWC Rangers 0-2; MAN CITY 1-0 (Murray); Albion 1-2 (Stobart); Preston 2-1 (Mannion, Stobart); BURNLEY 2-1 (Kirkham, Durandt); ECWC RANGERS 1-1 (Broadbent); Arsenal 5-1 (Stobart 2, Broadbent, Mason, Murray) & FULHAM 2-4 (Deeley, Stobart).

RECORD: PLD 49 W 26 D 10 L 13 F 113 A 85 (18-4-2 & 8-6-11).

SCORERS: Farmer 28, Murray 25, Broadbent 14, Deeley 9, Durandt 9, Mason 7, Flowers 5, Kirkham 5, Stobart 5, Horne 4, Mannion 1 & OG 1.

INTERNATIONALS: Flowers scored in two of England's matches while Kelly was selected for Eire. Apps: Flowers (E 9 + E v YE + FL 2), Kelly (ROI 3) & Kirkham (YE v E + E U23-2).

FAREWELLS: Brodie 1-0 (Northampton), Cocker 1-0, Horne 52-18 (Blackpool), Mannion 19-7 (Norwich) & Sidebottom 35-0 (Villa).

1961 - 62

DEBUTANTS: Chris Crowe (Blackburn), Fred Davies, Freddie Goodwin, John Harris, Mark Lazarus (QPR), Peter McParland (Villa),

Bobby Thomson, Terry Wharton & David Woodfield. McParland was born in Ireland.

SUMMARY: Off the field the Wolverhampton Wanderers Development Association was formed in 1962 but on it Wolves fell to their lowest ebb since 1933. The glory days were coming to an end and the worrying drop in attendances suggested fans had been spoiled by success, though 16,000 watched a joint-testimonial for Wright and Mullen in which a Farmer hatrick helped Wolves draw 4-4 with an International XI. The teenagers showed there was some light on the horizon by almost snatching the Youth Cup, Wolves participating in their fourth final of a competition that had only been in existence for a decade.

LEAGUE: 18th (36). Sheffield United marked their return to the top flight by beating Wolves, who immediately opened their account against West Ham. Then Villa came to Molineux on what was an unhappy day all-round for the hosts. John Harris broke his leg, there was a rare bottle-throwing incident and a brace by Dougan gave Villa their first point in nine derbies with Wolves. After toiling vainly in the sweltering heat of Blackburn there were more setbacks until the ninth match, when Slater inspired them to victory over Forest.

Wolves saw off Man Utd prior to having mixed fortunes in the second city of Birmingham. They lost to Everton in dense fog and were a poor 11th when fast-improving Ipswich arrived at Molineux. Wingers Wharton and Hinton sent them packing, the former scoring in the 69th minute of his debut though the East Anglians were still to be surprise champions. Confidence received another lift as Wolves were the first visitors to take a point off Burnley only to ruin it against Arsenal. A Murray goal did the trick at Fulham where Farmer was hurt having not played since the early part of 1961-62, in fact he broke a bone below the knee which amazingly was not discovered for five weeks. Wolves managed another fine victory before having what can only be described as a black spell in the next five games. One point was gained as Blackburn had their first Molineux success in their last 21 visits and Blackpool rammed seven past Wolves, a fate they had avoided since 1934-35.

A new-look team was fielded for the Spurs test and they responded well in front of a keen crowd, Crowe and McParland re-paying some of the £55,000 they had cost with goalscoring debuts. The Cardiff fixture was played on a Friday night to prevent a clash with a Welsh Rugby Union International and the switch did Wolves no harm at all. They made it three wins in a row and also 10 on the trot against their rivals that day, Birmingham.

Results were in and out until Albion exploited Wolves weaknesses to make the prospect of taking on the leading duo an awesome one, but Wolves were not disgraced against either Ipswich or Burnley. From then on the main interest centred around two meetings with Chelsea, nine goals being scored at Stamford Bridge and Woodfield making his debut in the return witnessed by just 14,597 supporters. People were clearly disappointed at Wolves not being in the top six for the first time in 10 seasons, in fact while they were never in danger their dismal run-in left them only four points ahead of relegated Cardiff.

F.A. CUP: Wolves were too strong for D4 Carlisle while Cullis sprang some surprises for the fourth round tie with Albion. In a bid to tighten up an ailing defence he gave debuts to Davies, Thomson and Goodwin, but the experience of Albion took them through.

RESULTS: Sheff Utd 1-2 (Flowers); WEST HAM 3-2 (Murray 2, Deeley); VILLA 2-2 (Farmer 2); Blackburn 1-2 (Farmer); BLACKPOOL 2-2 (Murray 2); Spurs 0-1; Forest 1-3 (Murray); CARDIFF 1-1 (Farmer); FOREST 2-1 (Kirkham 2); Man Utd 2-0 (Kirkham, Broadbent); Villa 0-1; Birmingham 6-3 (Mason 2, Deeley, Lazarus, Murray, Slater); EVERTON 0-3;Bolton 0-1; MAN CITY 4-1 (Lazarus, Hinton, Durandt, Murray); Leicester 0-3; IPSWICH 2-0 (Wharton, Hinton); Burnley 3-3 (Flowers, Hinton, Murray); ARSENAL 2-3 (Wharton 2); Fulham 1-0 (Murray); SHEFF WED 3-0 (Hinton, Lazarus, Wharton); SHEFF UTD 0-1; West Ham 2-4 (Murray 2); Albion 1-1 (Murray); FAC CARLISLE 3-1 (Wharton 2, Broadbent); BLACKBURN 0-2; Blackpool 2-7 (Murray, Wharton); FAC ALBION 1 –2 (Murray); SPURS 3-1 (Wharton, McParland, Crowe); Cardiff 3-2 (Wharton 2, McParland); BIRMINGHAM 2-1 (McParland, Wharton); MAN UTD 2-2 (Crowe, Murray); Everton 0-4; BOLTON 5-1 (McParland 2, Crowe, Broadbent, Murray); Man City 2-2 (Crowe, Wharton); LEICESTER 1-1 (Hinton); ALBION 1-5 (Broadbent); Ipswich 2-3 (Flowers, McParland); BURNLEY 1-1 (Crowe); Arsenal 1-3 (Murray); Chelsea 5-4 (Crowe 2, Wharton, Kirkham, McParland); FULHAM 1-3 (Broadbent); CHELSEA 1-1 (Broadbent) & Sheff Wed 2-3 (Flowers, Farmer).

RECORD: PLD 44 W 14 D 10 L 20 F 77 A 89 (9-7-7 & 5-3-13).

SCORERS: Murray 17, Wharton 13, Crowe 7, McParland 7, Broadbent 6, Farmer 5, Hinton 5, Flowers 4, Kirkham 4, Lazarus 3, Deeley 2, Mason 2, Durandt 1 & Slater 1.

YOUTH CUP: Birmingham 1-0, Northampton 3-1, STOKE 4-0, SHEFF UTD 3-0, Villa 4-1, Chelsea 1-0, CHELSEA 3-0, NEWCASTLE 1-1 (Galley/13,916) & Newcastle 0-1. Team: Barron, Rickerby, Thomson, Goodwin, Woodfield, Knighton, Povey, Attwood, Galley, Knowles & Calloway. In the second leg Kemp replaced Attwood.

SCORERS: Galley 6, Attwood 4, Knowles 3, Povey 3, Ford 1, Goodwin 1, Kemp 1 & Rickerby 1.

INTERNATIONALS: Flowers had another eventful campaign with some vital penalties amongst his five goals. He became their first player to score in four successive games from a non-forward position and in the 1962 WCF he was the only England man to score twice as he appeared in all their four matches. Farmer netted four for the Under 23 team which contained a hatrick in their 5-2 win in Holland, while McParland continued his Irish

International career. Apps: Farmer (E U23-2), Flowers (E 12 + E v YE + FL 3), Kelly (ROI 2) & McParland (NI 1).

FAREWELLS: Clamp 241-25 (Arsenal), Deeley 237-76 (Orient), Durandt 49-11 (Charlton), Jones 22-0 (Bristol Rovers), Kelly 18-0 (Norwich), Lazarus 9-3 (QPR), Mason 173-54 (Orient) & Stuart 322-1 (Stoke). EDDIE CLAMP hailed from Coalville in Leicestershire and made his debut in the 1953-54 championship season, though he was only chosen once more. In fact Clamp was not actually an automatic selection until Wolves regained the title in 1957-58, when he was one of three players to top the appearance chart with 45, also converting some valuable penalties. The hard-tackling wing-half was 27 when he was transferred for a massive fee of £35,000.

NORMAN DEELEY had not reached five feet in height when he was introduced to the first team, not growing that many inches afterwards. The Wednesbury ace was big in stature though and he was not deterred at making only 38 appearances in five seasons, the change from right-half to right-wing proving the turning point for him. In 1957-58 he played 45 times and was a belated successor to Hancocks whose original replacement Hooper had never properly settled at the club. From then on Deeley never looked back with a significant F.A. Cup contribution in 1959-60 and a year later he made the most Wolves appearances, 47, eventually being sold for £12,000 at the age of 28.

BOBBY MASON was a slightly built player from Tipton who also had to wait patiently before being regarded as one of the senior team members. He never stopped running and would have done well in the modern game, and he did do well in European Cup-ties. The inside-forward left Wolves for somewhere in the region of £10,000.

EDDIE STUART came from a place called Middleburg and his previous club was Johannesburg Rangers. He played twice in 1951-52 but a mystery illness kept him out of the first team in 1952-53 and his whole future looked in jeopardy. Stuart gradually established himself as a sound cog in the Wolves defence, usually at right-back, and he was involved in the four major friendlies. This man with a magnificent physique briefly took over the captaincy early in 1959-60 but the season ended on a sour note when he was omitted at Wembley, his stay at Wolves coming to an end with an £8,000 move.

1962 - 63

DEBUTANT: John Galley.

SUMMARY: James Marshall succeeded James Baker who had been Wolves Chairman since the war, while Flowers was appointed captain. Wolves made an impressive start as if to prove that 1961-62 was merely a temporary setback and though they did not quite maintain that form they finished a useful fifth, which meant over the last 20 seasons they had easily the best record of any Football League club. Wolves also completed a decade of floodlight friendlies at Molineux, 13 resulting in victory and the other four being drawn with all except Celtic being foreign opposition. Both the reserve and youth teams could perhaps claim to be amongst the best four in the country, the former being runners-up in the Central League for Midlands and Northern sides and the latter reaching the national Youth Cup SF.

LEAGUE: 5th (50). Farmer became the third Wolves man in seven years to strike four times against Man City in a tremendous opening day result. Wolves scored five goals in 15 minutes either side of the break, the Northerners lone reply being an unintentional effort from Showell. The team further indicated they meant business by giving West Ham a long-overdue drubbing, having lost all their previous eight matches at Upton Park.

The young Wolves went into their seventh fixture with only a point dropped, reaching a peak with a superb win at skilful Tottenham. Forest looked set to halt the march but Wolves salvaged a late equaliser, an enthusiastic crowd urging them on with the Molineux roar that had almost become a thing of the past. They were unable to complete the double over Spurs but two fine victories followed. The first was at Ipswich, where a Hinton rocket was sandwiched between two Town goals before McParland popped up with a brace to swing the game round. Then at home to Liverpool in the dying minutes Showell came from nowhere to clear when Jimmy Melia appeared to have levelled matters for the third time that day. The unlucky Farmer had made a blistering start to 1962-63 but was now hampered by a disc problem that was to put him on the sidelines for most of the season.

Wolves had 19/22 points with Everton second on 17, only to disappoint their fans in the top-of-the-table meeting. A week later Everton drew in the afternoon, while that Saturday night Wolves suffered their first away failure as they flopped at Bolton to fall a point behind the Toffees. Birmingham underlined that the rot had set in then came Highbury heartbreak, Wolves trailing by two goals before recovering to go ahead, only to finally lose 5-4. This put them fifth yet they were still within three points of leaders Everton and Spurs. Sheff Wed halted a run of 11 defeats at Molineux when they held Wolves to a 2-2 draw and the next visitors, Man Utd, won 3-2 after being 2-0 behind.

Wolves were drifting in the wrong direction until they found their touch with 12 goals in three away games. John Galley, nephew of Tom, collected a couple of them and Wolves recorded a 9-0 aggregate in London against Orient and Fulham. Wolves then drew at Man City having been 3-0 down to the irritation of their hosts who had not got the better of them in their most recent 16 attempts.

Weatherwise, it was the worst winter since 1946-47, only 10,484 braving the elements at Molineux for the first game there in seven weeks. Another eight weeks elapsed before the next one, wingers Wharton and Hinton providing a grandstand finish of five goals in the last 24 minutes to destroy Albion. The attack carried on where they left off against Bolton, but even an early goal gifted to Hinton at Hillsborough was not enough to earn a point. Mason and Deeley returned to Wolverhampton in the colours or Orient, who were having a brief D1 excursion, while any thoughts of revenge Albion had when they led 2-0 were removed.

Wright returned to Molineux as manager of Arsenal and for once was sad to see Wolves win at home, though the visit of Burnley was more memorable. Wolves were fortunate to be 2-1 up at half-time and were relieved as Hinton unleashed two thunderbolts within five minutes to make it 4-1, going on to make post-war history by scoring seven on three occasions in a D1 season. The Easter double over Villa that ensued raised Wolves hopes of a runners-up spot, Hinton then getting their 40th away goal before Leicester squared matters. The term petered out somewhat for Wolves and their fine points haul was five less than that of the second-placed team and 11 adrift of Champions Everton.

In 17/20 tables Wolves had occupied a top six position and without bias were the supreme club in England over this time-span. If we award 22 marks for the top team down to one mark for the 22nd team, Wolves have a staggering 30 marks more than anyone else. If a straightforward points count is taken the result is equally emphatic: Wolves 1,006; Arsenal 943 and Man Utd 920. The Red Devils were in D2 in 1937-38 though even maximum points would not have been enough to catch Wolves had they been in the top flight. Wolves also had one of the best defences and when it came to scoring goals it really was no contest: Wolves 1,769; Man Utd 1,532 and Arsenal 1,520.

F.A. CUP: Wolves stayed in the Cup for a while yet did not progress beyond the third round, the reason for this apparent contradiction being that the exciting tie they lost to Forest was postponed five times.

RESULTS: MAN CITY 8-1 (Farmer 4, Murray 2, Hinton, Wharton); West Ham 4-1 (Farmer 2, Crowe, Wharton); Blackpool 2-0 (Crowe 2); WEST HAM 0-0; BLACKBURN 4-2 (Hinton 2, Farmer, Crowe); Sheff Utd 2-1 (Farmer, Wharton); Spurs 2-1 (Wharton, Crowe); FOREST 1-1 (Wharton); SPURS 2-2 (Murray 2); Ipswich 3-2 (McParland 2, Hinton); LIVERPOOL 3-2 (Murray, Crowe, Wharton); EVERTON 0-2; Bolton 0-3; BIRMINGHAM 0-2; Arsenal 4-5 (Broadbent, Crowe, Flowers, McParland); SHEFF WED 2-2 (Kirkham 2); Burnley 0-2; MAN UTD 2-3 (Stobart 2); Orient 4-0 (Stobart 2, Crowe, Hinton); LEICESTER 1-3 (Hinton); Fulham 5-0 (Hinton 3, Stobart, Galley); Man City 3-3 (Crowe, Galley, Stobart); SHEFF UTD 0-0; FAC Forest 3-4 (Stobart 2, Broadbent); Liverpool 1-4 (Murray); Everton 0-0; Birmingham 4-3 (Broadbent, Kirkham, Stobart, Wharton); ALBION 7-0 (Wharton 3, Stobart 2, Hinton 2); BOLTON 4-0 (Wharton, Crowe, Stobart, Kirkham); Sheff Wed 1-3 (Hinton); ORIENT 2-1 (Stobart, Wharton); Albion 2-2 (Hinton, Stobart); ARSENAL 1-0 (Wharton); BURNLEY 7-2 (Broadbent 2, Hinton 2, Murray, Wharton, OG); VILLA 3-1 (Murray, Wharton, Hinton); Villa 2-0 (Wharton, Hinton); Leicester 1-1 (Hinton); Man Utd 1-2 (OG); FULHAM

2-1 (Flowers, Hinton); Forest 0-2; IPSWICH 0-0; BLACKPOOL 2-0 (Broadbent, Crowe) & Blackburn 1-5 (Farmer).

RECORD: PLD 43 W 20 D 10 L 13 F 96 A 69 (11-6-4 & 9-4-9).

SCORERS: Hinton 19, Wharton 16, Stobart 14, Crowe 11, Farmer 9, Murray 8, Broadbent 6, Kirkham 4, McParland 3, Flowers 2, Galley 2 & OG 2.

INTERNATIONALS: England's first European Nations Cup (now the European Championship) goal was scored by Flowers to make his total 10, of which six were penalties. Crowe and Hinton made their debuts to create the 24th and most recent example of three Wolves men in the England XI, excluding the two quartets. However, a warning sign that times were changing for the club came when nobody was selected for an England match for the first time since 1938 - a period covering nearly 150 Full Internationals. Flowers played for the FLXI against England as the format for the Cup Final curtain-raiser was altered temporarily, Hinton scoring that night against the FLXI. The Wednesbury winger also netted a hatrick as the Under 23 team won 4-2 in Yugoslavia, being narrowly denied another as he twice struck the woodwork while the other goal came from a penalty after his shot had been handled on the line. Apps: Crowe (E 1), Flowers (E 6 + FL 1 + FL v E), Hinton (E 1 + E v FL + E U23-2) & Thomson (E U23-2).

FAREWELLS: John Harris 3-0 (Walsall), McParland 21-10 (Plymouth) & Slater 338-25 (Brentford). BILL SLATER was born in the Lancashire town of Clitheroe and joined Wolves as an Amateur International, gaining six more caps before turning professional. He was a calm, elegant footballer who served Wolves well as a wing-half but his career looked on a downward spiral early in 1959-60 when he was demoted to the reserves. Slater fought his way back in as the centre-half and by the end of the season had clinched the captaincy, led Wolves at Wembley and won the 'Footballer of the Year' award. Later in 1960 he even qualified as a Bachelor of Science and was one of several Wolves stars of the 1950's who went on to prove their talents were not just confined to soccer. He was equal top of the appearance chart with 40 in 1961-62 and he remained with Wolves until shortly after his 36th birthday.

F.A. CUP WINNERS 1892 - 93

F.A. CUP WINNERS 1907 - 08

F.A. CUP WINNERS 1948 - 49

LEAGUE CHAMPIONS 1953 - 54

LEAGUE CHAMPIONS 1957 - 58

LEAGUE CHAMPIONS 1958 - 59

F.A. CUP WINNERS 1959 - 60

LEAGUE CUP WINNERS 1973 - 74

LEAGUE CUP WINNERS 1979 - 80

TOWN COAT OF ARMS

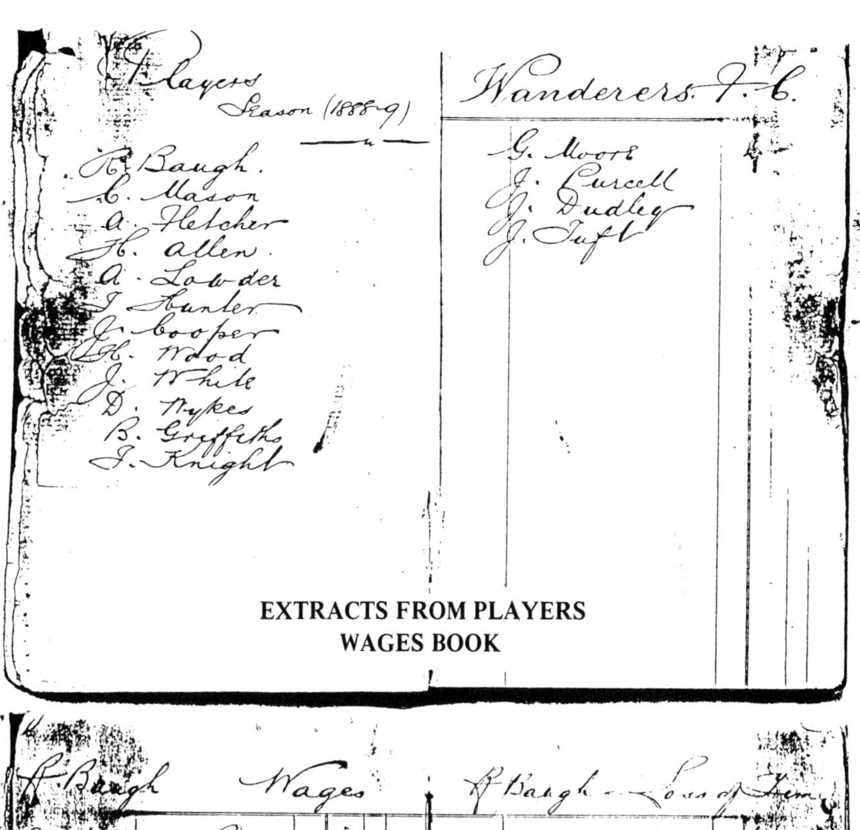

Players Season (1888-9) Wanderers F.C.

R. Baugh
C. Mason
A. Fletcher
H. Allen
A. Lowder
T. Hunter
J. Cooper
H. Wood
J. White
D. Wykes
B. Griffiths
T. Knight
G. Moore
J. Purcell
J. Dudley
J. Tuft

EXTRACTS FROM PLAYERS WAGES BOOK

R. Baugh Wages | R. Baugh – [illegible]

Date	Match		£ s d	Date			
Sept 1st	Notts Rangers	RB	1 0 0				
" 3rd	W.B. Albion	RB	1 0 0				
Sept 8th	Aston Villa	RB	1 0 0	Sep 8th		RB	[illegible]
" 15th	North End	RB	1 0 0	" 15th		RB	2 6
" 22nd	Burnley	RB	1 0 0				[illegible]
" 29th	Bo Rovers	RB	1 0 0				[illegible]
Oct 6th	Accrington		1 0 0	Oct 6th			[illegible]
" 13th	Burnley		1 0 0	" 13th			4
" 20th	Rovers		1 0 0	" 20th	Rovers		[illegible]
" 27th	North End		1 0 0	" 27th			4
Nov 3rd	Derby County		1 0 0				
" 10th	Bolton Wanderers		1 0 0				
" 24th	Aston Villa		1 0 0	" 24th	(10/ for previous week)		10 6
Dec 1st	Accrington		1 0 0				
" 15th	Albion		1 0 0				
" 22nd	Stoke		1 0 0				
" 24th	Shrewsbury Town		1 0 0				
" 26th	Newton Heath		1 0 0				
			£9 0 0				£1.12 0

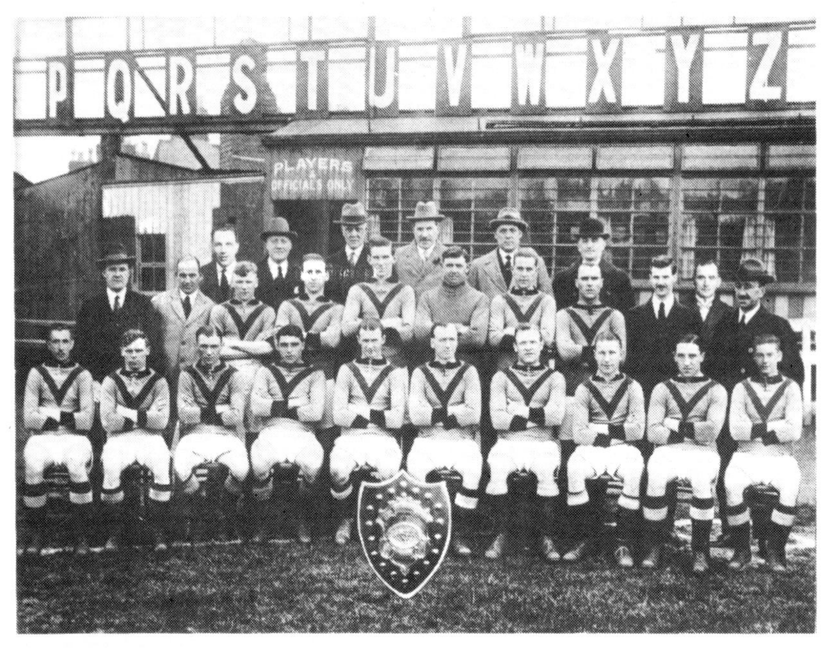

WOLVES TEAM 1923 - 24

WOLVES TEAM 1938 - 39

Wolves v Honved. Bert Williams and Eddie Stuart leave the field with Ferenc Puskas after Wolves won 3-2 at Molineux.

WOLVES v HONVED 1954 - 55

WOLVES v NEWCASTLE 1972 - 73

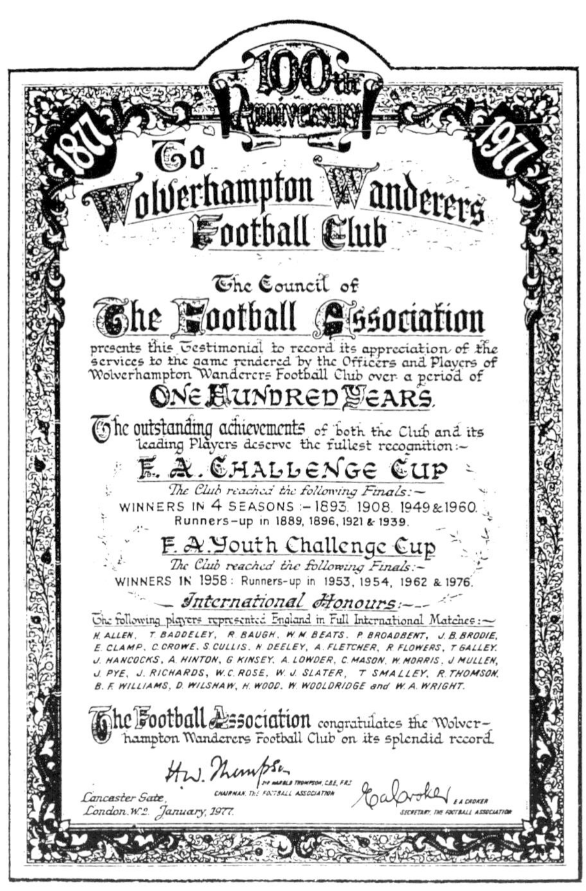

100th Anniversary

1877 1977

To Wolverhampton Wanderers Football Club

The Council of The Football Association presents this Testimonial to record its appreciation of the services to the game rendered by the Officers and Players of Wolverhampton Wanderers Football Club over a period of

ONE HUNDRED YEARS.

The outstanding achievements of both the Club and its leading Players deserve the fullest recognition:–

F. A. CHALLENGE CUP

The Club reached the following Finals:–

WINNERS IN 4 SEASONS :– 1893, 1908, 1949 & 1960.

Runners-up in 1889, 1896, 1921 & 1939.

F. A. Youth Challenge Cup

The Club reached the following Finals:–

WINNERS IN 1958 : Runners-up in 1953, 1954, 1962 & 1976.

International Honours:–

The following players represented England in Full International Matches:–

H. ALLEN, T. BADDELEY, R. BAUGH, W. M. BEATS, P. BROADBENT, J. B. BRODIE, E. CLAMP, C. CROWE, S. CULLIS, N. DEELEY, A. FLETCHER, R. FLOWERS, T. GALLEY, J. HANCOCKS, A. HINTON, G. KINSEY, A. LOWDER, C. MASON, W. MORRIS, J. MULLEN, J. PYE, J. RICHARDS, W. C. ROSE, W. J. SLATER, T. SMALLEY, R. THOMSON, B. F. WILLIAMS, D. WILSHAW, H. WOOD, W. WOOLDRIDGE and W. A. WRIGHT.

The Football Association congratulates the Wolverhampton Wanderers Football Club on its splendid record.

Sir Harold Thompson, C.B.E., F.R.S.
Chairman, The Football Association

E. A. Croker
Secretary, The Football Association

Lancaster Gate,
London. W.2. January, 1977.

WOLVES CENTENARY TESTIMONIAL 1977

BEFORE WORK AT MOLINEUX 1979

WOLVES v ORIENT 1987 - 88

WOLVES v SWANSEA 1987 - 88

STEVE BULL 1988

WOLVES TEAM 1988

Chapter 3

1963 - 64 to 1981 - 82

1963 - 64

DEBUTANTS: Jim Barron, Ray Crawford (Ipswich), Peter Knowles, Dick Le Flem (Forest), Jimmy Melia (Liverpool) & Bobby Woodruff (Swindon).

SUMMARY: Although the failure to attract 20,000 to Molineux after Christmas confirmed that Wolves days amongst the elite were clearly numbered they were by no means a bad team. While 16th was not exactly what they were used to, points-wise they were as near to the runners-up as the bottom club. Sadly, the victories at home were equalled by the defeats for the first time in 41 years, with the only real promise provided by the ball skills of Knowles and Pat Buckley, who found the net three times for Scotland's Youths.

LEAGUE: 16th (39). Wolves wore predominately gold socks with two black rings as if accepting that the past links were being severed though the Highbury result augured well for 1963-64. It was a different tale as Smith and Greaves caused havoc in Spurs visit to Molineux and a lively opening week was completed when Stuart and Clamp returned in the red and white stripes of newly-promoted Stoke. A seasonal best 43,217 were largely unaware of a strange incident as Wolves inadvertantly kicked-off in both halves.

Wolves then conceded 21 goals in five games with Blackburn running riot at Molineux. Finlayson made a sorry farewell at the end of this sequence but optimism was restored as Wolves embarked on a run of eight games without defeat. They had 16 points from the same amount of fixtures and were fortunate to be toppled by Burnley, a late shot going in off the post. Wolves were well beaten when they next travelled and the first half of the season was rounded-off at Fulham, where the defence looked decidedly shaky again.

Form improved until a 2-0 advantage over Forest was tossed away on a day Stobart scored his final first team goal, having netted over 100 for the reserves. January also saw the departure of promising 21-year-old Hinton, who for some reason was a victim of the boo-boys in the crowd. Farmer sustained his latest and most serious injury blow during this miserable month when he hurt his knee in a practice session. When Leicester came to Molineux three penalties were awarded with both sides scoring and City missing one, and though not fully fit Farmer was recalled for the next match at Albion. It was his 57th D1 outing and he could not add to his 44 goals, but more important his future comebacks were restricted to the junior teams and early in 1966 his contract was cancelled by mutual consent and his long battle was lost. Back to 1963-64 when Wolves were involved in another untidy affair at Bramall Lane, where Crawford replaced the injured keeper Davies only for the ball to be deflected past him off Thomson's foot to give United victory.

Wolves ended the season on a defiant note by notching a couple of 4-0 wins, the balding Melia scoring twice in the former. Portsmouth-born Crawford's hatrick at Bolton gave him 26 goals in 34 appearances, an incredible 18 being away from home. He also got two for Ipswich before his transfer to be fifth highest D1 scorer yet Wolves were still out of the top eight D1 scoring teams for the first time in 30 years. In their 25 seasons in the premier section they were now equal leaders on aggregate points with Arsenal.

F.A. CUP: Old Cup adversaries Arsenal made it a short stay for Wolves, two goals putting them in a commanding position before Wharton replied.

RESULTS: Arsenal 3-1 (Crowe, Hinton, Murray); SPURS 1-4 (Hinton); STOKE 2-1 (Crowe, Farmer); Spurs 3-4 (Hinton, Crowe, Kirkham); Forest 0-3; LIVERPOOL 1-3 (Flowers); BLACKBURN 1-5 (Farmer); Liverpool 0-6; Blackpool 2-1 (Crawford 2); CHELSEA 4-1 (Wharton 2, Crawford, Broadbent); ALBION 0-0; West Ham 1-1 (Hinton); Leicester 1-0 (Crawford); BOLTON 2-2 (Knowles, Broadbent); Birmingham 2-2 (Wharton, Hinton); MAN UTD 2-0 (Crawford, Wharton); Burnley 0-1; IPSWICH 2-1 (Crawford, Knowles); Sheff Wed 0-5; EVERTON 0-0; Fulham 1-4 (Crawford); ARSENAL 2-2 (Flowers, Crowe); Stoke 2-0 (Crawford 2); VILLA 3-3 (Crawford 2, Wharton); Villa 2-2 (Crawford, Crowe); FAC Arsenal 1-2 (Wharton); FOREST 2-3 (Broadbent, Stobart); Blackburn 1-1 (Crowe); BLACKPOOL 1-1 (Crawford); Chelsea 3-2 (Crawford 2, Le Flem); WEST HAM 0-2; LEICESTER 1-2 (Broadbent); Albion 1-3 (Le Flem); BIRMINGHAM 5-1 (Wharton 2, Crawford, Flowers, Le Flem); BURNLEY 1-1 (Wharton); Man Utd 2-2 (Crawford 2); SHEFF UTD 1-1 (Crawford); Sheff Utd 3-4 (Crawford 2, Melia); SHEFF WED 1-1 (Melia); Everton 3-3 (Crawford 2, Wharton); Ipswich 0-1; FULHAM 4-0 (Melia 2, Knowles, Le Flem) & Bolton 4-0 (Crawford 3, Knowles).

RECORD: PLD 43 W 12 D 15 L 16 F 71 A 82 (6-9-6 & 6-6-10).

SCORERS: Crawford 26, Wharton 10, Crowe 6, Hinton 5, Broadbent 4, Knowles 4,, Le Flem 4, Melia 4, Flowers 3, Farmer 2, Kirkham 1, Murray 1 & Stobart 1.

INTERNATIONALS: Flowers was England skipper for one match

and was joined in the defence by Thomson, who watched his colleagues blast in 18 goals during his first two Full Internationals. Apps: Flowers (E 3 + E v YE + FL 2), Hinton (E U23-1) & Thomson (E 4 + FL 2 + YE v E + E U23-3).

FAREWELLS: Crowe 85-24 (Forest), Farmer 61-44, Finlayson 203-0, Hinton 78-29 (Forest), Murray 299-166 (Man City) & Stobart 54-22 (Man City). MALCOLM FINLAYSON was plucked from D3 obscurity for £4,000 which proved to be money well spent. The big keeper was born in Dumbarton and was very agile for his size, tackling the challenge of following in the footsteps of Williams with great determination. He in turn had to make way for Davies and was called upon just once in 1962-63 and 1963-64, breaking a finger at Anfield in the latter and retiring at the end of the season.

JIMMY MURRAY was a dark-haired centre-forward from Dover whose greatest asset was simply scoring goals. In 1957-58 he enjoyed three hatricks in seven games and was equal top of the appearance chart. He was on target in the last seven matches of 1958-59 as well as the opening day fixture of 1959-60, when he led the appearances with 53, also sharing that distinction in 1961-62. Murray had to settle for a mere 17 strikes that term having totalled 112 in the previous four seasons, and as the ratio continued to fall gradually he was transferred for £27,000.

1964 - 65

DEBUTANTS: Pat Buckley (Third Lanark), John Farrington, Clive Ford, Graham Hawkins, Fred Kemp, Ken Knighton, Dave MacLaren (Plymouth), Hughie McIlmoyle (Carlisle), George Miller (Dunfermline), David Thompson, Dave Wagstaffe (Man City) & Joe Wilson (Forest). Buckley, MacLaren, McIlmoyle and Miller were born in Scotland, Kemp in Italy.

SUMMARY: Relegation and the sacking of Stan Cullis after 30½ years of wonderful service were two bitter pills for the public of Wolverhampton to swallow. John Ireland had taken over the chairman's seat relinquished by Marshall and the bombshell soon followed with Cullis being dismissed the day after Wolves first win. Results had been horrific but Cullis was working hard to repair the damage and had just recovered from illness when the shock news was announced, a decision that put some people off Wolves for life. It must be said that results were better under Caretaker-Manager Andy Beattie, who Wolves had secured from Preston, but he could not save them and Christmas gloom was heightened by the death of their old supremo Buckley.

LEAGUE: 21st (30). A 3-0 opening day home defeat and a bad injury to debutant Ford set the pattern for this miserable campaign. Only a point was mustered in seven games until West Ham were involved in a night of drama, particularly for Harris, as Wolves revived some memories with a gripping 4-3 success.

The town sank into despair as seven defeats left Wolves with a pathetic 3/30 points. Beattie was in charge when a long-range Woodfield shot sealed victory at Stoke, the fans being further lifted by a fine show against Spurs. The improvement continued with a draw at Burnley and two points at the expense of Sheff Utd, only for Wolves to crash to five more reverses.

Hopes were raised again by three nice results but trips to Liverpool and Manchester brought no reward. It was looking an impossible task when Wolves rallied, Villa just stopping them from claiming a quartet of Midland scalps. Wolves had to get back in the groove at White Hart Lane where it was 1-1 at the interval. Spurs led 3-1 then 4-2 then 5-3 before Wolves pulled one back and nearly equalised, but Spurs grabbed two late goals to complete 45 pulsating minutes.

Thomson, an ever-present since 1961-62, was rested for the Fulham match with Wolves knowing that victory would put the Londoners within reach. It was 0-0. Burnley made Wolves supporters accept the inevitable and despite two spirited wins in the North they were finished off by Everton at home.

Woodruff, who had a throw-in measured at over 40 yards during his stay, produced another rare feat when he converted a hatrick of headers against Sunderland. Wolves went to Nottingham and made it 15 points from 12 games but it was too late as they had to settle for overtaking Birmingham. The final embarrassment was still to come as Wembley-bound Liverpool fielded a virtual reserve team at Molineux and won 3-1 to graphically illustrate why there was a different journey ahead for Wolves, bottom three: Fulham 34, Wolves 30 and Birmingham 27.

F.A. CUP: Replays were required against D2 teams Portsmouth and Rotherham, then in the fifth round at Villa Park a fine 38th-minute move was rounded-off by Woodruff. Villa equalised and even extra-time in the replay failed to sort the matter out. In the snow of the neutral Hawthorns a hero emerged in McIlmoyle who got all three Wolves goals, adding two more a few days later in the QF with Man Utd. The Reds transformed the game with five goals thanks to some splendid attacking flair, though there was a suspicion of the Wolves keeper being held down at set pieces. By the time the home side got on the scoresheet again their dreams of salvaging something from 1964-65 had gone. The days of 55,000+ crowds at Molineux were over, in fact the 53,581 present were slightly above the official capacity of the ground.

RESULTS: CHELSEA 0-3; Leicester 2-3 (Wharton, Knowles); Leeds 2-3 (Knowles, Crawford); LEICESTER 1-1 (Crawford); ARSENAL 0-1; West Ham 0-5; Blackburn 1-4 (Thompson); WEST HAM 4-3 (Crawford 2, Knowles, Harris); BLACKPOOL 1-2 (Crawford); Sheff Wed 0-2; BIRMINGHAM 0-2; Albion 1-5 (Knowles); MAN UTD 2-4 (Crawford 2); Fulham 0-2; FOREST 1 -2 (Crawford); Stoke 2-0 (Wharton, Woodfield); SPURS 3-1 (Wharton, Le Flem, Crawford); Burnley 1-1 (Crawford); SHEFF UTD 1-0 (Woodfield); Everton 0-5; LEEDS 0-1; VILLA 0-1; Arsenal 1-4 (Crawford); Chelsea 1-2 (Crawford); FAC Portsmouth 0-0;

FAC PORTSMOUTH 3-2 (McIlmoyle 2, Crawford); BLACKBURN 4-2 (Woodruff 2, McIlmoyle, Crawford); Blackpool 1-1 (Wagstaffe); FAC ROTHERHAM 2-2 (Crawford, Flowers); FAC Rotherham 3-0 (Woodruff, Wharton, Wagstaffe); SHEFF WED 3-1 (Miller 2, Wharton); Liverpool 1-2 (Woodruff); FAC Villa 1-1 (Woodruff); FAC VILLA 0-0; Man Utd 0-3; FAC Villa 3-1 (McIlmoyle 3); FAC MAN UTD 3-5 (McIlmoyle 2, Knowles); Birmingham 1-0 (Wharton); ALBION 3-2 (McIlmoyle 2, Woodruff); STOKE 3-1 (Buckley, Woodruff, Wharton); Villa 2-3 (McIlmoyle, Woodruff); Spurs 4-7 (Buckley, McIlmoyle, Kirkham, Wharton); FULHAM 0-0; BURNLEY 1-2 (Flowers); Sheff Utd 2-0 (Knowles, Woodruff); Sunderland 2-1 (Knowles, McIlmoyle); EVERTON 2-4 (Wharton, Woodruff); SUNDERLAND 3-0 (Woodruff 3); Forest 2-0 (McIlmoyle, Buckley) & LIVERPOOL 1-3 (Miller).

RECORD: PLD 50 W 16 D 8 L 26 F 74 A 100 (9-4-12 & 7-4-14).

SCORERS: Crawford 15, McIlmoyle 14, Woodruff 13, Wharton 9, Knowles 7, Buckley 3, Miller 3, Flowers 2, Wagstaffe 2, Woodfield 2, Harris 1, Kirkham 1, Le Flem 1 & Thompson 1.

INTERNATIONALS: Flowers was again the main inspiration as he captained England twice more and made his 13th appearance in an Inter-League match, while Thomson repeated his 1963-64 achievement of being honoured at four different grades. Apps: Flowers (E 3 + E v YE + FL 1) & Thomson (E 4 + FL 1 + YE v E + E U23-5).

FAREWELLS: Barron 9-0 (Chelsea), Broadbent 498-145 (Shrewsbury), Crawford 61-41 (Albion), Ford 2-0 (Walsall), Galley 5-2 (Rotherham), Goodwin 46-0 (Stockport), Kemp 4-0 (Southampton), Kirkham 112-15 (Peterborough), Le Flem 19-5 (Middlesbrough), Melia 24-4 (Southampton), Showell 218-3 (Bristol City) & Thompson 10-1 (Southampton). PETER BROADBENT was another Dover-born product who emerged from the mines of Kent to develop into one of Britain's most talented footballers. He cost Wolves at least £10,000 which was then a considerable amount and often demonstrated the reasons why, with such passing skills and vision that he was sometimes too clever for his team-mates. Broadbent topped the list of appearances with 40 in 1955-56 and was prominent in the big four friendlies of the era. He could make or take goals, scoring 10 in the F.A. Cup, and had the gift of making his profession look easy. He had his own testimonial in 1964-65 which was a rare honour in those days and eyebrows were raised when Wolves released the 31 -year-old for a small fee.

JOHNNY KIRKHAM was an attacking wing-half who made the England Youth XI in 1958-59, further honours following. He made several first team appearances in 1961-62 and 1962-63 but the next season saw him mainly on the fringe of the action. The Wednesbury man never fulfilled his potential despite the occasional stirring performance and went for a modest sum.

GEORGE SHOWELL was a Bilstonian who was understudy to Wright, thus making just 46 appearances in five seasons. When Wright retired in stepped Showell yet he could not retain his long-awaited place, showing typical gritty qualities by then breaking through at right-back, where he continued to be a fine club servant.

1965 - 66

DEBUTANTS: Mike Bailey (Charlton), John Holsgrove (Palace), Ernie Hunt (Swindon) & Les Wilson.

SUMMARY: Ronnie Allen took the helm and although Wolves adapted well to their unfamiliar surroundings they never had more than an outside chance of promotion. The outfit of the team was also new as they were now clad in gold shorts to follow the latest trend of one-colour strips. Substitutes were introduced in the Football League but in the Cup Wolves endured something they had definitely seen before, as they again wasted a 2-0 lead at home to Man Utd.

LEAGUE D2: 6th (50). Any illusions that life would be more comfortable in this division were shattered within a few days. McIlmoyle's 58th-minute header was wiped out by an offside-looking Coventry goal with the game then slipping from Wolves grasp, while at Maine Road own goals by Miller and Thomson saved the City forwards any unnecessary exertion.

Knowles got the home programme off to a brighter start but the return with Man City led to a bleak night indeed. Harris gifted another own goal and Murray scored past his old colleagues to help City to their first win in their most recent 22 visits to the ground. Woodfield was the first Wolves player to be sent off at Molineux for approximately 30 years after his clumsy challenge resulted in Mike Summerbee tumbling over the Molineux Street boundary wall, though the City man later insisted it was unintentional.

If Wolves believed that 3/4 victories had solved their problems they were going to come down to earth with a bump, or nine to be precise. Yet after 12 minutes of frantic activity at The Dell they were level at 2-2 with a close battle seemingly in prospect. It was the Saints who went marching on though as Martin Chivers alone helped himself to four goals in a 9-3 massacre. Character was shown by Wolves as they buckled down to a quartet of 3-0 successes with Gordon Ferry of Orient doing them a favour with a brace of own goals, followed by a competent 1-1 draw at Huddersfield. Then came a 3.30 pm kick-off against Palace after the train from London was delayed, the patience of fans being rewarded as popular right-back Joe Wilson found the head of McIlmoyle, who steered it to Knowles who in turn lobbed in the winner. The real story of the afternoon was a series of breathtaking saves by Palace keeper John Jackson who somehow kept it down to 1-0.

There was a sequence of 2-2 draws, including the visit to Preston which was the first match in which the highlights were recorded on television on the Sunday. Wolves led Portsmouth 7-0 after an hour to extract some form of Hampshire retribution and increase their unbeaten run to 10 games, only for Bolton to spoil it all. Wolves used their heads to get that setback out of their system, all four strikes against Ipswich being nodded in. They also did well in the tense meetings with Bristol City at Christmas while a rivalry was developing between them and the second nearest team geographically, Coventry. In what was described as a four-pointer City attracted 44,718 to Molineux, and appropriately enough it was their centre-forward Ray Pointer who broke the deadlock shortly before the interval. Wolves dominated much of the proceedings but failed to score and their prospects of going up were never the same afterwards.

The closing weeks of the campaign saw Wolves go six games without defeat to re-join the leading pack, but a 2-0 reverse at Portsmouth was perhaps the last straw for them. They were not quite equipped to return to D1, their vulnerability being in evidence on the final day at Ipswich when they were 2-1 up only to trail 4-2 by the break, Hawkins adding his name to the own goal men. Wolves were four points behind the runners-up and were top D2 scorers with 87, Knowles being third best in the section on 19 in just 31 appearances.

F.A. CUP: Wolves faced two unusual situations en route to the fifth round, taking on a team from the Cheshire League and one from a higher division. Altrincham were easily dismissed while a twisting McIlmoyle header and a Knowles classic put Sheff Utd on their way out. Wolves were 2-0 up against D1 Man Utd after 10 minutes thanks to a couple of Wharton penalties, but in the second half a careless back pass by Knowles was intercepted and the whole pattern of the contest was changed, the attendance that day being 53,428.

RESULTS: Coventry 1-2 (McIlmoyle); Man City 1-2 (Knowles); CARLISLE 3-0 (Knowles 3); MAN CITY 2-4 (Wagstaffe, Woodruff); Cardiff 4-1 (McIlmoyle 2, Wagstaffe, OG); Rotherham 3-4 (Knowles, Wharton, Wagstaffe); DERBY 4-0 (Knowles 3, Woodruff); ROTHERHAM 4-1 (McIlmoyle, Woodfield, Wagstaffe, Knowles); Southampton 3-9 (OG, Woodruff, Knowles); BURY 3-0 (Wharton, Wagstaffe, Knowles); Norwich 3-0 (Wagstaffe, Wharton, Knowles); Orient 3-0 (Wagstaffe, OG 2); MIDDLESBROUGH 3-0 (Woodfield, Hunt, Knowles); Huddersfield 1-1 (Wharton); PALACE 1-0 (Knowles); Preston 2-2 (Knowles, Wharton); CHARLTON 2-2 (Hunt, McIlmoyle); Plymouth 2-2 (McIlmoyle 2); PORTSMOUTH 8-2 (Holsgrove 2, Woodruff 2, McIlmoyle 2, Flowers, Wagstaffe); Bolton 1-2 (McIlmoyle); IPSWICH 4-1 (Hunt, Woodruff, McIlmoyle, Wharton); Middlesbrough 1-3 (Knowles); BRISTOL C 1-1 (Buckley); Bristol C 1-0 (Knowles); ORIENT 2-1 (Wharton, Hunt); Charlton 1-1 (OG); HUDDERSFIELD 2-1 (Hunt, Woodruff); FAC ALTRINCHAM 5-0 (Hunt 2, McIlmoyle, OG, Woodruff); COVENTRY 0-1; Carlisle 1-2 (Wagstaffe); FAC SHEFF UTD 3-0 (Knowles 2, McIlmoyle); CARDIFF 2-1 (Wharton 2); Derby 2-2 (Hunt, McIlmoyle); FAC MAN UTD 2-4 (Wharton 2); SOUTHAMPTON 1-1 (Hunt); Bury 0-1; NORWICH 2-1 (Woodfield 2); PRESTON 3-0 (Hunt, Woodfield, McIlmoyle); Palace 1-0 (Woodfield); Birmingham 2-2 (Woodfield, Hunt); BIRMINGHAM 2-0 (Hunt, McIlmoyle); PLYMOUTH 0-0; Portsmouth

0-2; BOLTON 3-1 (Wharton, Knowles, McIlmoyle) & Ipswich 2-5 (Buckley, Knowles).

RECORD: PLD 45 W 22 D 10 L 13 F 97 A 65 (17-4-3 & 5-6-10).

SCORERS: Knowles 21, McIlmoyle 17, Hunt 12, Wharton 12, Wagstaffe 9, Woodruff 8, Woodfield 7, Buckley 2, Holsgrove 2, Flowers 1 & OG 6.

INTERNATIONALS: Flowers made his 49th England appearance which few had bettered and his total in all major representative matches reached 71. He was in the 22-man squad for the 1966 WCF but did not make the successful England XI. Apps: Flowers (E1), Hunt (E U23-2) & Thomson (E U23-3).

FAREWELLS: Gerry Harris 270-2 (Walsall), Miller 45-3 & Woodruff 72-71 (Palace). GERRY HARRIS was a sound tackling full-back from Claverley, adding to the list of Wolves stars born in the sparsely-populated county of Shropshire. He topped the appearances in 1958-59 with 45 and was a regular until 1960-61, being restricted to 26 outings over the next three seasons. Harris came back to the fore in 1964-65, particularly in the 4-3 win against West Ham in which he scored an own goal and conceded a penalty but redeemed himself by creating a goal for Wolves and netting their winner. He left for a nominal fee, taking the same road as his brother John.

1966 - 67

DEBUTANTS: Dave Burnside (Palace), Derek Dougan (Leicester), Bob Hatton, Phil Parkes & Gerry Taylor. Dougan was born in Ireland.

SUMMARY: Wolves used the extra year of re-building to good effect, gaining a well-deserved promotion. The club also entered the Football League Cup for the first time since it's inception in 1960-61, a competition that was slowly being accepted by the public. There was another F.A. Cup disappointment at Molineux but that was forgotten as Wolves finished second in D2, the reward being a summer tour of the United States where they won a prestigious tournament. Opposition from Brazil, Uruguay, Holland and Italy were brushed aside before Wolves beat Scotland's Aberdeen 6-5 in an astonishing final, Burnside hitting a hatrick. Another honour of 1966-67 was not quite so spectacular, Wolves collecting the SSC which was not as important as it had been in the past while the Central League highspot was the scoring of Buckley (33) and Alun Evans (24).

LEAGUE D2: 2nd (58). Wolves were humbled by Birmingham at Molineux as only one of their first five fixtures was won. An unusual feature about the latter concerned Bristol-born Burnside, a man who had been chiefly famous for his ball-juggling skills that had entertained crowds galore. Yet he was no more than an average footballer who made a scoring debut for Wolves - despite being listed in the programme line-up of opponents Crystal Palace as he was still with them when it went to press.

The team got into their stride with three goals at Carlisle, four versus Blackburn after fans had fought on the pitch and seven against

Cardiff. Only one out of 15 was lost and though Wolves did not repeat their thrashing of Portsmouth there was a goal for Hatton within 30 seconds of his debut. Wolves suffered defeat at Bury and then Coventry continued to hold the upper hand over them, before they made amends at Norwich. A 25-yarder from Bailey and a well-taken Wagstaffe goal gave Wolves a 2-0 lead at Birmingham in their 14th post-war visit, yet it was to be their only reverse in all that time. Some lethal finishing in the festive clashes with Derby re-consolidated Wolves position at the head of the table.

A single Hunt goal was all that Wolves could muster in the following four matches with the inevitable consequence that they were deposed as leaders, the frustrations spilling over as Wagstaffe was sent off at Blackburn. However, promotion was virtually assured as they responded by equalling their record of eight succesive League wins, two of which were televised. Knowles created something of a stir by kicking the ball out of the ground in celebration of his goal at Portsmouth and literally paying for it, while Dougan attracted better publicity in front of the cameras with a hatrick on his home debut. Easter was completed with a useful double over Huddersfield, the Molineux meeting pulling in 40,429 supporters.

Wolves dropped a point in a torrid afternoon for their players and followers alike at Millwall, but Rotherham were accounted for in a Saturday night affair. A huge number of fans cheered Hunt's brace at Preston as D1 loomed nearer, then a fine performance against Bury made it official.

Seeking a 15th match without defeat Wolves went to Coventry with the championship set firmly in their sights. The Highfield Road attendance of 51,456 was a record by more than 6,000 as the D2 giants battled it out. Wolves made the early running so it was no surprise when Knowles struck with an angled drive. Coventry, under the progressive guidance of Jimmy Hill, were a different proposition in the second half to thoroughly deserve the win that put them level on points with Wolves, who still led on goal-average. Norwich were tamed as Wolves said their Molineux farewell while Coventry could only draw. An inexplicable last day trouncing at Palace cost Wolves the title, City leaping above them as they beat Millwall 3-1. If the three-points-per win system had been in operation Wolves would have been first but instead they had to be content with being top scorers on 88, Hunt getting 20 in 37 appearances to be fifth in the individual D2 chart in a happy season for the club, top three: Coventry 59, Wolves 58 and Carlisle 52.

LEAGUE CUP: Wolves began their own Football League Cup story by scraping through against D3 Mansfield in the second round. Some of the outstanding teams in the country still refused to participate despite the final being moved to Wembley having always been played on a two-leg basis before. Wolves probably wished they had opted out for at least another year after their result at D1 Fulham.

F.A. CUP: D3 Oldham led Wolves 2-0 with five minutes to go, fortunately a couple of Wolves defenders ventured upfield to show the attackers how it should be done. The replay was a formality to give Wolves a tie against holders D1 Everton that produced a 53,439 turnout at

Molineux. Wharton made an early breakthrough and for most of the afternoon an upset was on the cards, but an alleged foul on Alan Ball in the later stages spoiled the party atmosphere, a spot-kick being the only way Everton were likely to equalise. Wolves tried hard at Goodison Park but even their fans sensed it was the end of the Cup road.

RESULTS: BIRMINGHAM 1-2 (McIlmoyle); Ipswich 1-3 (McIlmoyle); Cardiff 3-0 (McIlmoyle 2, Buckley); BRISTOL C 1-1 (Knowles); PALACE 1-1 (Burnside); Carlisle 3-1 (Hunt 2, Holsgrove); LC MANSFIELD 2-1 (Hatton, Wharton); BLACKBURN 4-0 (Hunt 2, Burnside, Wharton); CARDIFF 7-1 (Wharton 3, Hunt, Thomson, McIlmoyle, Wagstaffe); Bolton 0-0; CHARLTON 1-0 (McIlmoyle); LC Fulham 0-5; PORTSMOUTH 3-1 (Hatton, Hunt, Wharton); Hull 1-3 (Bailey); PLYMOUTH 2-1 (Woodfield, Hunt); Northampton 4-0 (Hunt 3, McIlmoyle); MILLWALL 2-0 (McIlmoyle 2); Rotherham 2-2 (McIlmoyle, Wagstaffe); PRESTON 3-2 (Wharton 2, McIlmoyle); Bury 1-2 (Hunt); COVENTRY 1-3 (Burnside); Norwich 2-1 (Wagstaffe, Knowles); Birmingham 2-3 (Bailey, Wagstaffe); DERBY 5-3 (Wharton 2, Hatton 2, McIlmoyle); Derby 3-0 (McIlmoyle, Wharton, Hatton); IPSWICH 0-0; Bristol C 0-1; CARLISLE 1-1 (Hunt); Blackburn 0-0; FAC Oldham 2-2 (Bailey, Thomson); FAC OLDHAM 4-1 (Hunt, Wharton, McIlmoyle, Woodfield); BOLTON 5-2 (Hunt 2, Hatton 2, Wagstaffe); Charlton 3-1 (Knowles, Hatton, Woodfield); FAC EVERTON 1-1 (Wharton); FAC Everton 1-3 (Wharton); Portsmouth 3-2 (Bailey, Knowles, Hunt); NORTHAMPTON 1-0 (Wagstaffe); Plymouth 1-0 (Knowles); HULL 4-0 (Dougan 3, Knowles); Huddersfield 1-0 (Wharton); HUDDERSFIELD 1-0 (Knowles); Millwall 1-1 (Dougan); ROTHERHAM 2-0 (Dougan, Hunt); Preston 2-1 (Hunt 2); BURY 4-1 (Dougan 2, Wharton, Burnside); Coventry 1-3 (Knowles); NORWICH 4-1 (Dougan 2, Wharton, Hunt) & Palace 1-4 (Hunt).

RECORD: PLD 48 W 27 D 10 L 11 F 98 A 61 (17-5-2 & 10-5-9).

SCORERS: Hunt 21, Wharton 17, McIlmoyle 14, Dougan 9, Hatton 8, Knowles 8, Wagstaffe 6, Bailey 4, Burnside 4, Woodfield 3, Thomson 2, Buckley 1 & Holsgrove 1.

INTERNATIONALS: For the first time in 31 seasons England did not call upon anyone from Wolverhampton though there was consolation at Under 23 level. Thomson equalled what was then the record 15 appearances, many as captain, also playing in the 8-0 slaughter of Wales at Molineux which remains their best result at this grade. The signing of Dougan retained Wolves Full International interest, as he added to his already long career for Ireland. Apps: Dougan (NI 1) & Thomson (YE v E + E U23-2).

FAREWELLS: Flowers 513-37 (Northampton), Hatton 13-8 (Bolton), Knighton 13-0 (Oldham), MacLaren 47-0 (Southampton), McIlmoyle 104-45 (Bristol City) & Joe Wilson 63-0 (Newport). RON FLOWERS joined the club in 1950-51 via the Wath Nursery as he came from the Yorkshire village of Edlington. He was a big, strong wing-half who settled down well in the area and made a major contribution to Wolves more illustrious years. Apart from a brief refusal to re-sign in 1960 he was always happy at the club and was still there when their great D1 era ended in 1964-65, being equal top of the appearances with 48. Flowers finally departed aged 33 near the beginning of 1967-68, though he returned to Molineux in 1970-71 when 21,000 enjoyed his belated testimonial as Wolves saw off an England XI 8-4.

HUGHIE McILMOYLE was born in Port Glasgow and was a typical old-fashioned type of centre-forward. He was good in the air and though not always so clever with his feet he notched 10 goals in the F.A. Cup for Wolves. His 44 appearances in 1965-66 put him equal top and he was well-like by the locals, inspiring many of the earliest songs and chants of the North Bank choir.

1967 - 68

DEBUTANTS: Alun Evans, Mike Kenning (Norwich), John McAlle, Frank Munro (Aberdeen), Derek Parkin (Huddersfield), Stewart Ross, Frank Wignall (Forest) & Evan Williams (Third Lanark). Munro and Williams were born in Scotland.

SUMMARY: Wolves returned to the major League and played admirably in their first two games at Molineux to make it 14 without defeat there, but the season developed into a struggle as Wolves fought to stave off a quick relegation. No attendance at home dropped below 25,000 while a sad note was the death of writer Ivan Sharpe, whose "Today's Topical Talk" had been a popular feature of the Wolves programme for decades.

LEAGUE: 17th (36). A vast Wolverhampton contingent were delighted with the opening day trip to Craven Cottage where Fulham were avenged. Molineux's 51,438 crowd were buzzing with excitement for the visit of Albion, who forced Parkes to make a penalty save in the sixth minute. Wolves were coasting at 2-0 when the linesman persuaded the referee that an Albion effort had crossed the line though when it was 3-2 near the end they scored a goal that was clear-cut enough — it was punched in! Parkes was then given his marching orders for protesting at a decision that robbed Wolves of maximum points for that first week as they then clipped Leeds 2-0. Dougan scored both within 12 minutes, despite briefly leaving the fray in between after a heavy challenge from Norman Hunter.

Hunt scored at Tottenham prior to his £80,000 transfer but it did not halt a run of three away defeats, watched by an aggregate of 135,000 fans. Wolves suffered a similar fate at home to Leicester before regaining their form at West Ham, where Evans made a fine debut that he followed up with last-gasp winner against Burnley. At Hillsborough both Evans (18) and Knowles (22) scored on their birthdays to earn a useful point.

The highlight so far came on a Monday night as Wolves pipped Arsenal 3-2 in a lively tussle. Goalkeeper Williams made an acrobatic debut while a tremendous tackle by Thomson in the dying seconds proved decisive, Wolves then drawing again in Sheffield. This put them 14th after 14 matches with 14 points! Then came a most welcome scoreline at home to Coventry, though the fans were not so pleased the next time they headed for the Molineux exits. Wolves had gradually inched their way back from 3-0 down to Stoke to 3-3, only to lose from virtually the last kick of the game. They were still out of luck at Liverpool, Williams seeing his great penalty save count for nothing as it was ordered to be re-taken.

At Christmas there were 63,450 at Old Trafford and 53,940 at Molineux, though again Wolves took more comfort from the gates than the results. Victory over Sunderland was the first in 10 for Wolves, who then showed it was no fluke at Highbury as they strove to get clear of the danger zone.

Suddenly, Wolves were back in trouble as both Sheffield clubs won at Molineux before Coventry rubbed it in, leaving them 21st having played one more than the team above them. Relegation seemed a long way off as Wolves raced to a 4-0 interval lead over Forest— the North Bank had even repelled one of the now frequent invasions of territory by visiting hordes. Dougan completed a hatrick and Wignall may well have followed suit if he had not been forced to limp off in the 70th minute. Wolves then picked up four points from as many games and their future remained in the balance with three to go.

McAlle made his debut at Chelsea as strike-partner to Dougan, though luckily Wignall was back to seize a hatrick in the return to guarantee Wolves D1 status. A win against Spurs kept them four points from relegation yet only three from the top half of the table, while 81 goals scored at Molineux made it the best place in the entire League for seeing the ball go in the net.

LEAGUE CUP: One goal scored by D2 opponents in Yorkshire was enough to end Wolves interest in the competition at the first hurdle.

F.A. CUP: See above!

RESULTS: Fulham 2-1 (Bailey, Dougan); ALBION 3-3 (Hunt, Bailey, Burnside); LEEDS 2-0 (Dougan 2); Albion 1-4 (Bailey); Everton 2-4 (Wilson, Wharton); Spurs 1-2 (Hunt); LEICESTER 1-3 (Knowles); LC Huddersfield 0-1; West Ham 2-1 (Dougan 2); BURNLEY 3-2 (Knowles 2, Evans); Sheff Wed 2-2 (Knowles, Evans); NEWCASTLE 2-2 (Wharton, Holsgrove); Man City 0-2; ARSENAL 3-2 (Dougan 2, Evans); Sheff Utd 1-1 (Dougan); COVENTRY 2-0 (Knowles 2); Forest 1-3 (Thomson); STOKE 3-4 (Holsgrove, Knowles, Buckley); Liverpool 1-2 (Evans); SOUTHAMPTON 2-0 (Dougan, Knowles); FULHAM 3-2 (Knowles 2, Woodfield); Leeds 1-2 (Dougan); Man Utd 0-4; MAN UTD 2-3 (Buckley, Bailey); EVERTON 1-3 (Knowles); Leicester 1-3 (Kenning); WEST HAM 1-2 (Dougan); FAC Rotherham 0-1; Burnley 1-1 (Dougan); Newcastle 0-2; LIVERPOOL 1-1 (Dougan); SUNDERLAND 2-1 (Dougan, Kenning); Arsenal 2-0 (Wignall, Holsgrove); SHEFF WED 2-3 (Wignall, Holsgrove); SHEFF UTD 1-3 (Farrington); Coventry 0-1; FOREST 6-1 (Dougan 3,

Wignall 2, Kenning); Stoke 2-0 (Wignall, Knowles); Sunderland 0-2; MAN CITY 0-0; Southampton 1-1 (Wagstaffe); Chelsea 0-1; CHELSEA 3-0 (Wignall 3) & SPURS 2-1 (Wignall, Parkin).

RECORD: PLD 44 W 14 D 8 L 22 F 66 A 77 (10-4-7 & 4-4-15).

SCORERS: Dougan 17, Knowles 12, Wignall 9, Bailey 4, Evans 4, Holsgrove 4, Kenning 3, Buckley 2, Hunt 2, Wharton 2, Burnside 1, Farrington 1, Parkin 1, Thomson 1, Wagstaffe 1, Wilson 1 & Woodfield 1.

INTERNATIONALS: Wolves remained off the full England scene though there were some bright spots. Apps: Bailey (FL 1), Dougan (NI 2) & Knowles (E U23-2).

FAREWELLS: Buckley 28-8 (Sheff Utd), Burnside 41-5 (Plymouth), Davies 172-0 (Cardiff), Hawkins 29-0 (Preston), Hunt 82-35 (Everton), Ross 1-0 & Wharton 242-79 (Bolton). FRED DAVIES was a Liverpudlian who was secured from Llandudno Borough United. He was a solid last line of defence for Wolves, though in 1965-66 he was restricted to eight appearances by MacLaren. The dedicated Davies emerged as Wolves main keeper in their promotion term but with competition from youngsters like Parkes and Williams he moved on for £12,000.

TERRY WHARTON was a fast direct winger, who often scored from outside the area. 1962-63 was his best season but he continued to be a useful member of the Wolves line-up until he was transferred to his home-town club for £60,000 after Wolves had originally wanted Francis Lee as part of the deal. In the ensuing years we were to lose count of the big names linked with Wolves, suffice to say few of them actually arrived.

1968 - 69

DEBUTANTS: Alan Boswell (Shrewsbury), Derek Clarke (Walsall), Hugh Curran (Norwich), Dave Galvin, Bertie Lutton, Jim McVeigh, Jimmy Seal & Paul Walker. Curran was born in Scotland and Lutton in Ireland.

SUMMARY: Wolves had a respectable season up to the last few weeks, ending one position higher than in 1967-68. Manager Allen departed in the autumn, the vacancy being filled by Bill McGarry who had just brought Ipswich back to D1. Coach Sammy Chung was also recruited having originally joined forces with McGarry at Watford in 1963, while another new manager at the club was folk singer Harvey Andrews, who was in charge of Wolves first souvenir shop situated at the rear of the North Bank. Administrator Jack Howley left Wolves after an association stretching back to 1923 while Alun Evans ended a much shorter career there when he was involved in Wolves biggest transfer deal, also becoming Britain's first £100,000 teenager. In the summer Wolves again won the American Championship though they only had to overcome sides from England and Scotland this year. Top scorers were Curran (6), Dougan (5) and Knowles (5) as they made such an impression under the name of Kansas City Wolves that a wealthy American citizen wished to purchase the team!

LEAGUE: 16th (35). Woodfield had a grim opening day as Wolves lost at Ipswich, breaking his nose and having a splendid header disallowed when a colleague was adjudged to have fouled the goalkeeper. Wolves trailed 3-0 to Man City before Wignall pulled a couple back, being denied a remarkable hatrick by the woodwork. The first home fixture heralded the publication of a new match-day magazine as the old-style programmes began to disappear, Wolves beating QPR. They had to make do with a point three days later against Arsenal, the North Bank receiving high praise in a national paper for their backing that night. In fact supporters all over the country recognised the 'Cowshed' as being one of the leading places for the new type of football atmosphere that had come to grounds in recent years — not that it was appreciated by everybody.

At Leeds there was a repeat of the previous visit, Wolves losing in the dying minutes after being ahead for an hour. The derby at West Brom was a drab goalless draw, with quality forwards from both sides absent though Wolves would have preferred that to happen again rather than the humiliation that followed, Evans scoring twice as Liverpool went on a 6-0 Molineux riot.

Dougan's brave, low header at Coventry eased the pain and the next seven games saw Wolves display mid-table form. This included a fixture at Notts County, neighbours Forest from across the River Trent forced to use the ground because of a fire at their stadium. Wolves were managerless when they pounded Newcastle 5-0, an overhead kick by Knowles being the pick of the bunch. There was a seventh defeat in a row of meetings with Man Utd but Wolves produced some fine play to overcome Tottenham. Both teams converted penalties on an icy surface at Stamford Bridge, Boswell stopping another Chelsea spot-kick in a 1-1 draw.

A seasonal best of 44,023 watched Wolves draw 2-2 with Man Utd and they were on 31 points after 32 games, with the £65,000 Curran looking a good buy. However, apart from an entertaining success against Man City there was little else for Wolves fans to enthuse about in 1968-69. It was the 70th season of the League and the first in which Wolves had failed to average a goal-per-game.

LEAGUE CUP: Brave minnows D4 Southend were given sporting applause at the final whistle as the Wolves supporters realised their team's late winner was unmerited. There was no repetition against D2 Millwall but in the fourth round the lights went out for Wolves on a windy October night at D2 Blackpool.

F.A. CUP: Wolves did a good job at D2 Hull only to be well and truly robbed at Tottenham. Television clearly indicated they were unlucky to have a Knowles effort ruled out and should also have been awarded a penalty, while the corner that led to a Spurs goal was dubious to say the least. The record books prove Wolves lost 2-1 though the unbiased observers from the Midlands claimed an unofficial 3-1 win!

RESULTS: Ipswich 0-1; Man City 2-3 (Wignall 2); QUEENS PARK 3-1 (Wignall, Bailey, Dougan); ARSENAL 0-0; Southampton 1-2

(Wagstaffe); LEICESTER 1-0 (Dougan); STOKE 1-1 (Bailey); LC SOUTHEND 1-0 (Farrington); Leeds 1-2 (Munro); SUNDERLAND 1-1 (Wignall); Albion 0-0; LC MILLWALL 5-1 (Farrington 2, Dougan, Munro, Kenning); LIVERPOOL 0-6; Coventry 1-0 (Dougan); Leicester 0-2; CHELSEA 1-1 (Knowles); LC Blackpool 1-2 (Wagstaffe); Sheff Wed 2-0 (Knowles, Dougan); EVERTON 1-2 (Knowles); Forest 0-0; WEST HAM 2-0 (Farrington, Bailey); Burnley 1-1 (Dougan); NEWCASTLE 5-0 (Knowles 2, Dougan 2, Wignall); Man Utd 0-2; SPURS 2-0 (Dougan, Wignall); Chelsea 1-1 (Kenning); SHEFF WED 0-3; FAC Hull 3-1 (Dougan 2, Wignall); FOREST 1-0 (Knowles); FAC Spurs 1-2 (Wagstaffe); Everton 0-4; BURNLEY 1-1 (Knowles); MAN UTD 2-2 (Dougan, Curran); Spurs 1-1 (Curran); IPSWICH 1-1 (Kenning); Queens Park 1-0 (Dougan); SOUTHAMPTON 0-0; Stoke 1-4 (Curran); West Ham 1-3 (Wilson); LEEDS 0-0; Liverpool 0-1; Arsenal 1-3 (Wilson); MAN CITY 3-1 (Knowles, Dougan, Munro); ALBION 0-1; COVENTRY 1-1 (Knowles); Sunderland 0-2 & Newcastle 1-4 (Curran).

RECORD: PLD 47 W 13 D 15 L 19 F 52 A 64 (9-10-4 & 4-5-15).

SCORERS: Dougan 14, Knowles 9, Wignall 7, Curran 4, Farrington 4, Bailey 3, Kenning 3, Munro 3, Wagstaffe 3 & Wilson 2.

INTERNATIONALS: Dougan scored twice for Ireland in 1968-69 and Knowles netted once for the English Under 23 team. Apps: Bailey (FL 1), Dougan (NI 6), Knowles (E U23-2) & Thomson (FL 1).

FAREWELLS: Boswell 10-0 (Bolton), Evans 20-4 (Liverpool), Galvin 5-0 (Gillingham), Kenning 40-6 (Charlton), McVeigh 2-0 (Gillingham), Seal 1-0 (Walsall), Thomson 299-3 (Birmingham), Wignall 35-16 (Derby) & Williams 15-0 (Villa). BOBBY THOMSON hailed from Smethwick and was a speedy, polished left-back who soon gained honours. He was Wolves only ever-present in 1962-63 and 1963-64 and during the next season he set up what was then a post-war club record of 131 consecutive League appearances, a stark contrast to Wolves other Bobby Thomson who was selected just once. He was equal top of the appearance chart in 1964-65 and 1965-66 and though he did not quite attain the standards first expected of him he rarely let Wolves down, so it was something of a shock when they released him when still only 25 years old.

1969 - 70

DEBUTANTS: Jim McCalliog (Sheff Wed), Mike O'Grady (Leeds), John Oldfield (Huddersfield) , John Richards & Bernard Shaw (Sheff Utd). McCalliog was born in Scotland.

SUMMARY: Wolves did themselves proud in the League for the majority of the campaign but had no real joy in the three Cups they entered. Behind-the-scenes news was even worse with the death of George Noakes who had scouted for them for 21 years, while Physiotherapist George Palmer retired having served Wolves well since 1946. A Wolves Supporters Club was formed in January to add to the North Bank Away Supporters Club, yet those in charge at Molineux continued to show an incredible dis-interest in such organisations. The inventive and amusing North

Bankers reached the final of a televised 'Kop Choir' competition despite having little to sing about after the first few weeks.

LEAGUE: 13th (40). Molineux's Golden Wanderers of the last four years resumed the tradition of wearing black shorts for the August 9th kick-off. Stoke were sent packing, as were Southampton, while another win at Sheffield was marred by the sending off of Dougan. He became the first person to receive a suspended sentence in the shape of a 14-day playing ban, as the game's rulers sought to rid football of the poor image it had acquired in recent times. There were more pleasant matters to report at The Dell as three Wolves defenders scored to complete a brilliant start to 1969-70, though Everton and Liverpool were both ahead of them on goal-average.

No wonder 50,873 were at Molineux for the visit of Man Utd which ended goalless, with the Merseyside pair having similar results. Wolves then shared the spoils again under their powerful new £20,000 floodlights as another large crowd took the average at Wolverhampton to over 40,000. Defeat at Coventry was bad enough, the repercussions being worse as that afternoon ended doubts that Knowles was harbouring over his future. He made an emotional farewell against Forest, the fact that Wolves lost 3-0 lead seeming trivial in comparison. It was Wolves turn to recover at Chelsea, two late Curran goals bringing them back from the dead.

Wanderers were clinging on to fourth spot and three 1-1 draws meant they were losing touch with leaders Everton who were due at Molineux. Dougan was harshly given his marching orders on the day that is remembered for all the wrong reasons, as we saw an example of crowd trouble being related to events on the field. People at the back of the North Bank surged down resulting in nearly 100 injuries and many arrests, while a six-week ban was imposed on Dougan in addition to his other offence.

Everton were going strongly with 32/36 points though Wolves did get to within two points of second-placed Leeds after beating Albion. At Liverpool, the Wolves fans were incensed by a body check on Paul Walker by the home goalkeeper when the only goal of the day seemed certain. Then Lutton scored one and made another against Arsenal to ensure Wolves got the reward they deserved on this occasion. The December highspot came when Wagstaffe cut in from the wing to dribble past some bemused Chelsea players, before letting fly from the edge of the area in a 3-0 win.

Munro was a victim of the stricter code of conduct when he was given a month's suspension while the unlucky Dougan had not long returned to action when he damaged his cheekbone which caused another eight-week lay-off, the accident ironically happening at Everton. Wolves were still challenging to finish third when they played their 1,000th post-war League fixture, drawing at Albion after one of the home strikers had equalised in the dying seconds when the ball appeared to go in off his bottom. That was the closest Wolves came to success in their last 13 games, despite the Easter penalty saves of Oldfield from men of the calibre of Peter Storey and

Tommy Smith. More injuries accelerated Wolves slide down the table with Curran deriving some satisfaction by being fifth top D1 scorer, netting 20 in 38 outings.

LEAGUE CUP: The tie with Tottenham was the first in this Cup to create any real interest in the town, the audience being increased as it was the first floodlight match to be televised in colour. Knowles had a magnificent first half having just announced his retirement, Wolves getting the solitary goal through McCalliog. Shaw made his debut at D3 Brighton as Wolves progressed only to fall weakly to D2 QPR.

F.A. CUP: Wolves held out for 73 minutes on the rock-hard Turf Moor pitch, until a Steve Kindon-inspired Burnley took the initiative.

ANGLO-ITALIAN CUP: This tournament seemed an utterly pointless venture as the best teams from both nations were excluded. Sunderland were the only other English side in Wolves group, though they did not meet. Foreign opposition returned to Wolverhampton when Fiorentina visited on a Friday night, Wolves winning 2-1 and coping equally well with a physical Lazio, but they narrowly failed to win the group after the return games in Italy.

RESULTS: STOKE 3-1 (Dougan 2, Knowles); SOUTHAMPTON 2-1 (Knowles, Munro); Sheff Wed 3-2 (Curran, McCalliog, Knowles); Southampton 3-2 (Parkin, Bailey, Wilson); MAN UTD 0-0; DERBY 1-1 (Dougan); Coventry 0-1; LC SPURS 1-0 (McCalliog); FOREST 3-3 (Curran 2, Dougan); Chelsea 2-2 (Curran 2); Ipswich 1-1 (Dougan); BURNLEY 1-1 (McCalliog); LC Brighton 3-2 (Curran 2, Woodfield); Newcastle 1-1 (McCalliog); EVERTON 2-3 (Curran 2); SHEFF WED 2-2 (Dougan, O'Grady); Spurs 1-0 (Curran); LC Queens Park 1-3 (Wilson); WEST HAM 1-0 (McCalliog); Man City 0-1; ALBION 1-0 (O'Grady); Liverpool 0-0; ARSENAL 2-0 (Curran, Lutton); Palace 1-2 (OG); SUNDERLAND 1-0 (Curran); Leeds 1-3 (Wilson); CHELSEA 3-0 (Curran 2, Wagstaffe); Forest 2-4 (McCalliog, Wilson); Man Utd 0-0; FAC Burnley 0-3; Burnley 3-1 (O'Grady, McCalliog, Bailey); NEWCASTLE 1-1 (Curran); IPSWICH 2-0 (Dougan, Curran); Everton 0-1; SPURS 2-2 (Bailey, Woodfield); Stoke 1-1 (Curran); MAN CITY 1-3 (Wilson); Albion 3-3 (Curran 2, O'Grady); Sunderland 1-2 (McCalliog); PALACE 1-1 (Curran); LEEDS 1-2 (Curran); Arsenal 2-2 (Dougan, Curran); LIVERPOOL 0-1; West Ham 0-3; Derby 0-2; COVENTRY 0-1; AIC FIORENTINA 2-1 (Dougan, Wagstaffe); AIC LAZIO 1-0 (Bailey); AIC Fiorentina 3-1 (Dougan, Curran, Richards) & AIC Lazio 0-2.

RECORD: PLD 50 W 17 D 16 L 17 F 66 A 69 (11-8-5 & 6-8-12).

SCORERS: Curran 23, Dougan 10, McCalliog 8, Wilson 5, Bailey 4, O'Grady 4, Knowles 3, Wagstaffe 2, Woodfield 2, Lutton 1, Munro 1, Parkin 1, Richards 1 & OG 1.

INTERNATIONALS: Despite the continuing absence of Wolves men in the England team it was heartening to see in a magazine that their players aggregate of 241 post-war appearances was a staggering 70 more than that of any other club. There was plenty more to enthuse about as Curran became Wolves only Full International for Scotland, 19-year-old Lutton lined-up for Ireland and Bailey scored for the FLXI. Apps: Bailey (FL 1), Curran (S 1), Dougan (NI 4), Lutton (NI 2), Munro (S U23-3) & Parkin (E U23-4).

FAREWELLS: Clarke 2-0 (Oxford), Farrington 37-5 (Leicester), Knowles 190-64 & Woodfield 274-15 (Watford). PETER KNOWLES was born in the small Yorkshire town of Frickley and carried on the Wath Wanderers link to Wolves. He scored in the 1964 International Youth Tournament Final as England beat Spain 4-0 and was to be Wolves most gifted discovery of the decade, although sometimes his temperament held him back. The inside-forward began 1969-70 displaying the sort of skills that would have at last established him as a household name and his attitude to football seemed good. He then stunned Wolves supporters by turning his back on the sport for religion, joining the Jehovah's Witnesses. For several years Wolves retained his registration but hopes of Knowles making a comeback gradually faded as he had obviously found something more important to him than fame and fortune — peace of mind.

DAVID WOODFIELD was a tough centre-half with dark, curly hair who was a fearsome sight when he rolled his sleeves up to do battle. Born in Leamington, he showed briefly in 1965-66 that he could do the business at the other end of the park when Wolves used him as an emergency centre-forward. Woodfield left for £30,000 and had to wait until 1973-74 for his testimonial, when he was remembered with sufficient affection for almost 15,000 to pay to watch it.

1970 -71

DEBUTANTS: Bobby Gould (Arsenal), Danny Hegan (Albion) & Ken Hibbitt (Bradford PA). Hegan was born in Scotland.

SUMMARY: Goal-average prevented Wolves from attaining third position after a splendid effort in the League, though at least they secured some silverware in the form of the Texaco Cup. Future prospects looked extremely rosy as McGarry endeavoured to guide the club back to greatness, another slightly optimistic sign being provided by certain individuals as Wolves reached the SF of the Youth Cup.

LEAGUE: 4th (52). A disastrous opening week made Wolves apparent relegation candidates, so it was a relief when Curran finished off a move he had started himself at Coventry. That was the first of three away trips before Wolves came back to Molineux to play Stoke, giving Dougan a run-out as centre-half.

A sweet left-foot volley from substitute Richards wrapped up the game with Huddersfield and commenced a spell of six consecutive wins. At Burnley it was Dougan who was on the bench, though he was brought on as Wolves prepared to take a free-kick. He sauntered into the middle and nonchalantly headed the cross in, which probably made him the first substitute to come on and score without kicking the ball! Newcomer Gould then scored a genuine hatrick against Man Utd, Wolves then coming from behind to beat both Southampton and Newcastle, finally trimming Man City 3-0.

Anfield continued to be an ill-fated stadium for Wolves who threatened to tear the Reds apart in the early exchanges, only to fade when a couple of decisions went against them. Wolves also felt aggrieved when McAlle's drive from at least 35 yards rocketed into the Albion net only to be cancelled out as McCalliog was standing in an offside position, although the ball was travelling so fast that nobody could have interfered with play. At least Wolves gained the points and earned another with two late strikes at West Ham to go fifth, but they could not hold Leeds before a seasonal best 41,318.

When Wolves beat Everton for the first time in 17 tries they must have believed anything was possible and they went to Leeds a few weeks later with faint title hopes. The top three were Leeds (28-43), Arsenal (27-40) and Wolves (28-36) though with the latter shortly to come to Molineux there was a chance to close the gap on the leading duo. Sadly, both Leeds and double-bound Arsenal crushed Wolves 3-0, with some consolation being derived as they beat Liverpool 1-0 in between those results. A banana shot by O'Grady did the trick, but the £80,000 buy had proved a sorry replacement for Knowles as he had been haunted by an achilles tendon problem which had not properly cleared up since his arrival.

Over the final 11 games the outstanding memory concerned the 100th League meeting with West Bromwich Albion. At half-time Wolves were 1-0 down but they attacked the Smethwick End after the interval where their fans were easily drowning the noise from the rest of the ground, the team responding with an enthralling performance to win 4-2. That put them third and though Spurs were to nudge them out of that place it did not detract from a fine campaign, top four: Arsenal 65, Leeds 64, Spurs 52 and Wolves 52.

LEAGUE CUP: Wolves first visit to the University city of D2 Oxford proved to be something of an education as their dismal League Cup record continued.

TEXACO CUP: This new event was sometimes referred to as the British Isles Cup, which was somewhat deceptive as the top sides were ineligible. Nevertheless, there was a useful English line-up of Albion, Stoke, Burnley, Forest and Spurs, yet Wolves progressed to the final by dismissing two of the six Scottish entrants and one of the four Irish teams involved. In the first leg in Edinburgh there was a sixth-minute setback for Wolves, but a brace by Curran helped them make it 4/4 Texaco away wins. Hearts won at Molineux, leaving a bemused American to present the trophy to 3-2 aggregate-winners Wolves to the cheers of the 28,462 crowd.

F.A. CUP: McCalliog's penalty gave Wolves a nice start only for D2 Norwich to level in the eighth minute. A flurry by Wolves after the break put paid to the Canaries and clinched a fourth round trip to Derby. Dougan struggled in the mud of The Baseball Ground, though he did manage a header that was palmed on to the bar, Richards stabbing in the rebound. This had apparently forced a replay but Derby had other ideas, getting a late decider they hardly deserved.

RESULTS: Newcastle 2-3 (Curran, Dougan); DERBY 2-4 (Dougan, Curran); SPURS 0-3; Coventry 1-0 (Curran); Forest 1-4 (Curran); Ipswich 3-2 (Curran 2, Gould); STOKE 1-1 (Curran); LC Oxford 0-1; Chelsea 2-2 (Hibbitt, McCalliog); TC Dundee 2-1 (Gould, McCalliog); HUDDERSFIELD 3-1 (Curran, Gould, Richards); Burnley 3-2 (McCalliog, Dougan, Gould); TC DUNDEE 0-0; MAN UTD 3-2 (Gould 3); Southampton 2-1 (Wagstaffe, Dougan); NEWCASTLE 3-2 (Bailey, Gould, Wagstaffe); TC Morton 3-0 (Gould 2, Dougan); MAN CITY 3-0 (Gould 2, McCalliog); Liverpool 0-2; TC MORTON 1-2 (Curran); ALBION 2-1 (Wagstaffe, Dougan); West Ham 3-3 (McCalliog 2, Gould); LEEDS 2-3 (Gould, Curran); Palace 1-1 (Curran); TC Derry 1-0 (Gould); BLACKPOOL 1-0 (OG); Arsenal 1-2 (Dougan); Spurs 0-0; EVERTON 2-0 (Dougan 2); FAC NORWICH 5-1 (McCalliog 2, Gould 2, Hibbitt); Derby 2-1 (Shaw, Gould); COVENTRY 0-0; FAC Derby 1-2 (Richards); PALACE 2-1 (Dougan 2); Blackpool 2-0 (Dougan, McCalliog); CHELSEA 1-0 (Hibbitt); Leeds 0-3; LIVERPOOL 1-0 (O'Grady); ARSENAL 0-3; Man City 0-0; WEST HAM 2-0 (Gould 2); Albion 4-2 (Curran 2, Bailey, Gould); TC DERRY 4-0 (Parkin, Curran, O'Grady, Gould); FOREST 4-0 (Curran 3, Gould); Stoke 0-1; Everton 2-1 (Bailey, Gould); Man Utd 0-1; TC Hearts 3-1 (Curran 2, Bailey); SOUTHAMPTON 0-1; Huddersfield 2-1 (Curran, McCalliog); IPSWICH 0-0; BURNLEY 1-0 (Dougan) & TC HEARTS 0-1.

RECORD: PLD 53 W 28 D 9 L 16 F 84 A 63 (15-4-7 & 13-5-9).

SCORERS: Gould 24, Curran 20, Dougan 13, McCalliog 10, Bailey 4, Hibbitt 3, Wagstaffe 3, O'Grady 2, Richards 2, Parkin 1, Shaw 1 & OG 1.

INTERNATIONALS: Scotland's sudden interest in Wolverhampton continued as they gave a debut to Munro, Curran scored for them at Wembley and McCalliog added to his appearances, thus the total number of Wolves men to play for Scotland rose to three. Parkin appeared for the FLXI, Dougan was on target in two of Ireland's matches and a trio of Under 23 Internationals completed the club's fine honours list. Apps: Curran (S 4), Dougan (NI 6), Hibbitt (E U23-1), McCalliog (S 1), Munro (S 4 + S U23-1) & Parkin (FL 1 + E U23-1).

FAREWELLS: Holsgrove 200-7 (Sheff Wed), Lutton 19-1 (Brighton) & Oldfield 19-0 (Crewe). JOHN HOLSGROVE was a Londoner who cost Wolves a fee of £18,000. He was a lanky, awkward opponent who usually turned out at left-half and in 1967-68 showed he could not only tackle but score the occasional goal as well, topping the appearances with 44. Towards the end of his Wolves career he netted at the wrong end of the field and a suicidal back-pass helped turn the crowd against him as his nine outings of 1970-71 were mainly unhappy, though Holsgrove did many good things for Wolves for which he should be remembered.

1971 - 72

DEBUTANTS: Steve Daley, Peter Eastoe & Alan Sunderland.

SUMMARY: UEFA Cup Finalists Wolves brought a taste of European glory back to the town in defeating top foreign clubs Juventus and Ferencvaros. Although their League position was lower they were only 11 points away from Champions Derby, which remains as close as they have been since 1963. For most of the season Wolves were invincible at Molineux, yet having gone through 21 games unscathed they lost 5/6 before depriving Leeds of the double.

LEAGUE: 9th (47). Wolves squandered a 2-0 hold on the Tottenham match, fell to a last-minute penalty at Liverpool and drew with Leeds at neutral Huddersfield in a lively opening week. There were visits from the Manchester duo with City beaten in a fine contest and United attracting a seasonal best of 46,479. Bailey scored with virtually his first kick of the campaign to subdue Palace while a Dougan hatrick was to foil Forest. In the 12th fixture a goal by Daley on his debut helped Wolves move up to 14 points, only for them to hit a sticky patch.

Young Richards was denied a hatrick by a fractional offside decision as Derby were ousted 2-1. An even better result ensued after Arsenal had led 1-0 at the interval, with Wolves in desperate need of some inspiration. Wagstaffe provided it with a stunning angled shot that was to be voted BBC's 'Goal of the month', though Hibbitt also unleashed a drive that was a worthy candidate. A snow blizzard was hardly noticed as rampant Wolves scored five times in 20 sensational minutes and they continued to strike freely at Albion. Wolves tremendous spell reached a peak in January with a superb first half display at Old Trafford that put them within four points of leaders United, a measure of their improvement being gauged by their disappointment at then drawing at home to Liverpool.

Wolves slumped to their first defeat in 11 games at Maine Road, leaving them sixth while City took over at the top. From then on they fought a losing battle to remain involved in the chase, the last dwindling hope going at Derby where Munro conceded a penalty for a foul on Kevin Hector for the third year running. At Southampton the Wolves spot-kick king McCalliog failed twice, Taylor floating in the winner to spare his blushes. There was a competent win at Crystal Palace before Wolves were robbed of an away hatrick at Everton as luck deserted them, though Hibbitt got a brace.

Leicester thwarted any ambitions Wolves had of finally going through a D1 term unbeaten at Molineux and Wolves struggled until they recorded successive victories at Huddersfield and Nottingham. A mere two days after their Wembley triumph Leeds came to Wolverhampton and lost a controversial affair 2-1. The official gate of 53,397 was never to be equalled at Molineux again while many more got in without paying or were locked outside or even turned back on arriving in town, one police estimate being that 70,000 wished to attend.

LEAGUE CUP: Aided by some scintillating football Wolves led Man

City 3-1, only to see all their efforts wasted in the last 10 minutes.

UEFA CUP: The Inter-Cities Fairs Cup was given a new title from 1971-72 as Wolves competed in it for the first time, having qualified by coming fourth in the League the previous season. It was open to the leading clubs who had not made it to the ECC or ECWC yet it was almost as difficult to win. Europe's stronger nations had three or four representatives, all of whom would be superior to most of the entrants in the other two tournaments and of course the best team in a country one year are not obliged to be the best in the next one. Also, there were 64 participants in this UEFA Cup so there was an extra round to negotiate.

Wolves comfortably removed a Portuguese University team, soured slightly by the sending off of Hegan, while Leeds and Southampton suffered first round exits. After a fine win in Holland there was a remarkable second leg at Molineux as shots by Hibbitt, Dougan and McCalliog were all deflected in for own goals. Bailey showed his qualities of leadership in the bitter cold of East Germany with Wolves seeing the job through to equal the feat of Leeds and Man Utd, the only other English representatives to ever win six consecutive European games.

A tough QF with Juventus was easily the stiffest test so far, Wolves soon falling behind in Turin. McGarry was warned for touchline coaching, then ordered back to the perimeter of the athletics track though he had the last laugh as Wolves gained a creditable draw. The return was spoiled by the late announcement that five of the Italian stars were unavailable, but nevertheless 40,411 cheered as Hegan's long-range shot and Dougan's deft flick put Wolves in control until Juventus reduced the arrears late on to make it a nail-biting finish. Yet another away first leg took Wolves to Hungary where Parkes stopped a penalty with his foot as they trailed 2-1, encouraging the British side to get back in the game and equalise when Munro headed in a Wagstaffe corner. Daley scored within 25 seconds of an entertaining match at Molineux that deserved a bigger audience than 28,262 as Ferencvaros at last demonstrated the sort of skills expected at this level, only for another Parkes penalty save to give Wolves a 4-3 aggregate. Tottenham, who came sixth in the League but had been far less impressive than Wolves in the UEFA Cup, defeated AC Milan 3-2 in the other SF.

Meeting an English team in the final detracted some of the glamour of the occasion, although Wolves can still proudly boast at being in the solitary all-British final of a European competition. Just 38,362 turned up for the first leg at Wolverhampton, when a Chivers thunderbolt and header outweighed a McCalliog penalty. At White Hart Lane 54,303 fans saw Alan Mullery increase the Spurs advantage with a close-in header, a Wagstaffe screamer reviving Midland hopes. It stayed 3-2 on aggregate to the Londoners despite the introduction of substitutes Bailey and Curran for Hibbitt and Dougan, Wolves having started both legs with the same XI. Team: Parkes, Shaw, Taylor, Hegan, Munro, McAlle, McCalliog, Hibbitt, Richards, Dougan & Wagstaffe.

F.A. CUP: The outlook was bright as a Richards backheel sent

McCalliog clear to open the score against Leicester, but from then on Wolves were forced on the retreat. It took until the 76th minute for justice to be done, Leicester duly winning the Filbert Street replay 2-0 so there was no hard luck story this year.

RESULTS: SPURS 2-2 (Gould, McCalliog); Liverpool 2-3 (Dougan, Hibbitt); Leeds 0-0; MAN CITY 2-1 (Hibbitt, McCalliog); MAN UTD 1-1 (Shaw); PALACE 1-0 (Bailey); Stoke 1-0 (Hegan); LC Man City 3-4 (McAlle, Hegan, Parkin); EVERTON 1-1 (Hegan); UC ACADEMICA COIMBRA 3-0 (McAlle, Richards, Dougan); Newcastle 0-2; FOREST 4-2 (Dougan 3, McCalliog); UC Academica Coimbra 4-1 (Dougan 3, McAlle); Chelsea 1-3 (McCalliog); SOUTHAMPTON 4-2 (Dougan 2, Parkin, Daley); Spurs 1-4 (Bailey); UC Den Haag 3-1 (Dougan, McCalliog, Hibbitt); West Ham 0-1; COVENTRY 1-1 (Munro); UC DEN HAAG 4-0 (Dougan, OG 3); Ipswich 1-2 (Dougan); DERBY 2-1 (Richards 2); ARSENAL 5-1 (Dougan 2, Wagstaffe, Hibbitt, McCalliog); UC Carl-Zeiss Jena 1-0 (Richards); Albion 3-2 (McCalliog, Wagstaffe, Richards); HUDDERSFIELD 2-2 (Dougan, Richards); UC CARL-ZEISS JENA 3-0 (Dougan 2, Hibbitt); Sheff Utd 2-2 (Richards, OG); STOKE 2-0 (Dougan, OG); Leicester 2-1 (Dougan, Munro); NEWCASTLE 2-0 (Parkin, Richards); Man Utd 3-1 (Dougan, Richards, McCalliog); FAC LEICESTER 1-1 (McCalliog); FAC Leicester 0-2; LIVERPOOL 0-0; Man City 2-5 (Richards 2); WEST HAM 1-0 (Richards); Coventry 0-0; IPSWICH 2-2 (Hibbitt, McCalliog); Derby 1-2 (McCalliog); UC Juventus 1-1 (McCalliog); Southampton 2-1 (McCalliog, Taylor); Palace 2-0 (Dougan, McCalliog); UC JUVENTUS 2-1 (Hegan, Dougan); Everton 2-2 (Hibbitt 2); LEICESTER 0-1; UC Ferencvaros 2-2 (Richards, Munro); Arsenal 1-2 (Richards); CHELSEA 0-2; ALBION 0-1; UC FERENCVAROS 2-1 (Daley, Munro); Huddersfield 1-0 (Daley); Forest 3-1 (Hegan, Richards, Hibbitt); SHEFF UTD 1-2 (Richards); UC SPURS 1-2 (McCalliog); LEEDS 2-1 (Dougan, Munro) & UC Spurs 1-1 (Wagstaffe).

RECORD: PLD 57 W 26 D 15 L 16 F 96 A 74 (15-8-5 & 11-7-11).

SCORERS: Dougan 24, Richards 16, McCalliog 15, Hibbitt 9, Hegan 5, Munro 5, Daley 3, McAlle 3, Parkin 3, Wagstaffe 3, Bailey 2, Gould 1, Shaw 1, Taylor 1 & OG 5.

INTERNATIONALS: Hegan joined Dougan in the Irish team despite being a Scot by birth and Richards scored on an Under 23 tour, while Wagstaffe gained some recognition at last. Apps: Dougan (NI 5), Hegan (NI 4), Richards (E U23-3) & Wagstaffe (FL 1).

FAREWELLS: Curran 90-47 (Oxford), Gould 50-25 (Albion), O'Grady 35-6 (Rotherham), Walker 22-0 (Peterborough) & Les Wilson 103-8 (Bristol City). LES WILSON was born in Manchester but spent most of his childhood years out in Canada. He was one of a new breed of utility men who stood in for Wolves in several positions, though he was more often to be found in defence because of his fiery tackling. The 42 appearances he made in 1968-69 were easily his highest total and a lot of supporters were sorry to see him go.

1972-73

DEBUTANTS: Derek Jefferson (Ipswich), Steve Kindon (Burnley), Brian Owen (Colchester) & Barry Powell.

SUMMARY: Consistent Wolves excelled in the three major competitions yet honours continued to elude them, being only the second team to bow out in the SF of both the League Cup and the F.A. Cup in the same season. They had kicked-off 1972-73 in July with their solitary appearance in the Watney Cup, a tournament for high-scoring teams from all divisions, though the initials probably summed up what Wolves thought of it after succumbing to D3 Bristol Rovers — despite the presence of their first £100,000 signing Kindon. Wolves longest unbeaten run of the term covered 10 matches while off-the-field they still dominated a national contest for social clubs that had been organised over the last four years, Wolves winning it for the third time.

LEAGUE: 5th (47). Former Rugby-man Kindon scored at Newcastle but it was not sufficient to halt the Geordies, with Wolves under-strength rearguard also unable to stem the tide of Arsenal's attacks in midweek. Molineux fans were treated to an exciting win over Spurs and then three late goals to overcome West Ham, Coach Owen helping Wolves injury crisis by joining their defence. Parkes then adopted the role of goalkeeping schemer, McCalliog fastening on to his long clearance to score at Southampton and Richards heading in another 'lofty' kick at Coventry.

When Richards grabbed a hatrick in the 11th match Wolves were two points adrift of the leaders, only to draw twice then fall to a late strike by Gould at The Hawthorns. Kindon began to justify his price-tag with two well-taken goals at West Ham before some patchy home form plunged Wolves down the table.

In January Emlyn Hughes inadvertantly beat his own goalkeeper as Liverpool had a fine two-month unbeaten spell ended by Wolves, not that it was to prevent them from taking the title. Bobby Charlton showed he could still produce the goods for Man Utd with a brace when Wolves went to Old Trafford, where the talented Hegan got his last goal for them before 1973 turned sour for him and he was sacked for persistent infringements of the club rules. Wolves were 11th with 15 games remaining, embarking on a good run highlighted by a 5-1 pounding of Man City. It culminated with a Richards hatrick against Everton, the best coming as he received the ball with his back to goal and flicked it up with his left foot before twisting round to volley it in with his right.

There was now the real incentive of a UEFA Cup place to aim for and it was virtually sealed after Wolves caned Norwich 3-0 in mudbath conditions. There was no joy at Stoke but the European spot was clinched as Wolves completed a seasonal treble over Coventry, with young forwards like Sunderland cheering the Molineux faithful. A mere point from visits to Tottenham and Derby cost them fourth position, while ever-present Richards was second top D1 scorer with 27.

LEAGUE CUP: Wolves took advantage of home draws against D2 Orient, D2 Sheff Wed and Bristol Rovers to reach their first League Cup QF. At that point D2 Blackpool tried their luck at Molineux, forcing Wolves to a replay which was settled by Dougan. In the first leg of the SF the Wolves defence were static as Martin Peters gave Spurs a third-minute lead, John Pratt rounding-off a move in lethal style to make it 2-0. A poor crowd of 28,327 saw Hibbitt give Wolves a glimmer of hope for the return which was played on the last Saturday of the year. An own goal and a late piece of opportunism from Richards gave Wolves a 2-1 verdict after 90 minutes, thus the total score was 3-3. A replay at a neutral ground would have been the fairest course of action despite the away 'wins' but Spurs had an extra 30 minutes of the advantage of playing at White Hart Lane, which they finally took with an equaliser to send them towards Wembley glory.

TEXACO CUP: Unable to defend the trophy in 1971-72 because of their UEFA Cup ventures, Wolves faced the Scots of Kilmarnock. They won 5-1 which was also the aggregate score, a meagre 8,734 fans attending the Molineux tie. Wolves were knocked out by their first English opponents in the competition, losing both legs of the second round to Ipswich.

F.A. CUP: Bailey scored a second-minute goal before breaking a bone in his foot as Wolves ousted a dull Man Utd, following it up against D2 sides Bristol City and Millwall when one strike proved enough again. The latter visitors were unfortunate which prompted a near-riot outside the ground, the air being a sea of missiles. There were 50,106 at Molineux for the QF as Dougan, obviously recovered from being knocked cold by a Kindon blast in the warm-up, headed on for Richards to race through and score a typical 1972-73 Wolves goal. Coventry were finished off by Hibbitt's penalty in the 49th minute so Wolves had to face Leeds at Maine Road, Bailey being 12th man having only just regained his fitness. His deputy young Powell wasted an early opportunity and shortly after half-time Billy Bremner broke the deadlock as Wolves conceded their only goal in five ties. Richards nearly levelled when he turned quickly to hit the inside of the post, the ball rolling agonisingly across the line. A speculative Wagstaffe punt landed on the roof of the net in the dying seconds as Wolves slipped to a sad defeat, Leeds losing the final to Sunderland.

RESULTS: WC Bristol R 0-2; Newcastle 1-2 (Kindon); Arsenal 2-5 (Richards, OG); SPURS 3-2 (Richards 2, Hibbitt); WEST HAM 3-0 (McCalliog, Richards, Dougan); Southampton 1-1 (McCalliog); Coventry 1-0 (Richards); BIRMINGHAM 3-2 (McCalliog 2, Munro); LC ORIENT 2-1 (Dougan, Richards); Liverpool 2-4 (Kindon, Richards); TC KILMARNOCK 5-1 (Dougan 2, Richards 2, McCalliog); MAN UTD 2-0 (Dougan, Richards); Leicester 1-1 (Hegan); TC Kilmarnock 0-0; STOKE 5-3 (Richards 3, Dougan, Hegan); LC SHEFF WED 3-1 (Hibbitt, Munro, Dougan); Man City 1-1 (Dougan); PALACE 1-1 (Dougan); Albion 0-1; TC Ipswich 1-2 (Richards); LEEDS 0-2; LC BRISTOL R 4-0 (Richards, Kindon, McCalliog, OG); West Ham 2-2 (Kindon 2); TC IPSWICH 0-1; LC BLACKPOOL 1-1 (McCalliog); ARSENAL 1-3 (Richards); IPSWICH

0-1; Sheff Utd 2-1 (Richards, Hibbitt); LC Blackpool 1-0 (Dougan); DERBY 1-2 (Richards); Everton 1-0 (Hibbitt); CHELSEA 1-0 (Sunderland); LC SPURS 1-2 (Hibbitt); Norwich 1-1 (Dougan); LEICESTER 2-0 (Dougan, Richards); LC Spurs 2-2 (OG, Richards); SOUTHAMPTON 0-1; FAC MAN UTD 1-0 (Bailey); LIVERPOOL 2-1 (OG, Richards); FAC BRISTOL C 1-0 (Richards); Man Utd 1-2 (Hegan); NEWCASTLE 1-1 (Hibbitt); FAC MILLWALL 1-0 (Richards); Birmingham 1-0 (Dougan); MAN CITY 5-1 (Dougan 3, Richards 2); Chelsea 2-0 (Dougan, Richards); Palace 1-1 (Munro); FAC COVENTRY 2-0 (Richards, Hibbitt); ALBION 2-0 (Hibbitt, Richards); Leeds 0-0; SHEFF UTD 1-1 (Richards); FAC Leeds 0-1; EVERTON 4-2 (Richards 3, Hibbitt); Ipswich 1-2 (Richards); NORWICH 3-0 (Sunderland 2, Richards); Stoke 0-2; COVENTRY 3-0 (Powell, Sunderland, Richards); Spurs 2-2 (Sunderland, Richards) & Derby 0-3.

RECORD: PLD 59 W 27 D 14 L 18 F 91 A 68 (21-4-7 & 6-10-11).

SCORERS: Richards 36, Dougan 17, Hibbitt 9, McCalliog 7, Kindon 5, Sunderland 5, Hegan 3, Munro 3, Bailey 1, Powell 1 & OG 4.

INTERNATIONALS: Dougan made his 26th appearance for Ireland since being at Wolverhampton, including some as captain. His striking partner at club level also received honours, Richards ending seven years of Wolves absence from the England team as well as playing in one of the final Inter-League fixtures. Apps: Dougan (NI 2), Hegan (NI 2) & Richards (E 1 + FL 1 + E U23-1).

FAREWELLS: Owen 5-0 & Shaw 153-2 (Sheff Wed). BERNARD SHAW was a well-established right-back when Wolves paid £70,000 for him but he did not quite fulfil his early promise. He did well in the UEFA Cup run, surprising some of his foreign opponents with tenacity that few people of his size could equal. Shaw produced some of his best football for Wolves during a stint in midfield in 1972-73 before returning to his home-city, though to a different team.

1973-74

DEBUTANTS: Jimmy Kelly (Cliftonville), Geoff Palmer, Gary Pierce (Huddersfield) & Peter Withe. Kelly was born in Ireland.

SUMMARY: The Football League Cup came to Molineux as Wolves captured their first big prize in 14 years. It was their fourth successive good season, a period in which Wolves were amongst the best six clubs in both League and Cups without getting the credit warranted. Although Wolves had no players in the 1974 WCF there were some Wolverhampton connections. The opening ceremony was filmed from the Goodyear airship; Dougan was on the T.V. panel; One of the Australian squad was born in the town and the final was refereed by local Butcher Jack Taylor.

LEAGUE: 12th (41). There was an opening day delay for net repairs at the North Bank end, caused by the Norwich keeper getting entangled in a vain attempt to stop a Dougan goal. Wolves maintained their form against Sheff Utd, only to crash to five defeats in a row. They were left a precarious

20th after their fifth reverse to Ipswich in the space of a year and were unable to even muster a goal in the next three outings.

As winter started to bite the prospect of four journeys running was a chilling one for Wolves, but a fine strike by Palmer at Tottenham helped put them on the road to a splendid haul of five points. A well-taken brace by Richards ended Chelsea's resistance and useful draws ensued at Leicester and Burnley. Wolves were not caught napping by the two pm kick-off against Southampton, extending their unbeaten run to eight to leave them well up the table.

When Wolves beat Ipswich 3-1 it was a perfect follow-up to their Wembley success though it was not one of the League Cup heroes who stole the show but a Merseysider named Withe, who had been plucked from the obscurity of South African football. Hibbitt was in the wars at Man City as Wolves drew 1-1, having a goal disallowed and even booking himself as the referee could not hear his name properly! Wolves also drew with Spurs before swamping Derby 4-0 and drawing at West Ham. There was another bright spell of attacking at home to Arsenal and as in the previous fixture at the ground the main stars were Kindon and Sunderland, both running half the length of the field to score.

The undefeated sequence reached seven before a setback in the final match at Derby, leaving Wolves with the belief that their youngsters could complete the transition of changing them from a useful side to one capable of challenging for the championship.

UEFA CUP: There was quite a shock in Portugal when Richards was dismissed for retaliation though Wolves still won, Eastoe scoring in the second leg as they strolled to the next stage. Wolves had to come unstuck on their foreign travels eventually but a 3-0 tanning in East Germany was most unexpected, Wolves fighting back to win the return 4-1. However, they were eliminated by what is curiously referred to as the away goals counting double rule, which means that when the aggregate scores are level the team getting most in their away leg qualifies. Leeds progressed one round further, Ipswich got to the QF and Spurs fell at the final hurdle.

LEAGUE CUP: The path to Wembley commenced at the home D3 Halifax, where Wolves had no real problems. D3 Tranmere took them to a replay while it needed a second half scoring burst to dampen the enthusiasm of D4 Exeter. The power crisis forced Wolves to have to play both this and the QF tie on midweek afternoons, suffering the consequence at the turnstiles with a mere 7,623 at the Exeter match. The missing fans were denied the pleasure of a fine solo goal by Richards as Liverpool were pipped, Wolves coming under some very heavy pressure in the closing minutes. It was Richards who did the trick again in the SF meetings with Norwich, a crowd of 32,605 watching the Molineux leg while Man City were beating Plymouth 3-1.

FINAL: Terrace tickets cost 80p as the 97,886 attendance paid receipts of £161,500 for a game that kicked-off at 3.30 pm. Pierce replaced the injured Parkes knowing that his inexperience would be tested by a star-studded City forward-line, the Mancunians being favourites although their season was to peter out and leave them 14th in the League. In the first half Wolves were more than holding their own and a 43rd-minute volley from HIBBITT put them in front. After the break City were only defied by the heroics of birthday-boy Pierce until BELL finally equalised. Wolves came back strongly despite the limping Wagstaffe having to make way for substitute Powell and in the 81st minute there was some neat approach work between Captain Bailey and Sunderland, the ball then running kindly for RICHARDS to steer it home and place Wolverhampton back on the footballing map. Team: Pierce, Palmer, Parkin, Bailey, Munro, McAlle, Hibbitt, Sunderland, Richards, Dougan & Wagstaffe.

F.A. CUP: One of the few ties to determine who finished third in the F.A. Cup was played as a seasonal curtain-raiser, Wolves beating the other 1973 SF losers Arsenal. The outcome of the 1973-74 competition was something of an injustice as Wolves again succumbed to Leeds having had the better of two gripping struggles, a harsh penalty award angering most of the 38,132 at Molineux while the referee did Wolves no favours at Elland Road either. In the final there was a 3-0 winning margin for Liverpool, the clearest since Wolves did the same in 1960.

RESULTS: FAC Arsenal 3-1 (Dougan 2, McCalliog); NORWICH 3-1 (Dougan 2, McCalliog); SHEFF UTD 2-0 (Dougan, McCalliog); Southampton 1-2 (Dougan); Leeds 1-4 (Dougan); BURNLEY 0-2; LEEDS 0-2; Newcastle 0-2; EVERTON 1-1 (Dougan); UC Belenenses 2-0 (Dougan, Richards); Chelsea 2-2 (McCalliog 2); UC BELENENSES 2-1 (Eastoe, McCalliog); MAN UTD 2-1 (McCalliog, Dougan); LC Halifax 3-0 (Sunderland, Dougan, Richards); Birmingham 1-2 (Richards); QUEENS PARK 2-4 (Richards, OG); UC Lokomotive Leipzig 0-3; Ipswich 0-2; LC Tranmere 1-1 (Sunderland); MAN CITY 0-0; UC LOKOMOTIVE LEIPZIG 4-1 (Kindon, Munro, Dougan, Hibbitt); Liverpool 0-1; LC TRANMERE 2-1 (Dougan, Powell); WEST HAM 0-0; LC EXETER 5-1 (Hibbitt 2, Richards 2, Dougan); Spurs 3-1 (Powell, Palmer, Hibbitt); Arsenal 2-2 (Dougan, Richards); Coventry 0-1; Stoke 3-2 (Munro, Richards, Hibbitt); LC LIVERPOOL 1-0 (Richards); CHELSEA 2-0 (Richards 2); Leicester 2-2 (Sunderland, Richards); Burnley 1-1 (Powell); SOUTHAMPTON 2-1 (Wagstaffe, Richards); FAC LEEDS 1-1 (Richards); FAC Leeds 0-1; NEWCASTLE 1-0 (Richards); Norwich 1-1 (Dougan); LC Norwich 1-1 (Richards); LC NORWICH 1-0 (Richards); STOKE 1-1 (OG); Sheff Utd 0-1; Everton 1-2 (Sunderland); BIRMINGHAM 1-0 (Munro); Man Utd 0-0; LC Man City 2-1 (Hibbitt, Richards); IPSWICH 3-1 (Sunderland, Withe, Dougan); Queens Park 0-0; LIVERPOOL 0-1; Man City 1-1 (Kindon); SPURS 1-1 (Powell); DERBY 4-0 (Kindon 2, Sunderland, OG); West Ham 0-0; ARSENAL 3-1 (Sunderland 2, Kindon); COVENTRY 1-1 (OG); LEICESTER 1-0 (Sunderland) & Derby 0-2.

RECORD: PLD 57 W 23 D 18 L 16 F 77 A 62 (17-7-4 & 6-11-12).

SCORERS: Richards 18, Dougan 17, Sunderland 9, McCalliog 7,

Hibbitt 6, Kindon 5, Powell 4, Munro 3, Eastoe 1, Palmer 1, Wagstaffe 1, Withe 1 & OG 4.

INTERNATIONALS: Wolves had nobody selected at full level for the first time since 1929-30 though there was much to savour regarding the England Under 23 team. Only Chelsea (19) had supplied more players as a new Wolves trio took their contingent up to 18, while Richards completed a quartet. Apps: Palmer (E U23-1), Powell (E U23-1), Richards (E U23-2) & Sunderland (E U23-1).

FAREWELLS: Eastoe 6-1 (Swindon), Hegan 65-8 (Sunderland) & McCalliog 204-47 (Man Utd). JIM McCALLIOG cost £70,000 and was a neat, thoughtful midfielder who was also capable of some Glasgow-style aggression. He was a fine one-touch player and in 1970-71 topped the Wolves appearance chart with 51. McCalliog scored in five successive games during 1971-72, an exceptional feat for a non-striker especially as four of them were away. He helped Dougan dominate the club's early goalscoring of 1973-74 before being sold for £60,000 at the age of 27.

1974 - 75

DEBUTANTS: Willie Carr (Coventry), John Farley (Watford), Don Gardner & Nigel Williams. Carr was born in Scotland and Gardner in Jamaica.

SUMMARY: Wolves received a pre-season boost by winning the televised 'All in the game' trophy, their squad of Pierce, Bailey, McAlle, Parkin, Hibbitt and Sunderland beating the likes of Derby and Chelsea as well as hosts Bristol City in a contest covering a variety of soccer skills. This gave Wolverhampton a little national prestige but when it came to the real thing Wolves did nothing to enhance the area, failing to sustain their League challenge and crashing out of three Cups at Molineux.

LEAGUE: 12th (39). Richards had been out of action since Wembley but proved his sharpness with a fine opening day goal at Burnley. Wolves had the edge in a goalless affair with Liverpool and capped the first week with this result: Hibbitt 4, Newcastle 2. His efforts included a penalty and a long-range special and he remains the only Wolves man to score four in a match since 1962.

Spurs visited Molineux and a Chivers brace took his tally to 10 against Wolves in five years. Pierce was in brilliant form at Newcastle though his team were finding points hard to come by and drew 0-0. One sorry week saw them slump to their first defeat in 15 trips to London while Sunderland received a double-fracture to his leg in a training session. Peter Shilton made a wonderful debut for Stoke at Molineux, though even he could not keep out a Powell volley and Hibbitt penalty. Wolves were heartened by this showing and Kindon hit a purple patch, treating the fans to five home goals in December. A fine Boxing Day win over Everton lifted Wolves to 25 points from 23 games, just over four behind the leaders of a wide-open title race and in their present mood anything was possible.

Alas, Wolves deteriorated rapidly as four setbacks sent them to mid-table mediocrity. They nudged Arsenal 1-0 than led at Stoke through another Hibbitt penalty before Munro got the final touch to an inswinging Farley corner, only for the Potters to strike twice in the last three minutes to go top. The visit of Chelsea brought the smiles back as Carr crowned his debut with an early goal and Wolves recorded the biggest D1 victory of 1974-75. They had now scored seven or more in 19 post-war League fixtures, all except two being in the premier division. Number 20 was on schedule as they led Luton 5-2 after an hour despite the absence of their two main strikers, but that was how it stayed.

Hibbitt converted his ninth penalty of the term against Middlesbrough as well as reminding everybody that he could still find the target from 30 yards too. His 17 goals in 41 appearances made him fourth top D1 scorer and left him well ahead of any other midfielders. As for Wolves, their lowest position in six seasons had been 13th which was an achievement equalled by only four teams in the country.

LEAGUE CUP: A diving header by Richards gave Wolves the edge in the early stages against D2 Fulham, but the Cup holders were not to reign for very long.

UEFA CUP: Having qualified by virtue of their League Cup exploits, Wolves once again went to Portugal in the first round where they collapsed 4-1 to Oporto. They made a valiant attempt to wipe out the deficit and would have succeeded if not for a tragic Palmer own goal, not to mention some strange interpretations of the rules by the officials. England fared badly in the Cup, Ipswich and Stoke suffering a similar fate to Wolves and Derby going out in the third round.

F.A. CUP: Ipswich pulled off a freak result after Wolves had dominated matters, being repeatedly dogged by ill-fortune and poor finishing.

RESULTS: Burnley 2-1 (Richards, Palmer); LIVERPOOL 0-0; NEWCASTLE 4-2 (Hibbitt 4); Liverpool 0-2; Birmingham 1-1 (Richards); LEICESTER 1-1 (Richards); LC FULHAM 1-3 (Richards); Everton 0-0; UC Oporto 1-4 (Bailey); SPURS 2-3 (OG, Parkin); SHEFF UTD 1-1 (Daley); Chelsea 1-0 (Richards); UC OPORTO 3-1 (Bailey, Daley, Dougan); Middlesbrough 1-2 (Dougan); CARLISLE 2-0 (Withe, Parkin); Newcastle 0-0; Leeds 0-2; QUEENS PARK 1-2 (Hibbitt); Arsenal 0-0; IPSWICH 2-1 (Hibbitt, Munro); West Ham 2-5 (Richards, Kindon); STOKE 2-2 (Powell, Hibbitt); COVENTRY 2-0 (Kindon 2); BURNLEY 4-2 (Kindon 2, Richards 2); Man City 0-0; EVERTON 2-0 (Hibbitt, Kindon); Luton 2-3 (Powell, Munro); FAC IPSWICH 1-2 (Richards); Coventry 1-2 (Kindon); DERBY 0-1; Ipswich 0-2; ARSENAL 1-0 (Hibbitt); Stoke 2-2 (Hibbitt, Munro); WEST HAM 3-1 (Richards 2, Kindon); BIRMINGHAM 0-1; Sheff Utd 0-1; CHELSEA 7-1 (Richards 2, Carr, Hibbitt, Bailey, Kindon, Wagstaffe); Leicester 2-3 (Kindon, Richards); Spurs 0-3; MAN CITY 1-0 (Hibbitt); LUTON 5-2 (Hibbitt 3, Carr, Withe); Queens Park 0-2; Derby 0-1; MIDDLESBROUGH 2-0 (Hibbitt 2); Carlisle 0-1 & LEEDS 1-1 (Richards).

RECORD: PLD 46 W 15 D 11 L 20 F 63 A 64 (13-5-6 & 2-6-14).

SCORERS: Hibbitt 17, Richards 15, Kindon 10, Bailey 3, Munro 3, Carr 2, Daley 2, Dougan 2, Parkin 2, Powell 2, Withe 2, Palmer 1, Wagstaffe 1 & OG 1.

INTERNATIONALS: Munro returned to the Scottish scene after being ignored for perhaps his best three seasons, being particularly unlucky to miss the 1974 WCF. Apps: Munro (S 5), Palmer (E U23-1) & Powell (E U23-3).

FAREWELLS: Dougan 306-123, Gardner 1-0, Powell 71-7 (Coventry) & Withe 9-3 (Birmingham). DEREK DOUGAN was a lanky centre-forward from Belfast who settled down in Wolverhampton after a much travelled and eventful career. He cost £50,000 and immediately helped secure promotion then did his bit in keeping Wolves D1 status in the following two campaigns. In 1969-70 he represented the UK XI who took on Wales and in 1971-72 responded brilliantly to stories that he was past his peak, notching 20 goals by Boxing Day including two hatricks in four days. In 1972-73 Dougan became the first Irishman to score 200 Football League goals and by 1973-74 he was even chairman of the Professional Footballers Association. He also netted for an all-Ireland XI who were beaten 4-3 by the mighty Brazil and collected an overdue domestic honour thanks to the League Cup win. In 1974-75 he grabbed his 12th UEFA Cup goal but it was a frustrating period for the crowd favourite who was chosen on just six occasions. A seasonal best 34,875 turned out for the final match wishing to see Dougan go our in style before retiring, but they were greeted by the news he was substitute and had to wait until the 78th minute for him to enter the fray. Almost 26,000 were to watch his testimonial in 1976-77, which really speaks for itself.

1975 - 76

DEBUTANTS: Norman Bell, Maurice Daly, Bob McNab (Arsenal), Gerry O'Hara & Martin Patching. Daly was born in Eire.

SUMMARY: Wolves made a bad start and simply never recovered to disprove the notion they were too good to go down to D2. There was modest consolation from an F.A. Cup run and a fifth Youth Cup Final, a number only surpassed by Man Utd (six) though Albion outclassed Wolves in both legs. The public relations image of the club sank lower throughout 1975-76 thus a summer shake-up was inevitable with McGarry parting company as expected, the job surprisingly going to Chung. Director Harry Marshall who was the principle share-holder took on work previously undertaken by his father when he became chairman, Ireland occupying a new role as president. Wolves did manage a Wembley triumph this season in the indoor arena where they were national five-a-side champions. They drew 1-1 (Sunderland) with Ipswich and also 1-1 (Sunderland) against Stoke, winning both on penalties to set up a 2-1 (Sunderland, Bailey) SF defeat of Orient. A superb night was completed by a 3-1 (Hibbitt, Bailey,

Carr) success over Spurs, other members of the six-man squad being Pierce and McAlle.

LEAGUE: 20th (30). Britain's richest club Manchester United had somehow tumbled into D2 though the experience had done them no real harm as Wolves found to their cost on the first day. A cannonball drive by Carr helped Wolves to a 2-0 lead at Stoke only for it to be thrown away again, the Molineux men having to wait until their seventh match to get off the mark.

One swallow does not make a summer and four bad results indicated that Wolves were in for a harsh winter. They responded defiantly against Sheff Utd and almost wiped out a 3-0 deficit at Derby, where they received fantastic backing from their fans when their task seemed hopeless. There was considerable doubt about the legality of Everton's winner while Wolves were deprived of a point at Tottenham when Pat Jennings brilliantly tipped a fierce Bailey shot over the bar. Then Daley's late strike compensated for a dreary encounter with Ipswich before Wolves gained their first away League joy in 14 months. Richards scored one of Wolves fastest-ever goals after 18 seconds as they planted the ball in the Burnley net an astonishing eight times, the efforts of Farley, Kindon and Hibbitt being disallowed.

The changing face of football frowned on Wolves as seven fixtures yielded just two points to plunge them back into the bottom three, that being the number of teams now relegated. Luck tends to go against sides in trouble and Man Utd had only pierced their defence after several minutes unjustified injury-time. Wolves were in danger of losing touch with 19th-placed Birmingham until a Carr spot-kick at St. Andrews reduced the gap to a couple of points, as well as bringing Wolves a seasonal treble over the Blues. Only a point separated them as Wolves drew 1-1 with Leeds, McAlle netting an own goal when struck by a hasty clearance from Munro while Gould scored at the right end. He had been purchased from West Ham to become the first post-war player to return to Wolves senior team, having departed four seasons ago. McAlle had a goal scrubbed out against Stoke after much discussion, though at least Wolves won a tense game.

Over the next 10 matches a mere two victories were salvaged, both over rivals in distress. The worst period saw them concede late winners to Spurs and Man City then fail to exert pressure on a Leicester side once their keeper had been carried off. With five games left time was fast running out for Wolves, but five second half goals dazed Newcastle on a day Birmingham lost to further stir the passions of the crowd. They were level with the Brummies on points having played one more, while Burnley were still fighting in 21st spot with Sheff Utd already down. Disappointments at Arsenal and Coventry seemed to have put paid to Wolves yet they worked hard to overcome Norwich, so it all depended on the last match.

It was a tall order for Wolves who had to rely on Sheff Utd beating Birmingham and defeat Liverpool themselves to stay up on goal-average, unfortunately the Reds needed a victory or a draw of less than 3-3 to deny QPR the title. Kindon raced through to score and when the news filtered in that Sheffield were 1-0 up the miracle was on. The excitement was unbearable as Wolves held out until the 77th minute but the absence of central defenders Munro and McAlle told as Liverpool began a three-goal burst. Many of their hordes of fans in the official gate of 46,097 had behaved shamefully during the day but they were now all ecstatic and it was sheer agony to watch the Scouse celebrations on one of the town's saddest soccer nights, although Birmingham had equalised anyway.

The fact that in their previous eight seasons in D1 Wolves wins had just outnumbered their defeats counted for nothing as they became the third team to come 20th and be relegated. The ruling cast doubts that the 22 D1 clubs were the best 22 in England, and two of the three promoted sides were to find life very difficult in 1976-77. Wolves were probably unique in suffering the drop after scoring five on three occasions and conceding five only once, Richards being fourth= D1 scorer with 17 in 38 appearances. Amazingly, Wolves still headed the overall goal charts in their 35/37 seasons in the top flight, amassing 2,731 which was 50 more than ever-presents Arsenal. In May the Sporting Star invited the comments of readers on Wolves plight, the fans demanding improved toilet and catering facilities at the ground as well as a supporters club linked to the football club and the inevitable list of players Wolves should sign. The massive response underlined that people cared about football in Wolverhampton which was a pleasing factor following a dismal D1 campaign, bottom four: Birmingham 33, Wolves 30, Burnley 28 and Sheff Utd 22.

LEAGUE CUP: A late rally saved Wolves at D3 Swindon, not that the replay was exactly a walkover. Hibbitt showed his mettle at Birmingham and a QF place loomed when Wolves came out of the hat after D3 Mansfield. Their opponents were bottom of that particular section and it could be said that Wolves were truly 'staggered' by the outcome.

F.A. CUP: Wolves were delighted to give Arsenal an early exit and then knock out Ipswich in a replay, Gould scoring with an attempted cross while local lad O'Hara made a splendid debut. When D2 Charlton came to town Richards was on the bench for the first time since coming into the team, replacing Wagstaffe in the 20th minute and promptly being the first substitute to hit an F.A. Cup hatrick. He also gave Wolves a shock lead at Old Trafford, where Parkes was magnificent under pressure until foiled by a late deflection. Memories of the 1960's were unfortunately revived in the replay as Wolves struck two fine goals but Man Utd brought it back to 2-1 by the interval, then after Kindon had rocked the post with a vicious 58th-minute drive they equalised to force extra-time. The large crowd gasped as Parkin released a thunderbolt that hit the woodwork only for United to snatch a heart-rending winner. They were to slip up in the final to Southampton.

RESULTS: MAN UTD 0-2; Stoke 2-2 (Carr, Richards); Middlesbrough 0-1; QUEENS PARK 2-2 (Richards, Hibbitt); ARSENAL 0-0; Leeds 0-3; LC Swindon 2-2 (Sunderland, Richards); BIRMINGHAM 2-0 (Carr 2); LC SWINDON 3-2 (Sunderland, Richards, Hibbitt); Newcastle

1-5 (Daley); VILLA 0-0; WEST HAM 0-1; Liverpool 0-2; LC Birmingham 2-0 (Hibbitt 2); SHEFF UTD 5-1 (Richards 2, Hibbitt 2, Carr); Derby 2-3 (Kindon, Richards); EVERTON 1-2 (Hibbitt); Spurs 1-2 (Daley); IPSWICH 1-0 (Daley); LC Mansfield 0-1; Burnley 5-1 (Richards 2, Daley 2, Hibbitt); DERBY 0-0; MAN CITY 0-4; Leicester 0-2; MIDDLESBROUGH 1-2 (Hibbitt); Man Utd 0-1; COVENTRY 0-1; Norwich 1-1 (Bell); FAC ARSENAL 3-0 (Bell, Richards, Hibbitt); Birmingham 1-0 (Carr); LEEDS 1-1 (Gould); FAC Ipswich 0-0; FAC IPSWICH 1-0 (Gould); STOKE 2-1 (Carr, Bell); Queens Park 2-4 (Gould 2); FAC CHARLTON 3-0 (Richards 3); Ipswich 0-3; BURNLEY 3-2 (Richards 2, Bell); Villa 1-1 (Richards); Everton 0-3; FAC Man Utd 1-1 (Richards); FAC MAN UTD 2-3 (Kindon, Richards); Sheff Utd 4-1 (Kindon 2, Richards, Palmer); SPURS 0-1; Man City 2-3 (Daley, Kindon); LEICESTER 2-2 (Richards, Hibbitt); West Ham 0-0; NEWCASTLE 5-0 (Richards 3, Hibbitt, Carr); Arsenal 1-2 (Richards); Coventry 1-3 (Bell); NORWICH 1-0 (Richards) & LIVERPOOL 1-3 (Kindon).

RECORD: PLD 52 W 15 D 13 L 24 F 68 A 77 (11-6-9 & 4-7-15).

SCORERS: Richards 25, Hibbitt 12, Carr 7, Daley 6, Kindon 6, Bell 5, Gould 4, Sunderland 2 & Palmer 1.

YOUTH CUP: Birmingham 1-1, BIRMINGHAM 2-1, Fulham 1-1, FULHAM 3-2, Spurs 2-2, SPURS 4-0, Queens Park 1-0, Newcastle 2-1, NEWCASTLE 2-1, ALBION 0-2 (11,871) & Albion 0-3. Team: Walker, Duncombe, Tysall, Moss, Hazell, Berry, Singh, Patching, Crompton, Todd & Black. In the second leg substitute Loftus came on for Singh.

SCORERS: Crompton 6, Todd 4, Aston 2, Patching 2, Berry 1, Black 1, Moss 1 & Singh 1.

FAREWELLS: Jefferson 51-0 (Hereford), McNab 16-0, Taylor 188-1 (Swindon), Wagstaffe 401-31 (Blackburn) & Williams 11-0 (Gillingham). GERRY TAYLOR was born in Hull and came to Wolverhampton by courtesy of the Wath nursery. He spent most of his Molineux career in the reserves until he formed a steady full-back partnership with Shaw, making 49 appearances in 1972-73. His first team outings were spread over a decade but as they became less frequent the sturdy defender decided to move on.

DAVE WAGSTAFFE was a Mancunian who cost £30,000 and was a left-winger of the old-fashioned mould. He was a good dribbler who could waltz past opponents on his day, and though he sometimes tended to overdo it he always made Saturday afternoons more entertaining. He was a regular scorer in D2 and made the highest number of Wolves appearances, 48, in 1966-67. It was a pity that he was constantly hampered by injuries to his slim ankles which received a pounding from less-talented defenders, this being partly why Wagstaffe never had the confidence to match his ability. He certainly deserved his 1974 League Cup reward although even that did not go completely smoothly and his testimonial the following season attracted over 14,000 fans.

1976 -77

DEBUTANTS: George Berry, Colin Brazier & Kenny Todd. Berry was born in West Germany.

SUMMARY: Wolves celebrated their centenary year by winning the D2 title and reaching the last eight of the F.A. Cup again. Reaping the benefits of a settled side they lost just one of their first 23 away games including friendlies, and in competitive matches had runs of 16 without defeat and 10 wins in a row at home. In May the D1 runners-up Man City visited Molineux in a centenary friendly that pulled in almost 15,000 supporters. Television viewers had again watched Wolves clinch the five-a-side title, nobody else having ever won it twice let alone retained it. They trimmed Bristol City 3-0 (Sunderland 2, Carr) then required penalties after a stalemate with Ipswich. In the SF Wolves put a stop to the North of the border challenge of Rangers 1-0 (Daley) to ensure a final meeting with Stoke. Wolves were a shade fortunate to win 2-1 (Hibbitt, Daley) but were surely the equal of any British team at this event, their squad being completed by Pierce and Patching.

LEAGUE D2: 1st (57). With Parkes, Kelly and Jefferson still playing out in America the Wanderers opened with a dull performance on a sunny day against Burnley. After drawing with the other demoted side at Bramall Lane they came good at Nottingham, where a crowd disturbance caused a brief delay. Charlton were sent packing before Wolves went to London as almost 26,000 assembled to see George Best make a comeback in the colours of Fulham. Wolves kept a tight grip on him and they thrashed Oldham, one newspaper giving Kindon 10/10 in the individual ratings. Wolves were top of the heap on goal-difference, goal-average no longer being the criterion.

Luton reminded Wolves it would not be roses all the way, a lesson that looked to be heeded as they ran riot at Hereford — as did some of their followers. Incredibly, Wolves were hit for six themselves at home three days later and defeat at Hull left them a point clear of the 16th team of a closely-bunched D2 pack. The situation was improved when Sunderland, revelling in his attacking role, blasted Carlisle with a hatrick. A useful 2-2 draw at Blackpool was marred by the antics of Wolves supporters, their missile-throwing forcing the players off for several minutes.

After 15 games Wolves were six points adrift of leaders Chelsea and four behind the third club, but Richards was back after a lengthy lay-off and his influence soon began to tell. Wolves disposed of Orient and Plymouth, with only two late defensive errors preventing Chelsea from going the same way. Wolves were fifth when they tackled Bolton, who produced some neat football in atrocious conditions. Yet Gould got the only goal in the 77th minute, on a day when Black notched the one that decided Wolves Reserves match. Note the connection? A romp at Bristol made Wolverhampton the highest scorers in the country with 50 in 20 games and they reached the halfway stage by drawing at Millwall. Chelsea were still first with 32 points from 23 games followed by Bolton (22-30), Wolves (21-27), Forest (21-27) and Blackpool (22-27).

In February Wolves recorded their sixth success by four or more goals when Fulham were the visitors, although it was the first time in 1976-77 they had been at full strength. Wolves finally topped D2 after the Bristol Rovers win, not that the goals were flowing so freely now, one player suggesting that the false teeth found on the terraces afterwards had been left to add some bite to the attack! Notts County came to Molineux at Easter and the result was 2-2, the first time in which the team opening the scoring at the ground had not won all season. Richards scored a vintage goal versus Notts, adding another at Blackburn as Wolves made it 32/40 points to virtually guarantee promotion.

The 39th step of the campaign was at Plymouth, where Wolves gained the point that clinched an early managerial success for Chung. After faltering at Southampton the destiny of the title was still in doubt as Wolves had 54 points to Chelsea's 52, while the battle for third place was between Bolton, Blackpool and Forest. Thousands of Chelsea fans were in town but despite over 100 arrests there were no major incidents, Tommy Langley firing them in front on a day Berry made his debut and for most of the afternoon the championship seemed to be slipping from Wolves grasp. Their supporters sighed with relief at a 78th-minute equaliser with Chelsea also content as the point secured their promotion.

The 42nd fixture was vital to the Bolton outfit managed by Ian Greaves, while 8,000 travelled from the Midlands to swell the gate to 35,603. Some hefty early challenges by Bolton players increased Wolves determination and when Carr lobbed a free-kick over the defensive wall Hibbitt swept the ball home. Sid Kipping drove the coach back before retiring from the job after 20 years, unaware that the result was to have a bearing on the 1979 ECC as it meant Forest went up instead of Bolton.

Wolves topped a division for the sixth time and they had been leading scorers on 13 occasions, although their total of 84 was disappointing in the end. They were unbeaten against their main five rivals and completed six doubles while in D1 Liverpool had become the first team to retain the title since Wolves did it in 1959. The most remarkable aspect of it all was that Wolves had made a quick return with basically the same men who went down, Chung making no new signings and restricting the youngsters introduced to a miserly aggregate of six appearances which was a policy that paid off, top five: Wolves 57, Chelsea 55, Forest 52, Bolton 51 and Blackpool 51.

LEAGUE CUP: Wolves vainly appealed for offside as D3 Sheff Wed sealed victory at Molineux, thus their League Cup jinx against teams from lower divisions continued.

F.A. CUP: The third round tie was the first in 26 in which Wolves had not met opponents from the premier two divisions in the F.A. Cup, though D3 Rotherham were no pushovers. Wolves were next paired with favourites D1 Ipswich, whose keeper retrieved the ball from behind the line to deprive Richards of a hatrick and Wolves of an excellent win.

Brazier had a fine debut as Wolves edged an open replay 1-0, despite Hibbitt thumping the post with a 47th-minute penalty. He made amends against D3 Chester who had kept Wolves under control for 81 minutes, and the home side had now won 9/10 of their ties at the ground against teams from the lower two divisions. Wolves were dominant in the early exchanges of their QF with D1 Leeds only to be caught on the break, after which they never really looked dangerous. It was frustrating for the majority of the last-ever 50,000 Molineux crowd, especially as Wolves had now won just 1/21 tussles with Leeds.

RESULTS: BURNLEY 0-0; Sheff Utd 2-2 (Carr, Sunderland); Forest 3-1 (Gould 2, Daley); LC SHEFF WED 1-2 (Parkin); CHARLTON 3-0 (Gould 2, Sunderland); Fulham 0-0; OLDHAM 5-0 (Kindon 2, Sunderland, Daley, Hibbitt); LUTON 1-2 (Hibbitt); Hereford 6-1 (Gould 2, Carr, Daley, Sunderland, Kindon); SOUTHAMPTON 2-6 (Hibbitt, Daley); Hull 0-2; CARLISLE 4-0 (Sunderland 3, Carr); Blackpool 2-2 (Hibbitt, Munro); MILLWALL 3-1 (OG, Sunderland, Daley); Notts Co 1-1 (Gould); BLACKBURN 1-2 (Sunderland); Orient 4-2 (Richards 3, Gould); PLYMOUTH 4-0 (Richards 2, Hibbitt, Sunderland); Chelsea 3-3 (Richards 2, Gould); BOLTON 1-0 (Gould); Bristol R 5-1 (Sunderland 2, Hibbitt, Kindon, Daley); Millwall 1-1 (Hibbitt); FAC ROTHERHAM 3-2 (Richards 2, Daley); Burnley 0-0; FAC Ipswich 2-2 (Richards 2); FAC IPSWICH 1-0 (Richards); FOREST 2-1 (Carr, Richards); SHEFF UTD 2-1 (Sunderland, Richards); Charlton 1-1 (Patching); FULHAM 5-1 (Daley 2, Hibbitt 2, Richards); FAC CHESTER 1-0 (Hibbitt); BLACKPOOL 2-1 (Daley, Hibbitt); Luton 0-2; HEREFORD 2-1 (Todd, Hibbitt); Oldham 2-0 (Sunderland, Daley); FAC LEEDS 0-1; HULL 2-1 (Richards, Hibbitt); BRISTOL R 1-0 (Daley); Cardiff 2-2 (Daley, Hibbitt); NOTTS CO 2-2 (Daley, Richards); Blackburn 2-0 (Hibbitt, Richards); Carlisle 1-2 (Hibbitt); ORIENT 1-0 (Richards); CARDIFF 4-1 (Palmer, Sunderland, Patching, Hibbitt); Plymouth 0-0; Southampton 0-1; CHELSEA 1-1 (Richards) & Bolton 1-0 (Hibbitt).

RECORD: PLD 48 W 25 D 14 L 9 F 92 A 52 (18-3-5 & 7-11-4).

SCORERS: Richards 20, Hibbitt 18, Sunderland 15, Daley 14, Gould 10, Carr 4, Kindon 4, Patching 2, Munro 1, Palmer 1, Parkin 1, Todd 1 & OG 1.

INTERNATIONALS: Richards qualified for what was now the Under 21 team by the strange ruling that allowed a couple of over-age players, writing in the Sporting Star that his selection was a surprise 'not least to my mum', while Sunderland also took full use of the rule in the abysmal 0-0 draw with Wales at Molineux. Apps: Richards (E U21-2) & Sunderland (E U21-1).

FAREWELLS: Bailey 431-25, Gould 31-14 Total 81-39 (Bristol Rovers), Munro 365-19 (Celtic) & O'Hara 9-0. MIKE BAILEY was a snip at £40,000 having already played twice for England. The barrel-chested attacking right-half hailed from Wisbech but soon gained respect in the area, being voted Midlands 'Footballer of the Year' in 1966-67. Bailey was firm in the tackle and possessed a powerful shot, though occasionally his passing let him down. After all the near misses he happily lifted the League Cup at Wembley and when he did begin to struggle for his form in 1975-76 it was significant that the team suffered too. Approximately 20,000 enjoyed his testimonial in 1976-77 as Wolves beat Albion 3-0 with some assistance from special guest George Best, who scored twice. Bailey was transferred to Minnesota Kicks for £15,000 as he took on a new challenge across the Atlantic, leaving Wolves fans with some fond memories.

FRANK MUNRO was noticed by Wolves in Los Angeles when he scored a hatrick against them in the final of the American Championship. He cost £55,000 and the Dundee-born inside-forward was soon made welcome by the locals. He was converted to half-back, ironically after Wolves 1969 tour of the United States, and his coolness in defence gave the crowd some very entertaining moments — as well as a few worrying ones. Munro was very skilful for such a hefty man, so the fans were sorry to see him return to his native country for £20,000.

1977 - 78

DEBUTANTS: John Black, Paul Bradshaw (Blackburn), Mel Eves, Bob Hazell & Billy Rafferty (Carlisle). Black and Rafferty were born in Scotland.

SUMMARY: Shortly after a Molineux 'open-day' had attracted 10,000 fans, news of a £10m super-stadium was announced, stressing Wolves intentions of embarking on an era of success. They just about avoided relegation to keep the ambitions intact, an oddity being that the 3-1 scoreline cropped up in 7/11 matches, compared to 7/131 previously. It was Wolves biggest season on the transfer front as Bradshaw (£150,000), Rafferty (£125,000) and Daniel (£185,000) became the club's three most expensive purchases, the latter arriving at the end of 1977-78. Fees were generally getting out of hand as Wolves still managed to break even, the £240,000 departure of Sunderland being chiefly responsible.

LEAGUE: 15th (36). There were four penalties on the opening day at Bristol with City converting two and Carr netting one for Wolves as well as missing one, though the rebound was tapped in by Sunderland. It was a relief to see the affair settled by a spectacular Patching goal. At Molineux four balls were used before one of them was smashed into the QPR net by Richards in the 67th minute and Kindon's fine header against Arsenal put Wolves fifth. They continued to play well at Goodison Park, being unlucky not to take maximum points in a 0-0 draw.

Wolves first defeat came after their first team change as the cameras took their first look at them. It was also their first reverse in 16 Molineux games despite goals from Bell and Daley, the former being in action for the first time in 17 months and the latter taking advantage of his first penalty for Wolves. Misfortune continued at Albion where they were denied two clear-cut spot-kicks and had five key men injured yet the reserve lads helped them achieve a creditable draw. A similar result was on the cards at Villa Park until Parkes rolled the ball out to Brazier in the 75th minute, only for the lanky defender to lob it into his own net. Richards second half hatrick against Leicester gave Wolves nine points from eight games and remained the most recent one by any of their players until May, 1987.

Derby gained their only away success in 18 months at Wolves expense, then Norwich finally lowered their colours at the 15th attempt. Wolves pulled back two goals against West Ham and then turned on the style at Maine Road, being the first League visitors to win there for a year. Mick Ferguson of Coventry spoiled all that by becoming the first opponent to score a hatrick at Molineux for 16 years, then came four mixed results.

Talk of relegation suddenly filled the air after a couple of 3-1 setbacks and a hiding at McGarry's Newcastle, the former result being at Old Trafford as Wolves seventh trip to Lancashire in 1977 saw them concede their only goals there. At Christmas Leeds led 1-0 but were foiled by a superb Wolves fightback, before Bradshaw was beaten by a re-taken penalty at Anfield having apparently made a legitimate save. The next bright note was victory in the mud over second-placed Everton which was even more emphatic than the 3-1 score suggested. Wolves fell to bottom team Leicester who had won 1/26 then drew 3-3 with Norwich, but Hibbitt who had been sharing most of the recent goals with fellow-midfielder Daley fractured his ankle in the act of beating the East Anglian defence.

Wolves eased the pressure 2-1 at West Ham, the recalled Parkes having a tremendous last match for the club. A goal in the dying seconds from Albion stopped Wolves in their tracks and dismal shooting against Man City meant they had to be content with another 1-1 home draw, after Hazell had become the first coloured person to score for Wolves at Molineux. Suddenly, four defeats in eight days hurtled Wolves towards the danger zone and the rot was extended at Derby. West Ham had picked up 8/10 points to go above Wolves, who now led QPR by a mere three points having played twice more while Leicester and Newcastle were doomed. Richards weakly missed a penalty v. Middlesbrough while Rafferty had a stunning individual goal ruled out, the outcome being 0-0.

At Stamford Bridge poor Rafferty pulled the ball back from the bye-line for Eves to turn it in yet the referee deemed that the Scotsman was technically offside, a decision that reporters described as amongst the worst they had seen. Wolves drew and were 20th as they trailed 1-0 at half-time to Man Utd. The younger members swung the game round and with their main rivals losing the picture had dramatically improved in 45 minutes. Only a point was required for safety from two fixtures, both being tough ones indeed. Villa had to win to qualify for Europe so there would be no kindly neighbouring act from them on a night when supporters were segregated by a fence on the South Bank for the first time, the consequence of several terrace incidents since the more vociferous Wolves element had moved from the North Bank.Villa cancelled out Richards's 16th-minute strike but Eves restored Wolves lead, a late glancing header by Rafferty removing any lingering fears for most of the 30,664 crowd.

A surprise win at Ipswich made it 6/6 points after those nine games without victory, pushing Wolves up to a deceptive 15th four points ahead of relegated West Ham. Clarke came on as substitute and hit the woodwork, raising hopes that he would emulate brother Allan in ability as well as appearance. Wolves won a prize in 1977-78 in the Daily Mail/Vernons Pools Fair-Play League despite having a player dismissed and conceding five penalties. They gave away easily the lowest number of free-kicks and their 16 bookings was also the best total in D1, Wolves taking the title by 103 points which did not say much for the behaviour of the rest.

LEAGUE CUP: Wolves wanted revenge over D2 Luton who were one of the few thorns in their side in 1976-77, but after drawing first blood they buckled under to them again.

F.A. CUP: A late Daly goal spared Wolves blushes at D3 Exeter and they made no mistake in the replay. They were level at Highbury thanks to a curler by Hibbitt when Richards failed to hit the target when clean through. In the final minute the burly Hazell was sent off and the game restarted with an Arsenal corner that was headed in by Malcolm MacDonald - who Hazell had kept in check all afternoon. Wolves had a habit of going out to leading clubs by single-goal margins, favourites Arsenal reaching the final. Ipswich did well to beat them 1-0, so in three years of F.A. Cup activity the Suffolk team had only succumbed to Wolves.

RESULTS: Bristol C 3-2 (Carr, Sunderland, Patching); QUEENS PARK 1-0 (Richards); ARSENAL 1-1 (Kindon); LC LUTON 1-3 (Richards); Everton 0-0; FOREST 2-3 (Bell, Daley); Albion 2-2 (Bell, Daley); Villa 0-2; LEICESTER 3-0 (Richards 3); DERBY 1-2 (Hibbitt); Norwich 1-2 (Sunderland); WEST HAM 2-2 (Richards, Hibbitt); Man City 2-0 (Richards 2); COVENTRY 1-3 (Hibbitt); Birmingham 1-2 (Patching); NEWCASTLE 1-0 (Patching); Middlesbrough 0-0; IPSWICH 0-0; Man Utd 1-3 (Richards); CHELSEA 1-3 (Carr); Newcastle 0-4; LEEDS 3-1 (Richards 2, Patching); Liverpool 0-1; Queens Park 3-1 (Bell 2, Daley); BRISTOL C 0-0; FAC Exeter 2-2 (Carr, Daly); FAC EXETER 3-1 (Richards, Hibbitt, Daley); Arsenal 1-3 (OG); EVERTON 3-1 (Hibbitt 2, Daley); FAC Arsenal 1-2 (Hibbitt); Forest 0-2; Leicester 0-1; NORWICH 3-3 (Daley 2, Hibbitt); West Ham 2-1 (Rafferty, Carr); ALBION 1-1 (Daley); MAN CITY 1-1 (Hazell); LIVERPOOL 1-3 (OG); Leeds 1-2 (Daley); Coventry 0-4; BIRMINGHAM 0-1; Derby 1-3 (Patching); MIDDLESBROUGH 0-0; Chelsea 1-1 (Eves); MAN UTD 2-1 (Patching, Eves); VILLA 3-1 (Richards, Eves, Rafferty) & Ipswich 2-1 (Rafferty 2).

RECORD: PLD 46 W 13 D 13 L 20 F 58 A 72 (8-8-7 & 5-5-13).

SCORERS: Richards 13, Daley 9, Hibbitt 8, Patching 6, Bell 4, Carr 4, Rafferty 4, Eves 3, Sunderland 2, Daly 1, Hazell 1, Kindon 1 & OG 2.

INTERNATIONALS: Daly graduated to the full Eire XI while the England 'B' team was revived after a couple of decades, several withdrawals from a tour of the Far East making it more like a D team. Wolves had a trio lining-up in one match though with Richards unfit and Eves unproven only Daley was there with true justification after a fine season. The latter duo both scored while Bradshaw received recognition at Under 21 level. Apps:

Bradshaw (E U21-2), Daley (E 'B' 5), Daly (ROI 2 + ROI U21-1), Eves (E 'B' 3) & Richards (E 'B' 3).

FAREWELLS: Daly 30-1, Farley 38-0 (Hull), Kelly 21-0 (Walsall), Kindon 131-31 (Burnley), Parkes 382-0, Sunderland 175-33 (Arsenal) & Todd 4-1 (Port Vale). STEVE KINDON was born in Warrington and what he lacked on the technical side he made up for with his sheer enthusiasm. He was either very good or awful as he willingly occupied most forward positions for Wolves. The well-built Kindon won a 75-metres sprint contest for professional footballers in 1976 and he was often stopped by unfair means when in full cry. He even had his own special 'Tank T-Shirts' and Molineux was slightly duller after he returned to Turf Moor for £80,000.

PHIL PARKES was from West Bromwich, joining Wolves in 1962-63 but as 1966-67 began he had not progressed beyond fourth-choice goalkeeper. He concentrated hard to make the first team that term and over the next few years he was to turn in a real variety of performances for Wolves, producing unbelievable saves yet being beaten by some comparitively straightforward efforts. He was an ever-present in 1971-72 and 1972-73, going on to create a club record of 170 successive appearances the next season when he sadly missed the trip to Wembley. Parkes was omitted for the entire 1976-77 campaign and made nine appearances in 1977-78, plus his testimonial, before deciding to try his luck with Vancouver White Caps.

ALAN SUNDERLAND was another Wath product, hailing from Mexborough in Yorkshire. He was usually part of the midfield line-up at first but then had a long spell at right-back before finally making his mark— as a striker. Sunderland was something of an enigma at Molineux as he was obviously very skilful with terrific ball control yet he often failed to do himself justice, but Arsenal were clearly aware of his capabilities and made Wolves an offer they could not refuse.

1978 - 79

DEBUTANTS: Ian Arkwright, Wayne Clarke, Peter Daniel (Hull) & Craig Moss.

SUMMARY: The official Molineux capacity was reduced to 41,900 to comply with the 'Safety at sports grounds act' with the massive South Bank going from holding 30,000 to 23,000-still one of the largest terraces in Britain. This prompted another pre-season statement from Wolves that the new stadium would be a cantilevered complex with 30,000 seats and room for 5,000 to stand at each end. It was said that this space-age arena would be ready for 1984 but like past plans it did not materialise, the only space link that year was to be that Molineux had no atmosphere! These schemes were briefly forgotten as Wolves made their worst-ever start to a season, ultimately leading to the dismissal of Chung. Ex-Arsenal and Forest star John Barnwell had resigned as manager of Peterborough and he got the job, Richie Barker being appointed as his number two after being in charge at Shrewsbury. Once the duo had settled in Wolves easily escaped the threat of relegation and almost got to Wembley, after 15/20 defeats there was only

4/20 though a less-gratifying statistic was the unique failure of any player to score a brace all season. Barnwell's fortunes also took a turn for the worse when he fractured his skull in a road accident in April.

LEAGUE: 18th (34). Andy Gray gave Villa the first-day points against Wolves and the rot quickly set in. Not only did Chelsea win a drab Molineux game, some of their so-called fans invaded the North Bank to cause a seven-minute delay. Wolves returned from Leeds as the only pointless or goalless D1 team before a Bristol player inadvertantly opened their account. Blunders at the back cost Wolves dear as Ipswich won 3-1 at Wolverhampton, when home players Clarke, Bell and Patching all struck the woodwork.

Wolves won their eighth match thanks to a Daniel penalty and there was no shame in defeat at Nottingham, the Forest duly equalling the D1 record of 35 without loss. Derby was developing into a dreaded venue for Wolves as they suffered their eighth beating in a row there, while they had lost on all seven journeys made in 1978-79. Coach Brian Garvey briefly took over, dropping the in-form Daley for Moss only for the misery to increase as Villa humiliated them 4-0 at Molineux which brought back memories of Man City doing exactly the same the last time Wolves were relegated.

There was a welcome result under new management at Bristol though the joy was short-lived. Bradshaw saved two penalties at Tottenham only for Spurs to score in the scramble that followed the latter, the keeper also receiving a knock with Hibbitt then taking his place between the sticks. Wolves lost at Bolton and were thoroughly outplayed by Albion to give Barnwell a grim home start.

Wolves pipped the only team below them, Birmingham, and slowly confidence grew culminating in them being only the second side to defeat Everton with a 13th-minute drive by Daley in the Molineux snow. They let slip a 3-1 advantage at QPR in the closing stages but on a quick return to London they triumphed over second-in-the-table Arsenal. Nobody believed Wolves could go down after that, their new fighting spirit being in evidence as they twice trailed to Spurs yet won 3-2. There was a lack-lustre display against Man City before Wolves played their hearts out only to somehow lose 1-0 to Liverpool, being denied a blatant penalty when Richards was fouled with seconds remaining.

Berry cleverly foiled the Derby offside-trap with a chip and a chase and probably Molineux's best goal of the term as Wolves made a mockery of the fact they had not overcome Derby since 1973-74, both results being 4-0. The home programme was completed with a neat and richly-deserved winner in the 89th minute against Brian Clough's ECC Finalists and it now seemed laughable that relegation had looked inevitable a few months previously.

LEAGUE CUP: Wolves interest here was brought to a conclusion by a team from a lower division for the ninth time. The fact that it was

D4 Reading meant that Wolves early season form had reached crisis proportions.

F.A. CUP: Drawn away to three leading D2 teams Wolves found themselves in the curious situation of being underdogs in each round. However, they came from behind at Brighton, won a 10-times postponed replay with Newcastle by when everyone seemed to have lost interest in the tie, and they were undeterred by Bell breaking his leg at Palace. Graham Turner's D3 Shrewsbury were the unlikely QF opponents and their first visit to Molineux attracted 40,946. Rafferty had apparently secured victory for Wolves late on but in the very last minute the Shropshire side levelled from the penalty-spot. Shrewsbury had been formidable at Gay Meadow all season and 16,479 crammed into the tiny ground to see Wolves reveal their superiority, going 3-0 up before the Shrews got a consolation. In a tedious SF at Villa Park the general verdict was that Wolves just did not play as an unimpressive Arsenal grabbed two decisive second half goals. Patching had a rasping shot tipped over by Jennings, this solitary decent attempt happening right at the end. Sunderland hit Arsenal's second goal and to rub it in got the decider at Wembley some weeks later.

RESULTS: Villa 0-1; CHELSEA 0-1; Leeds 0-3; LC Reading 0-1; BRISTOL C 2-0 (OG, Hibbitt); Southampton 2-3 (Bell, Daniel); IPSWICH 1-3 (OG); Everton 0-2; QUEENS PARK 1-0 (Daniel); Forest 1-3 (Eves); ARSENAL 1-0 (Eves); Middlesbrough 0-2; MAN UTD 2-4 (Hibbitt, Daley); Derby 1-4 (Carr); VILLA 0-4; LEEDS 1-1 (Daniel); Bristol C 1-0 (Daley); Spurs 0-1; Bolton 1-3 (Berry); ALBION 0-3; BIRMINGHAM 2-1 (Hibbitt, Daniel); COVENTRY 1-1 (Daley); FAC Brighton 3-2 (Bell, Daley, OG); SOUTHAMPTON 2-0 (Carr, Bell); Ipswich 1-3 (Berry); FAC Newcastle 1-1 (Hibbitt); EVERTON 1-0 (Daley); Queens Park 3-3 (Bell, Clarke, Patching); FAC NEWCASTLE 1-0 (Bell); Arsenal 1-0 (Richards); FAC Palace 1-0 (Patching); MIDDLESBROUGH 1-3 (Richards); Norwich 0-0; FAC SHREWSBURY 1-1 (Rafferty); FAC Shrewsbury 3-1 (Carr, Rafferty, Daniel); Liverpool 0-2; Chelsea 2-1 (Richards, Rafferty); MAN CITY 1-1 (Carr); FAC Arsenal 0-2; SPURS 3-2 (Richards, Daley, Hibbitt); Man City 1-3 (Hibbitt); LIVERPOOL 0-1; Birmingham 1-1 (Richards); NORWICH 1-0 (Hibbitt); Albion 1-1 (Richards); DERBY 4-0 (Rafferty, Berry, Daley, Daniel); BOLTON 1-1 (Richards); FOREST 1-0 (Richards); Coventry 0-3 & Man Utd 2-3 (OG, Richards).

RECORD: PLD 50 W 17 D 10 L 23 F 54 A 76 (11-5-7 & 6-5-16).
SCORERS: Richards 9, Daley 7, Hibbitt 7, Daniel 6, Bell 5, Carr 4, Rafferty 4, Berry 3, Eves 2, Patching 2, Clarke 1 & OG 4.

INTERNATIONALS: A distant relative enabled Berry to become only the second coloured man to represent Wales though he was actually born in Germany, where his Jamaican father was serving in the R.A.F., and bred in England. International football was turning into something of a farce as other players had been known to appear for countries they had never even visited! There were winning goals abroad for Daley in the 'B' team and Hazell at Under 21 level. Apps: Berry (W 1), Daley (E 'B' 1) & Hazell (E 'B' 1 + E U21-1).

FAREWELLS: Arkwright 3-0 (Wrexham), Black 5-0 (Bradford City), Daley 220-41 (Man City), Hazell 34-1 (QPR) & Pierce 111-0 (Bury). STEVE DALEY was a Barnsley man who needless to say arrived via the Northern link to Wolves set up by Mark Crook. In 1971 he helped England beat Portugal 3-0 in the IYT Final, Eastoe scoring twice. He was a tigerish player who could tackle and shoot well, although he had originally made his name as a left-winger. Daley was one of a quartet of Wolves ever-presents in 1976-77 as he began to fulfil his early promise at last, which was why he was to leave Wolves in sensational circumstances early in 1979-80.

GARY PIERCE was a £40,000 buy who will always be remembered for his 14th appearance — that being at Wembley. He also excelled at many of the minor events Wolves won as well as the real thing in 1976-77, when he was an ever-present and kept 14 clean sheets. Prior to 1977-78 he cracked a bone in his wrist and then had it in plaster on three separate occasions, thus failing to register a first team appearance. Once fully recovered Pierce found it difficult to dis-lodge Bradshaw and was restricted to three games in 1978-79 before joining his home-town team.

1979 - 80

DEBUTANTS: Hugh Atkinson, Andy Gray (Villa), Emlyn Hughes (Liverpool), John Humphrey, Mick Kearns (Walsall) & Dave Thomas (Everton). Atkinson was born in Eire and Gray in Scotland.

SUMMARY: Wolverhampton had become something of a music-hall joke in the 1970's but all was not gloom as it brewed some of the best beer in the country, printed one of the top provincial newspapers, broadcast a fast-improving local radio station, provided good shopping facilities and in 1979-80 boasted a leading football club again. Wolves won the League Cup and were sixth in D1 and September saw them involved in two incredible transfer deals. To receive £437,500 for Daley and pay £469,000 for Gray would be staggering enough but a £1m was added to those fees! Only Bryan Robson and Peter Beardsley have since cost an English club more and some Wolves fans argued that the money spent on Gray should have gone on three or four players and they might have been cheering the champions, although the £325,000 paid for Thomas did them no good. Other big deals concerned the sales of Hazell (£200,000), Rafferty (£175,000) and Patching (£100,000) in a season that saw Wolves constantly in the news — even the club programme was larger than ever. The Molineux Street stand and 71 houses had been demolished to make way for the new 9,500-seater that contained 42 executive boxes as the ground at last saw some modernisation. Although the pitch was moved over it was still a considerable distance from the stand and with Molineux less enclosed the home advantage was slightly reduced. Attendances were the highest for eight years but 43/80 Wolves goals were on their travels, in fact there were 15 wins at away or neutral venues including seven in succession Wolves were tipped to lose. Barnwell, who had returned to his desk early in the season, was voted Midlands 'Sports personality of the Year' by the Variety Club which underlined how Wolves had captured football's imagination in 1979-80.

LEAGUE: 6th (47). The opening fixture with Liverpool was postponed as the stand was not quite ready, forcing Wolves to commence at Derby on the Wednesday night when they duly caught up with Saturday's winners. They played efficiently in their first home match to tame Ipswich 3-0 but it was in the fifth game at Everton that they hinted something special was in store. Gray made his debut while Richards came back after another lay-off, both scoring in a fine 3-2 win.

The new strike-force starred in a fine defeat of Man Utd and Gray bagged a couple more at Highbury to give Wolves 11/14 points — all this after the normally-reliable bookmakers had tipped them for relegation. They ceased to set the soccer world alight in their next six matches but Hibbitt gave them victory at Stoke, leaving Wolves sixth after a third of the season, the leaders being just three points clear having completed one extra fixture.

Any genuine title prospects vanished on a snowy Friday night at Christmas as Brighton's Peter Ward notched a Molineux hatrick. The slide carried on to such an extent that Wolves were 14th when they visited a Man Utd side who had not had their colours lowered at Old Trafford. Richards put Eves through to change all that, then Hibbitt converted two penalties in a resounding 4-0 win at Norwich. Wolves were back on the warpath even if it was too late to make an impression on champions-to-be Liverpool who were 10 points ahead of them. An immaculate piece of finishing by Richards narrowed the gap on an emotional night significant for the fact that Hughes was the subject of the 'This is your life' television show, which in days gone by had featured the likes of Wright and Dougan.

Middlesbrough came away from Molineux with both points for the eighth time in 14 post-war raids, though Wolves immediately made amends at Villa Park despite fielding several reserves as Wembley loomed. Wins at Coventry and then Southampton on an Easter morning made it five away League successes on the trot and a goal aggregate of 14-2, equalling Wolves similar runs of 1938 and 1962. Wolves flopped in the easier-looking task at Brighton the next day but gained a draw on the short trip to Albion as Kearns blocked a penalty, the big keeper making his D1 debut at the age of 29. Wolves went out on a timid note against Arsenal to miss out on the fifth position in an excellent season, as they defeated all of the top five and nobody could improve on their 10 away victories.

LEAGUE CUP: The second round was now played over two legs and the shooting power of Palmer was the downfall of D2 Burnley. Wolves won at an in-form Crystal Palace and then needed a replay to eliminate D2 QPR. The QF at D3 Grimsby ended up goalless before Gray struck in the 22nd minute at Molineux, only for Palmer to slice the ball into his own net. Wolves were lucky to survive extra-time and in the decider at Derby they only qualified because of a controversial Hibbitt penalty and a Richards shot that was deflected in off a defender. Wolves cautiously welcomed a SF pairing with D3 Swindon but soon trailed in the first leg, Daniel wiping it out with a looping header in the 29th minute, though after a glaring miss by Richards the Wiltshire side stole a late winner. Record Molineux receipts of £80,839 were paid by 41,031 fans who saw Richards atone for his blunder as Wolves stumbled through 4-3 overall, Forest beating Liverpool 2-1 in the other SF.

FINAL: The rising cost of watching football was reflected by the £625,000 forked out by the 96,527 present, the charge to stand up being £3.50 now. If there was a replay it would be at Old Trafford, though the stand-by venue for the 1974 final, Stoke, would have been geographically ideal. Not that the Forest team who had held the trophy for two years expected such problems, on the other hand Captain Hughes was determined to prove his £90,000 move to Wolves would not be the anti-climax to his career predicted as he sought an honour that eluded him at Anfield. The well-organised Wolves rearguard frustrated Forest and always had players on the line during a goalmouth scamble, though Bradshaw was covering things adequately himself. Shortly after the break Wolves had cause for complaint as the ball was bundled in when Richards and Carr challenged,only for a foul to be awarded against Shilton. In the 66th minute a long kick by Daniel led to a mis-understanding in the Forest defence, leaving GRAY with the simplest of chances. Forest, who were to finish fifth in D1, pressed hard again though Berry was nearer to scoring when he hit the woodwork at the other end, so Wolves just about deserved to join the small band of teams who had won the League Cup more than once. Team: Bradshaw, Palmer, Parkin, Daniel, Hughes, Berry, Hibbitt, Carr, Gray, Richards & Eves.

F.A. CUP: An astonishing mix-up in the third round draw deprived Wolves of being at home, but they were still too strong for D2 Notts County. A superb replay victory at Norwich ensured a tie with D2 Watford that seemed to be petering out into a 0-0 draw. It all went wrong for Wolves as Kearns made an unhappy debut and substitute McAlle broke his leg within seconds of coming on, thus dreams of being the first club to reach both Wembley finals evaporated. Wolves had not been knocked out by a non-D1 team since 1967-68, easily the longest anyone in the country had gone without such a reverse.

RESULTS: Derby 1-0 (Clarke); IPSWICH 3-0 (Carr, Daniel, Eves); LC Burnley 1-1 (Palmer); Bristol C 0-2; LC BURNLEY 2-0 (Hibbitt, Palmer); PALACE 1-1 (Clarke); Everton 3-2 (Gray, Daniel, Richards); MAN UTD 3-1 (Hibbitt, Gray, Richards); LC Palace 2-1 (Hibbitt, Eves); Arsenal 3-2 (Gray 2, Hibbitt); Forest 2-3 (Richards, Daniel); DERBY 0-0; NORWICH 1-0 (Carr); Middlesbrough 0-1; VILLA 1-1 (Gray); LC Queens Park 1-1 (Hibbitt); Liverpool 0-3; LC QUEENS PARK 1-0 (Carr); Stoke 1-0 (Hibbitt); COVENTRY 0-3; ALBION 0-0; Man City 3-2 (Gray, Hibbitt, Daniel); LC Grimsby 0-0; BOLTON 3-1 (Gray 2, OG); LC GRIMSBY 1-1 (Gray); Leeds 0-3; LC Grimsby 2-0 (Hibbitt, OG); BRIGHTON 1-3 (Eves);

SOUTHAMPTON 0-0; Ipswich 0-1; FAC Notts Co 3-1 (Berry, Carr, Richards); BRISTOL C 3-0 (Gray, Richards, Daniel); Palace 0-1; LC Swindon 1-2 (Daniel); FAC NORWICH 1-1 (Gray); FAC Norwich 3-2 (Eves, Richards, Berry); EVERTON 0-0; Man Utd 1-0 (Eves); LC SWINDON 3-1 (Richards 2, Eves); FAC WATFORD 0-3; Norwich 4-0 (Hibbitt 2, Eves, Richards); LIVERPOOL 1-0 (Richards); MIDDLESBROUGH 0-2; Villa 3-1 (Brazier, Bell, Daniel); LC Forest 1-0 (Gray); STOKE 3-0 (Gray, Eves, Richards); Coventry 3-1 (Richards 2, Atkinson); SPURS 1-2 (Richards); Southampton 3-0 (Gray 2, Bell); Brighton 0-3; MAN CITY 1-2 (OG); Albion 0-0; Spurs 2-2 (Hibbitt, Bell); LEEDS 3-1 (Richards, Eves, Hibbitt); Bolton 0-0; FOREST 3-1 (Hibbitt, Richards, Palmer) & ARSENAL 1-2 (Richards).

RECORD: PLD 57 W 27 D 14 L 16 F 80 A 61 (12-8-7 & 15-6-9).

SCORERS: Richards 17, Gray 15, Hibbitt 13, Eves 9, Daniel 7, Carr 4, Bell 3, Palmer 3, Berry 2, Clarke 2, Atkinson 1, Brazier 1 & OG 3.

INTERNATIONALS: The icing on the cake of Wolves season was to have players represent four different nations — something they had not achieved even in their glory days. Hughes ended another seven years without any England connections for the club, being surprisingly re-instated as skipper for one match and twice coming on as substitute. Gray also trotted off the bench in the Scotland-England clash as well as hitting a cracker in another game, while Berry continued to turn out for Wales. Kearns completed the foursome, the Banbury-born goalkeeper adding to his Eire appearances though as with the other Molineux men who made their mark for that country he was never a first team regular at the club. Wolves could now proudly boast 57 Full Internationals (England 32, Wales 9, Ireland 8, Eire 4 & Scotland 4) who had made an aggregate of 425 appearances and scored 58 goals. Apps: Berry (W 3), Gray (S 2), Hughes (E3) & Kearns (ROI 2).

FAREWELLS: Patching 85-10 (Watford) & Rafferty 47-8 (Newcastle).

1980 - 81

DEBUTANTS: Mick Hollifield, Mick Matthews, John Teasdale & Rafael Villazan. Teasdale was born in Scotland and Villazan in Uruguay.

SUMMARY: After the euphoria of 1979-80 this season was a flop within a dozen games as Wolves were out of two Cups and on a losing streak in the League. Hughes was an O.B.E. recipient, as was Commercial Manager Jack Taylor, yet he showed more irritation than honour as he was booked seven times in 11 matches. 1981 began more pleasantly with Wolves unbeaten until their 10th outing then retaining their D1 status and doing well in the F.A. Cup. Joe Gardiner retired after approximately 50 years of tremendous service as player, trainer and scout while Barnwell sought foreign talent in a bid to revive the great occasions Gardiner enjoyed. Villazan cost £140,000 following protracted negotiations with the Spaniards Heulva, the South American International being lured to the Black Country by the pursuasive tongue of Barnwell. It was later revealed that Frenchman

Platini, soon to be regarded by most judges as the world's greatest footballer, may have joined Wolves if not for a broken ankle this term. Equally bad timing concerning problems in his homeland interrupted talks with Polish striker Boniek, who had a similar desire to parade his talents in England.

LEAGUE: 18th (35). Hibbitt pulled a muscle and his replacement Brazier had a shot cleared off the line on the opening day, Brighton scoring either side of this incident. Man Utd employed uncharacteristic negative tactics at Molineux so it was a victory for the sport when Berry and Carr cleverly combined to foil their offside-trap in the 85th minute. Wolves were in command during the first half at The Hawthorns though the pattern changed after an injury to the outstanding Gray, with Albion finally levelling when an effort went in off the chest of Hughes. There was another competent display against Palace before troubles began to pile up for the Wanderers.

There had been only three points collected from seven tries when a Hughes header sent them on the way to success against Leeds, so Wolves fans caught a glimpse of that famous smile before he began a suspension. A Clarke brace saw off the next visitors despite the sending off of Palmer, signs of an improvement continuing as a youthful Wolves XI drew at White Hart Lane and Old Trafford. Those hard-earned points were thrown away at home to Brighton, leaving little cause for optimism at their chances against a Liverpool side unbeaten in 22 games. It was 1-1 at the interval but a second half blitz was responsible for one of the shock scorelines of 1980-81 as the Merseysiders received a rare hiding. Bell then lost his boot in the process of netting the winner versus Stoke and his powerful drive rattled the bar at Arsenal, a Richards 20-yarder giving Wolves a share of the spoils.

Fortunes dipped again when they dropped a point to Southampton while only a spectacular performance by Bradshaw kept Liverpool down to one at Anfield. Wolves showered Forest with festive gifts as Palmer and Brazier scored own goals, the latter also conceding a penalty. Gray returned from two months on the sidelines as Wolves held out for an hour at Man City, but were sunk by a familiar collapse. A couple of headers by Eves and a Hibbitt 35-yarder against Middlesbrough were greeted with relief by the Wolves crowd, while the Albion game was swung by the arrival of substitute Bell. It looked destined to stay at 0-0 until he joined the fray and created both Wolves goals, almost getting one himself. A good recovery from 2-0 down at Coventry kept Wolves clear of the bottom trio, though they were far from safe.

Leaders Ipswich defied Wolves, who next faced the other main title contenders Aston Villa. It was a bad day as Daniel broke his leg, Wolves were further angered by the refusal of a Richards goal and Villa sneaked a late winner after Gray had blazed wildly over the bar. A year had passed since Wolves last success on enemy soil and they had not won any of their last 15 contests at Elland Road, but for once they had the upper hand against Leeds this season to put both records straight. On their next journey substitute Gray had a goal laid on by debut-boy Teasdale to give Wolves maximum points at Sunderland. Then three defeats put them back in the mire though they had games in hand and just about managed to survive, with only two points to spare over relegated Norwich.

LEAGUE CUP: Wolves tamely surrendered the trophy despite the fact that a tie staged over two legs reduced the likelihood of an upset. They lost 3-1 at D2 Cambridge, the embarrassment being completed when Bradshaw made an error in the 36th minute of the return.

UEFA CUP: The 1980 League Cup win gave Wolves a fourth crack at this Cup and they took on PSV Eindhoven in their modern Dutch stadium. Thomas made his solitary appearance of the season in midfield, a rumour circulating that his failure to settle in Wolverhampton revolved around his insistence on playing with his socks rolled down! Trailing 1-0 at half-time Wolves soon equalised thanks to a glorious Gray header, but PSV punished slackness at the back to restore their lead. Number three resulted from a harsh penalty award and fate further conspired against Wolves in the second leg, a mains power fault plunging the town centre into darkness as they were getting on top. The crowd reacted well with much humour and patience before action resumed and an Eves goal made it 12 successive home wins against foreign opposition, but it was not enough. Man Utd also fell by the wayside in the first round in contrast to Ipswich who actually won the Cup.

F.A. CUP: Stoke went 1-0 up but by the interval it was Wolves who had their noses in front at The Victoria Ground before the hosts had the last word. In the replay a sizzling Hibbitt volley sealed Stoke's fate after they had led at the break. Wolves drew at D2 Watford in the fourth round then won at home, with the visitors counting themselves unlucky on both occasions as Wolves avenged their conquerers of 1979-80. At 4.15 pm substitute Bell came on with Wolves 1-0 down to D2 Wrexham and he netted twice within eight minutes to guarantee a tough QF at high-riding Middlesbrough.

Gray's downward header in the seventh minute was cancelled out midway through the first half but Wolves, in the QF for the 25th time, comfortably held on. At Molineux they dictated the early play with Eves giving them some reward to please many of the 40,524 fans. It was the third year running a near-capacity crowd had been present for a Cup-tie at the ground and it is sad to reflect that Molineux has not even accommodated 30,000 since. Boro came back forcibly to equalise and as extra-time commenced they looked a good bet to reach their first-ever F.A. Cup SF. It was all slipping away from Wolves when Richards stunned the North-Easterners, super-sub Bell getting the clincher as Middlesbrough fell apart and later slid down the table. The experienced Hughes was recalled in place of McAlle for the Hillsborough SF with Tottenham, who quickly justified their free-scoring reputation. A fine drive by Hibbitt in the 11th minute made it all-square but a dubious free-kick decision gave Spurs a 2-1 advantage after an entertaining first half. Bradshaw made some good saves though Wolves were always in with a shout and in the last minute Hibbitt was tripped according to Welsh referee Clive Thomas, to enable Carr to casually stroke the ball home.

Controversy or not Wolves were well worth a draw and may have won with a more positive attitude in extra-time, soccer's image then being dented by several action-replays of Hibbitt's alleged dive and few of his goal. Wolves inexplicably agreed to Highbury as the replay venue and many of the vast majority of Spurs fans had probably walked to the 'neutral' stadium. Gray failed a fitness test while Barnwell and Barker were unable to work their magic as they steered Wolves to their 35th Cup-tie in around 28 months. Spurs won 3-0, carrying on to be the 29th finalists and 17th victors to have knocked Wolves out of the competition, while the Midlanders had still not had a decent Cup run since at the end of 1987.

RESULTS: Brighton 0-2; MAN UTD 1-0 (Berry); Albion 1-1 (Gray); LC Cambridge 1-3 (Daniel); PALACE 2-0 (Gray, Richards); LC CAMBRIDGE 0-1; Everton 0-2; COVENTRY 0-1; UC Eindhoven 1-3 (Gray); Villa 1-2 (Eves); IPSWICH 0-2; UC EINDHOVEN 1-0 (Eves); BIRMINGHAM 1-0 (Richards); Southampton 2-4 (Gray, Richards); Norwich 1-1 (Hibbitt); LEEDS 2-1 (Hughes, Richards); Leicester 0-2; SUNDERLAND 2-1 (Clarke 2); Spurs 2-2 (Atkinson, Richards); Man Utd 0-0; BRIGHTON 0-2; Middlesbrough 0-2; LIVERPOOL 4-1 (Eves, Richards, Bell, Hughes); STOKE 1-0 (Bell); Arsenal 1-1 (Richards); SOUTHAMPTON 1-1 (Bell); Liverpool 0-1; FOREST 1-4 (Richards); Man City 0-4; FAC Stoke 2-2 (Eves, Bell); FAC STOKE 2-1 (Eves, Hibbitt); MIDDLESBROUGH 3-0 (Eves 2, Hibbitt); Palace 0-0; FAC Watford 1-1 (Richards); FAC WATFORD 2-1 (Richards, Parkin); ALBION 2-0 (Eves, Gray); Coventry 2-2(Richards, Gray); FAC WREXHAM 3-1 (Bell 2, Richards); Ipswich 1-3(Gray); VILLA 0-1; FAC Middlesbrough 1-1 (Gray); FAC MIDDLESBROUGH 3-1 (Eves, Richards, Bell); NORWICH 3-0 (Palmer, Richards, OG); Birmingham 0-1; Leeds 3-1 (Richards, Clarke, Gray); LEICESTER 0-1; Sunderland 1-0 (Gray); FAC Spurs 2-2 (Hibbitt, Carr); FAC Spurs 0-3; MAN CITY 1-3 (Richards); Forest 0-1; ARSENAL 1-2 (Richards); SPURS 1-0 (Gray); Stoke 2-3 (OG, Hibbitt) & EVERTON 0-0.

RECORD: PLD 55 W 18 D 13 L 24 F 62 A 75 (16-2-9 & 2-11-15).

SCORERS: Richards 17, Gray 11, Eves 9, Bell 7, Hibbitt 5, Clarke 3, Hughes 2, Atkinson 1, Berry 1, Carr 1, Daniel 1, Palmer 1, Parkin 1 & OG 2.

INTERNATIONALS: Gray continued to fly the flag for Wolves with a little support from Atkinson. Apps: Atkinson (ROI U21-1) & Gray (S 4).

FAREWELLS: Hughes 75-2 (Rotherham), Kearns 10-0 (Walsall), McAlle 496-3 (Sheff Utd) & Thomas 16-0. JOHN McALLE was a Liverpudlian who arrived at Molineux in 1965-66, though he did not become a regular member of the first team until 1970-71. He was a very difficult opponent who tackled exceptionally well but his distribution sometimes left a lot to be desired. In 1971-72 he was an ever-present as well as scoring the only three goals of his career which against all the odds were in successive Cup-ties. McAlle was also chosen for the England Under 23 squad next term, only for a League Cup replay to deny him the opportunity but he played often enough for Wolves, topping their appearance chart with 54 in 1973-74, 51 in 1975-76 and 44 in 1977-78. Wolves defeated Spurs 2-1 in his 1978-79 testimonial with the aid of Birmingham's Argentinian Tarantini, while the Londoners paraded his fellow-countrymen Ardiles and Villa. McAlle proved his fighting spirit by ending a long absence from the side when he stepped into the shoes of Hughes, being unfortunate to then find himself out in the cold again and therefore having to leave for a fee of £10,000.

1980 - 81 ENDPIECE

It is almost impossible to establish a fair method that determines who have been the most successful clubs in the history of the game, though it does seem that up to and including 1980-81 Wolves had been amongst the six best in England. Using this particular system for the main three domestic competitions Wolves are in the top 10 each time, the only other teams which such a claim being Villa and Tottenham.

Wolves have been Football League Champions three times (1954, 1958 & 1959); runners-up on five occasions (1938, 1939, 1950, 1955 & 1960); third six times (1889, 1898, 1947, 1953, 1956 & 1961) and fourth four times (1890, 1891, 1900 & 1971). If we award the title-winners five points, the second-placed team three, the third team two and the fourth team one then Wolves score a total of 46. This puts them seventh behind Liverpool 85, Everton 74, Villa 68, Man Utd 65, Sunderland 63 and Arsenal 59.

Wolves have lifted the F.A. Cup four times (1893, 1908, 1949 & 1960); been finalists on four occasions (1889, 1896, 1921 & 1939) and lost in the SF five times (1890, 1951, 1973, 1979 & 1981). If we give the Cup-winners four points, the finalists two and the semi-finalists one then Wolves score a total of 29. This leaves them eighth behind Villa 40, Albion 38, Arsenal 36, Blackburn 36, Newcastle 36, Everton 31 and Man Utd 31.

Wolves have twice collected the League Cup (1974 & 1980) and once been beaten in the SF (1973). Using the same marks as in the F.A. Cup Wolves score a total of nine. This means they are fifth behind Villa 17, Man City 12, Spurs 11 and Forest 10.

Wolves total points tally is 84, which puts them sixth behind Villa 125, Liverpool 115, Everton 107, Arsenal 100 and Man Utd 99. Only the big-city clubs have done better than Wolverhampton who would have been even higher with any luck. They appeared set to dominate the wasted seven war-time seasons and during the first 15 post-war years were the hardest hit by international call-ups, in days when country definitely came before club. It should finally be mentioned that Wolves championship successes were by margins of four points or more while in eight campaigns they were within four of the top team, so they could easily have won D1 far more often than they did.

1981 - 82

DEBUTANTS: Alan Birch (Chesterfield), Bob Coy, Joe Gallagher (Birmingham), Tony Kernan & John Pender. Kernan was born in Eire.

SUMMARY: Richie Barker departed to manage Stoke before Wolves endured a terrible season to justify the air of pessimism that had been in the town when it began. The expensive purchases of Gallagher (£350,000) and Birch (£200,000) could not prevent relegation being a foregone conclusion by January, with the team hindered by constant bad publicity, action groups, pitch protests and other ugly behind-the-scenes activities. Barnwell terminated his contract on legal advice allowing Ian Greaves to make a troublesome exit from Oxford to take over but only the club's juniors gave him any real cheer, reaching the Youth Cup SF and providing five players for the Eire v. Ireland match. It was a sad way for Jack Dowen to go out after 50 years as groundstaff lad, player, scout, trainer, kitmaster and odd-job man, especially as Wolves were heading towards a financial crisis. Soaring interest rates on the John Ireland Stand they had surprisingly loaned a lot of money for, along with big signings and high salaries were to blame. Yet even the turmoil of 1981-82 did not prepare us for the shock announcement on June 6th that Wolves were £2m in debt, prompting Marshall to resign having borne the brunt of the criticism. Villa man Doug Ellis became chairman and within days recommended liquidation though it came to light later that such action was not essential as the club's assets comfortably outstripped it's debts. The official Receiver was called in on July 2nd as news spread throughout the football world of the unthinkable prospect of Wolverhampton Wanderers going out of existence.

LEAGUE: 21st (40). Wolves started brightly when Matthews headed the afternoon's only goal against a Liverpool side destined to win the title. A 28,001 crowd watched Birch, whose career had been mainly confined to the lower divisions, and Gallagher, who appeared the tall central defender Wolves had long needed, make competent debuts. A victory now merited three points in a bizarre attempt to rid football of the modern negative attitudes, but the only certainty was that the record books would have to be revised and making comparisons with past seasons would be harder. After losing to a Kevin Keegan-inspired Southampton it looked as if Wolves would salvage something at Leeds until Gallagher fractured his wrist, Arthur Graham then slamming a hatrick. Barnwell made six changes for the visit of Spurs to no avail and even an encouraging draw at Sunderland could not halt the slump to the bottom.

The new minimum £2 admission coupled with the fact that the recession was beginning to bite resulted in two meagre Molineux attandances. Supporters were obviously not going to be so patient and they would hardly be enticed back by the wretched affair with Mike Bailey's Brighton, though Wolves did beat Notts County 3-2 after trailing twice. Wolves then suffered their first defeat by a five-goal margin since 1968 and a further illustration of how times were changing came at Ipswich when substitute Bell missed a simple tap-in. The meeting with Middlesbrough lived down to expectations before Villa won at Molineux with alarming ease as Gray began a four-match ban.

Wolves suddenly strung together five fixtures without conceding a goal to jump up to 16th. Like England they had many players of a similar standard and few automatic selections, but in this spell the value of a more settled line-up was confirmed. It all commenced at Swansea where no previous visitors had gained a point although the 0-0 draw meant Wolves had not scored in 9/10 games, the late winner by Eves against Coventry ending a blank 535 minutes.

Wolves were confident of extending their run to six after a goalless first half at Albion, only for them to slip back into their bad old habits and finish relieved that three goals was all Albion managed. A vicious winter took it's icy toll and 23 days passed before Wolves tried to regain their pride, but classic goals by Trevor Francis and Kenny Dalglish meant two more setbacks as they tumbled to 19th. In January Coach Ian Ross temporarily took charge when he looked good enough to be in the side as Wolves produced some abysmal performances. The problems Greaves had inherited were underlined at Tottenham where they were crushed 6-1 before receiving an unprecedented eighth League defeat in a row.

Despite being firmly rooted in the bottom trio Wolves had an even record over the next six games and actually played some neat possession football, veterans Hibbitt and Carr both enjoying a new lease of life. A severe blow was inflicted by a Swansea outfit who poached a goal then killed the match as a spectacle when they stubbornly refused to do anything except hang on for the points, while a draw at Highfield Road kept Wolves in 20th position. Arsenal's last-minute equaliser was another nail in the coffin and the result at West Ham put the writing on the wall.

Easter saw a low diving header by Gray give Wolves some holiday happiness at Forest, then 48 hours later came a four-goals-in-17-minutes burst that was completely out of context with the events of 1981-82. Instead of the usual half-time inquest in the North Bank's open-air urinal there was jokes and laughter, though Man City did muster a consolation goal. Wolves leapt to 17th but the five below did have games in hand, while Gray continued his long-awaited scoring spree as Wolves drew with Blues to make it just three defeats in 11 fixtures.

Disaster struck at Stoke after Wolves had led 1-0 at the interval and looked a class above their opponents. The referee did them no favours by awarding Stoke a penalty and sending off Gray, who could have kept Wolves in D1 had he remained quiet. Hibbitt, Richards and Eves were booked for dissent while the names of Carr and Berry were added for fouls as Wolves lost their heads as well as the battle to a clearly inferior side. Albion delivered what was virtually the last rites and a young Wanderers team could make no impression at Brighton as the overdue pruning of the staff gained momentum. Wolves did well at Everton with Clarke netting superbly and Richards twice being desperately unlucky but the 1-1 draw was not enough, Eves and Richards then ensuring that Wolves at least went out on a winning note.

Victory at Stoke would have saved Wolves, whose main cause of failure was a pathetic total of 32 goals which made them the lowest scorers in their section for the first time this century. Following 4/5 seasons in the lower reaches of the table there could be few overall complaints about relegation, a fate that would hardly have been forecast two years ago. Wolves average League position had been 14th over the last 15 seasons which was deceptive as only eight teams had gathered more D1 points, 1981-82 bottom seven: Birmingham 44, Albion 44, Stoke 44, Sunderland 44, Leeds 42, Wolves 40 and Middlesbrough 39.

MILK CUP: This was actually the League Cup under sponsorship with Wolves given a tricky task against shock European Champions Aston Villa. Gray returned to his old ground to open the scoring, blotting his copybook by being dismissed, yet Gallagher still made it 2-0. Villa recovered to win and increased the lead in the second leg at Molineux, substitute Richards heading the equaliser on the night but Villa restored their two-goal aggregate advantage. It was only the third time Wolves had been removed from this Cup by a D1 club.

F.A. CUP: Gray scored from an acute angle but weak Wolves never got another look-in, Leeds knocking them out for the fourth occasion in a decade of F.A. Cup heartbreak. Ignoring comments about it mistakenly facing the pitch, the new stand had been highly-praised and it was significant that had one of the SF ties ended all-square Molineux would have staged the replay.

RESULTS: LIVERPOOL 1-0 (Matthews); Southampton 1-4 (Clarke); Leeds 0-3; SPURS 0-1; Sunderland 0-0; BRIGHTON 0-1; NOTTS CO 3-2 (Eves 2, Daniel); Man Utd 0-5; MC Villa 2-3 (Gray, Gallagher); Ipswich 0-1; MIDDLESBROUGH 0-0; VILLA 0-3; MC VILLA 1-2 (Richards); Swansea 0-0; COVENTRY 1-0 (Eves); Birmingham 3-0 (Gray, Richards, Brazier); SOUTHAMPTON 0-0; STOKE 2-0 (Palmer, Matthews); Albion 0-3; Man City 1-2 (Daniel); FAC LEEDS 1-3 (Gray); Liverpool 1-2 (Atkinson); EVERTON 0-3; SUNDERLAND 0-1; Arsenal 1-2 (Hibbitt); Spurs 1-6 (Hibbitt); MAN UTD 0-1; FOREST 0-0; Notts Co 0-4; IPSWICH 2-1 (Clarke 2); Middlesbrough 0-0; Villa 1-3 (Clarke); LEEDS 1-0 (Eves); SWANSEA 0-1; Coventry 0-0; ARSENAL 1-1 (Eves); West Ham 1-3 (Richards); Forest 1-0 (Gray); MAN CITY 4-1 (Gray, Clarke, Hibbitt, Eves); BIRMINGHAM 1-1 (Gray); Stoke 1-2 (Hibbitt); ALBION 1-2 (Gray); Brighton 0-2; Everton 1-1 (Clarke) & WEST HAM 2-1 (Eves, Richards).

RECORD: PLD 45 W 10 D 10 L 25 F 36 A 71 (8-5-10 & 2-5-15).
SCORERS: Eves 7, Gray 7, Clarke 6, Hibbitt 4, Richards 4, Daniel 2, Matthews 2, Atkinson 1, Brazier 1, Gallagher 1 & Palmer 1.

INTERNATIONALS: Gray retained Wolves interest in this sphere of football when he added a couple of appearances to his Scottish tally. Apps: Gray (S 2).

FAREWELLS: Atkinson 43-3 (Exeter), Bell 73-24 (Blackburn), Berry 160-6 (Stoke), Birch 16-0 (Barnsley), Brazier 75-2, Carr 283-26 (Millwall), Hollifield 25-0 (Hull), Kernan 1-0, Moss 5-0, Parkin 608-10 (Stoke), Teasdale 6-0 (Walsall) & Villazan 24-0. GEORGE BERRY had a love-hate relationship with the crowd as the Rostrup-born central defender could be somewhat erratic. Once he headed the ball into his own net from Gray's off-the-line clearance but on other occasions he summoned up fighting displays when the best forwards in the country had little joy against him. Berry topped the appearance list with 56 in 1979-80 and was one of the economic cuts at Wolverhampton when released on a free transfer.

WILLIE CARR cost Wolves around £80,000 apparently, though the original estimates were substantially greater. The diminutive ginger-haired midfielder was from Glasgow and sadly his international career was restricted to his pre-Wolves days. He produced that form only in spasms but nevertheless did a useful job for Wolves until he sought pastures new, when they recouped £10,000 on him.

1981 - 82 ENDPIECE

SEASON	APPS	GOALS
67-68	15	1
68-69	47★	0
69-70	50★	1
70-71	50	1
71-72	42	3
72-73	22	0
73-74	52	0
74-75	45★ =	2
75-76	39	0
76-77	48★ =	1
77-78	42	0
78-79	50★	0
79-80	54	0
80-81	28	1
81-82	24	0

Derek Parkin deserves a more detailed account than the other players making their farewells to Wolves simply because he has made more competitive first team appearances than anyone else in the club's history. He still has got no real challenger in sight and heads a top 10 completed by Hibbitt, Wright, Flowers, Broadbent, McAlle, Palmer, Mullen, Richards and Bailey.

Parkin signed for Wolves on February 14th, 1968, the £80,000 involved making him Britain's costliest full-back. His former team, Huddersfield, had a tradition for supplying players in that position though he was born in the Tyne and Wear city of Newcastle. The blonde defender, whose high-pitched shouting quickly earned him the nickname of Squeak, settled into the Wolves team and ventured upfield to score the last goal of the season. He participated in every League and Cup match during both 1968-69 and 1969-70 and his qualities were rewarded with representative honours in the latter, which he expanded on in 1970-71. All this was primarily down to his ability to read the game and not commit himself to a tackle too soon, a ploy that annoyed the crowd when it did not work out but that was the exception rather than the rule.

A mystery illness in 1972-73 was originally diagnosed as a heart complaint and kept Parkin on the sidelines for five long months, in fact at one point it was thought that more than just his sporting career was in doubt. The virus was soon forgotten as he resumed training and within a fortnight got the winner for Wolves third team, graduating through the reserves and continuing his soccer at top level as if nothing had happened. A year later he was at Wembley and his perserverance had not been in vain.

Parkin was an ever-present in 1976-77, though his image as a cultured player took a dent when he was sent off at West Ham in 1977-78, but in the next season he was a model of consistency and good behaviour again as he appeared in all Wolves fixtures. His testimonial in 1979 was held on a bitterly cold night which meant the attendance was a disappointing 7,261 as a Midlands Select XI beat Wolves 4-1, Hibbitt scoring, and within a few months Parkin enjoyed another League Cup success.

It was in 1981-82 that Parkin passed Wright's record of 490 appearances for Wolves in the Football League, going on to reach 501 including just one as substitute. He left Molineux after 14 years in which he had scored six goals in D1, two in the League Cup, one in the Texaco Cup and one in the F.A. Cup, but he had prevented Wolves from conceding many more. Parkin still possessed a fair amount of speed and coupled with the knowledge acquired during his career it helped him play a significant role against Wolves in that stormy Victoria Ground match, when although he would perhaps have liked to help his old collegues he proved he was a true professional.

Chapter 4

1982 - 83 to 1985 - 86

1982 - 83

DEBUTANTS: John Burridge (QPR), Paul Butler, Ian Cartwright, Alan Dodd (Stoke), Billy Kellock (Luton), Billy Livingstone, Dale Rudge, Gordon Smith & Dave Wintersgill. Kellock and Smith were born in Scotland.

SUMMARY: The players reported back for pre-season training unsure of their futures as Wolves were given a seven-day stay-of-execution having failed to meet the original deadline. Just three minutes remained when Derek Dougan and Property Developer Doug Hope fronted a successful bid of £2.3m for the club and at the time it seemed there would have been no Wolves otherwise. Consortiums led by Walsall's Ken Wheldon and Ellis had been favourites to take over if anyone did but the mystery backers on July 30th were Allied Properties, for whom the infamous Bhatti Brothers pulled the strings. The new regime dismissed victim-of-circumstances Ian Greaves in favour of Shrewsbury Assistant Manager Graham Hawkins, out went long-serving Phil Shaw as well as Jack Taylor and in came shrewd Villa administrator Eric Woodward. Greaves is still regarded by many Wolves fans as their best manager since Cullis though Darlaston-born Hawkins who had left Molineux 15 years earlier proved the doubters wrong. He not only guided them back to D1 but also helped them create a bit of history with three unbeaten runs stretching into double-figures, the total games numbering 10, 11 and 12. The team was sponsored by Tatung and their success was in contrast to the reserves who came bottom of the new D1 of the Central League, suffering a backlash of the 1981-82 events as several lads were blooded before being ready for that grade.

LEAGUE D2: 2nd (75). Wolves had only spent three seasons outside D1 in 50 years, yet few experts believed they could return there in the near future. Not only had many players departed but Hibbitt was still in America, Gray was suspended and Bradshaw had been badly hurt in a pre-season accident. However, the town breathed a huge sigh of relief at the opening fixture with Blackburn even taking place. Wolves paraded teenagers Wintersgill and Livingstone, the latter having been signed on a job opportunities scheme promoted by the Manpower Services Department, while another untried youngster was 12th man. Blackburn led 1-0 at the break but television recorded two headers by Eves that won the day in story-book fashion, substitute Butler crossing the ball for the decider.

The popular verdict was that the euphoria of the occasion had carried Wolves to that victory, the lads responding by passing stern tests at Chelsea and Leeds. It was their seventh game without defeat at Stamford Bridge while at Elland Road there was a debut for ex-Villa and Tottenham defender Smith. Wolves biggest win since 1976 lifted the tension, winger Butler producing some vintage stuff in his 20-minute appearance to demoralise Charlton. The season was barely a fortnight old when a couple of second half goals against Barnsley took Wolves to the top of D2. The on-loan Burridge made his move permanent to avert one crisis, celebrating with another clean sheet at Bolton. Right-back Humphrey was catching the eye with his attacking overtures, heading in from inches off the ground when Rotherham visited Molineux. Wolves became the first of the 92 League clubs to reach 20 points after the long trek to Carlisle though they were closely pressed by Sheff Wed, Grimsby and QPR. Even the free-scoring Wednesday could not penetrate a Wolverhampton defence that incredibly had not conceded a goal in eight and a half matches, the opening chapter of 1982-83 exceeding the wildest of their expectations.

Leicester brought Wolves down to earth though a firm Gray header v. Derby relieved any anxieties, Butler finally making his full debut. The lowest gate at a competitive Wolves fixture since 1927, just 4,571, saw them slip-up at Cambridge but they immediately produced 90 minutes of non-stop running to crush Grimsby with the new-look front trio of Gray, Eves and Clarke all on target. QPR, Fulham and Sheff Wed each briefly headed the table and Wolves travelled to Oldham hoping to re-claim the position, where with 10 minutes to go they were searching for an equaliser yet lost 4-1. Wolves were 2-1 up after a fine first half with Fulham only for the course of the game to be changed by a tragic mix-up between Gallagher and Coy, leaving Wolves out of the top three. Gallagher was soon to depart after a newspaper article in which he admitted he could not give full effort for the club as he was in dispute with them, making only three appearances this season.

Brierley Hill youngster Cartwright joined Dodd in being a debutant at Crystal Palace, the decline of Wolves rearguard continuing in the first four minutes as they went 2-0 down. Matthews encouraged them to a splendid comeback, then Eves and Cartwright hit tremendous goals against Middlesbrough to confirm Wolves were back in the groove. With much-fancied Sheff Wed faltering they were behind QPR and Fulham, and managed a competent 1-1 draw at Newcastle. Leaders QPR came to town and were stunned by a four-goal blast after the break which put Wolves second, three points adrift of the Londerers with a game in hand.

Lethal finishing by Clarke at Shrewsbury and a less-convincing win over Burnley saw Wolves leading D2 again, 10 points clear of the fourth team which was the position they had occupied a month previously. Wolves dealt with Fulham and Leeds, the latter pulling in 22,567 fans to Molineux, so they had gathered 12 points in eight days to bring their goal aggregate to 23-3 since those early shocks at Palace. The top four after 23 fixtures was Wolves 49, QPR 43, Fulham 41 and Leicester 36. Facing a strong wind at Blackburn they changed ends 2-0 in arrears, Wolves recovering well to draw level through Dodd who had done much to tighten up the defence in recent weeks. An interesting encounter with Chelsea practically ensured promotion as Wolves now led the fourth team by 15 points with 15 games to play.

Complacency set in with two unsatisfactory efforts followed by a 5-0 hiding at Leicester, although goal-difference still kept Wolves in front of QPR. Sheff Wed were well supported at Molineux knowing a win was essential to give them any chance of catching the likes of Wolves. Burridge saved a penalty and Clarke scored from one, yet that was not the conclusion of the spot-kick drama. In the closing stages Wednesday attacked fiercely with one forward getting his marching orders for a foul on Burridge, who sensationally stopped another penalty to clinch Wolves seventh home win on the trot.

A run of draws was happily interrupted by victory at Burnley, with Wolves then taking a 2-0 lead over Shrewsbury to indicate they might round-off the season in style after all, only to be glad of a point at the final whistle. Nobody would have suspected at Christmas that Wolves would be booed off the field by a sparse crowd in April but that was precisely what happened after Bolton's visit, another 0-0 stalemate at Middlesbrough giving them 8/9 draws which was hardly D1 material. With four matches remaining QPR were guaranteed promotion while Wolves had a four-point advantage over Fulham and a mere six over fast-improving Leicester. April 30th was a significant date as Gray got back on the goal trail and Burridge kept his 20th clean sheet of the term, Wolves defeating Palace 1-0 as their rivals made mistakes to erase fears they would not make a swift return to the elite.

Champagne rarely flows after the surrender of a 3-0 lead yet that was the May Day message to Wolverhampton. Memories of recent tentative play were buried as Wolves blazed ahead, the Charlton fightback being irrelevant as Fulham lost to QPR and Leicester drew to ensure Wolves went up. The long-anticipated meeting with QPR at Loftus Road had suddenly became meaningless as the boys from Shepherd's Bush were now champions, though there was still pride at stake so Wolves were dejected when the home side got a late unmerited winner. The most delicate of lobs by Matthews and a near-post flick by Gray after a lovely build-up put Wolves 2-0 to the good against Newcastle. It was squandered, but at least Wolves were pegged back by two outstanding goals as the teams fought out a 30th successive contest without an away win. It was an exciting final act to an exceptional season, during most of which Wolves had proved themselves to be very much alive and well, top four: QPR 85, Wolves 75, Leicester 70 and Fulham 69.

MILK CUP: D1 Sunderland broke down Wolves mean defence with a penalty before Eves levelled matters, the score staying at 1-1 with the Midlanders doing enough to suggest they could win the tie at Roker Park. Hibbitt made a belated start to 1982-83 and must have felt in an even bigger daze than his colleagues after 15 minutes, by when Wolves were 4-0 down and as good as out as they lost the discipline that had been serving them so well.

F.A. CUP: Hibbitt settled a tough battle at D4 Tranmere to give Wolves a fourth round trip to Villa Park. Injury ruled out Clarke and 43,121 watched Withe get the solitary goal with a mis-hit, as unlucky Wolves succumbed to D1 Villa for the seventh consecutive time.

RESULTS: BLACKBURN 2-1 (Eves 2); Chelsea 0-0; Leeds 0-0; CHARLTON 5-0 (Eves, Gray, Palmer, Clarke, Matthews); BARNSLEY 2-0 (Humphrey, Eves); Bolton 1-0 (Livingstone); ROTHERHAM 2-0 (Clarke, Humphrey); Carlisle 2-0 (Smith, Livingstone); MC SUNDERLAND 1-1 (Eves); Sheff Wed 0-0; LEICESTER 0-3; MC Sunderland 0-5; DERBY 2-1 (Palmer, Gray); Cambridge 1-2 (Eves); GRIMSBY 3-0 (Gray, Eves, Clarke); Oldham 1-4 (Hibbitt); FULHAM 2-4 (Clarke, Gray); Palace 4-3 (Matthews 2, Clarke, Gray); MIDDLESBROUGH 4-0 (Eves 2, Cartwright, Dodd); Newcastle 1-1 (Eves); QUEENS PARK 4-0 (Humphrey, Clarke, Palmer, Dodd); Shrewsbury 2-0 (Clarke 2); BURNLEY 2-0 (Eves, Gray); Fulham 3-1 (Pender, Clarke, Eves); LEEDS 3-0 (Clarke, Gray, Eves); FAC Tranmere 1-0 (Hibbitt); Blackburn 2-2 Matthews, Dodd); CHELSEA 2-1 (Eves, Clarke); FAC Villa 0-1; Barnsley 1-2 (Smith); CARLISLE 2-1 (Eves, Livingstone); Leicester 0-5; SHEFF WED 1-0 (Clarke); CAMBRIDGE 1-1 (Eves); Derby 1-1 (Kellock); Grimsby 1-1 (Eves); OLDHAM 0-0; Burnley 1-0 (Palmer); SHREWSBURY 2-2 (Palmer, Eves); Rotherham 1-1 (Hibbitt); BOLTON 0-0; Middlesbrough 0-0; PALACE 1-0 (Gray); Charlton 3-3 (Kellock 2, Eves); Queens Park 1-2 (Gray) & NEWCASTLE 2-2 (Matthews, Gray).

RECORD: PLD 46 W 21 D 16 L 9 F 70 A 51 (14-6-2 & 7-10-7).

SCORERS: Eves 19, Clarke 12, Gray 10, Matthews 5, Palmer 5, Dodd 3, Hibbitt 3, Humphrey 3, Kellock 3, Livingstone 3, Smith 2, Cartwright 1 & Pender 1.

INTERNATIONALS: Gray made it 13 appearances for Scotland since joining Wolves, scoring three goals this season including both in the 2-0 win in Canada. Apps: Gray (S 5).

FAREWELLS: Gallagher 34-1 (West Ham) & Richards 461-193.

1982 - 83 ENDPIECE

SEASON	APPS	GOALS
69-70	6	1
70-71	5	2
71-72	46	16
72-73	59★ =	36★

John Richards has the distinction of being the all-time highest competitive goalscorer for Wolves, the top 10 are completed by Hartill, Murray, Hancocks, Broadbent,

73-74	37	18★
74-75	37	15
75-76	47	25★
76-77	32	20★
77-78	41	13★
78-79	23	9★
79-80	41	17★
80-81	53★	17★
81-82	32	4
82-83	2	0

Westcott, Dougan, Wood, Swinbourne and Hibbitt.

Richards was born in Warrington and though that is in Cheshire he attracted the talent-spotters by hitting all six for Lancashire Boys against an English Public Schools XI. He signed as a professional for the Wolves in July, 1969, within months getting all five in a Central League match at Blackburn. Richards was top reserve scorer in 1969-70 and 1970-71, making the odd first team appearance. He became a regular in 1971-72 when only Dougan scored more for the club, grabbing his most important goal to date in the UEFA Cup SF in Budapest. Although he missed much of the early part of the season only 28 D1 marksmen were above him in the scoring list for the premier three English competitions.

Richards shot to first place in 1972-73, five clear of his nearest rival with a total that has rarely been equalled since and it was no wonder he was voted Midlands 'Footballer of the Year' and national 'Young player of the Year'. He had already gained representative honours when he was chosen for the full England team against Ireland. Despite being played out of position on the left-wing he had a hand in both English goals and was desperately unlucky not to be selected again, particularly when injury ruled him out of a tour. Some forwards were given several opportunities without ever setting the international scene alight, while Richards had scored more than the entire squad for one early-season England match.

In the opening weeks of 1973-74 he struggled, emerging from his first barren spell to consistently find the net until his Wembley winner. Pelvis problems hindered him as his main asset was turning sharply then speeding towards goal, and he did not play after the League Cup Final yet was still ninth top scorer. He dropped to 15th in 1974-75, trailing behind team-mate Hibbitt, and having been the perfect foil for Dougan he was no doubt sorry that they were seldom allowed to perform their double-act, some critics even suggesting Richards was ineffective without the big Irishman. He crushed that theory in 1975-76 by coming third in the goal charts, doing well over the last two months despite having to contend with a new injury for which surgery was delayed in view of Wolves relegation battle.

Richards had a frustrating summer culminating in a cartilage operation three days before the 1976-77 kick-off, which kept him out of the first 15 fixtures. He did not look too confident on his return against Blackburn and once more the experts decided he was finished. Richards then netted 14 in 12 games, continuing his recent domination of Wolves F.A. Cup scoring. Season 1977-78 saw his sixth hatrick as well as a brace for a Midlands XI who defeated England 2-1 in a testimonial for Referee Taylor. However, a long period without success sent him down to 25th in the D1 list.

After playing twice early on in 1978-79 Richards suffered a recurrence of the knee trouble which put him on the sidelines until February, so he was again written off by many. There must have been a lump in the throat of every Wolves fan at Highbury as he crowned his latest comeback with a majestic header to give his team a shock victory. He even went on to retain his record of always being amongst the top 30 goalscorers but after a spectacular volley at Nottingham in 1979-80 things turned sour for our modest hero, who did not add another for three months. During this bad patch he was sent off in England for the only time in his career although the way we saw it was that the Villa defender hit Richards's elbow with his nose! Seriously, the impetus of jumping for the ball rather than any malicious intent did the damage, leaving him to reflect on the players who had given him rough treatment over the years and escaped punishment. Richards had never had an outstanding partnership with the likes of Kindon, Bell, Sunderland and Rafferty so there were high hopes that Gray would be the answer, but it soon became obvious their styles did not complement one another. Nevertheless, it was impossible to keep Richards down for long and after Christmas he scored frequently enough to rise to 10th in the chart as well as breaking Westcott's Wolves record of 19 F.A. Cup strikes.

In 1980-81 he was 12th, reaping the benefits of an unusual injury-free campaign, not that the discomfort of the knee injury would ever completely go away and his training was restricted. He had developed into more of a creator of chances, often patiently retaining possession before releasing a perfectly-timed pass. Richards had been top Wolves marksman for 8/9 seasons, in fact only the penalties from Hibbitt prevented a clean sweep. Sadly, 1981-82 saw his first real failure although his colleagues fared little better, with Richards looking tired on occasions as he edged towards his 200-goal target. He did find the net in his testimonial when almost 13,000 watched a slick Moscow Dynamo win 4-2, but his competitive total left him seven short of the milestone. Richards is the Wolves fourth highest League scorer with the full breakdown as follows: 129 (D1), 24 (FAC), 17 (LC/MC), 15 (D2), 4 (UC), 3 (TC) and 1 (AIC). His average did not compare with several past stars but Richards played in a more defensive era and often lacked support in the Wolves attack.

He was not in the team when 1982-83 began and found himself in dispute with both Hawkins and Dougan. He went on loan to Derby, scoring twice, before finally donning a Wolves shirt at Easter. Richards was the best player on the park yet was chosen just once more for a side who had been unable to net many goals since Christmas, leaving in circumstances that left a bitter taste in the mouth. He joined Portugal's Maritimo on a free transfer and enjoyed two years in the sunshine, coming out of retirement in 1985-86 to make a belated farewell to Wolves supporters in a benefit match, though his goal could not stop the modern Wolves beating an ex-players XI 4-1 in front of 5,000 people for whom Richards was a reminder of happier days. Perhaps if he had been more greedy and selfish he would have achieved even more success, number nine MacDonald had the perfect attitude for a striker and if a member of his team wearing six on his back scored with an overhead kick then MacDonald would probably claim it! Richards endeared himself to the folk of Wolverhampton with his conduct both on and off the field and had a very good career, which with a bit of luck would have been a great one.

1983 - 84

DEBUTANTS: Martin Bayly, Mike Bennett (Bolton), Andy Blair (Villa-loan), Mark Buckland, Danny Crainie (Celtic), Paul Dougherty, Joe Jackson, Steve Mardenborough (Coventry), Scott McGarvey (Man Utd-loan), Graham Rodger, Tony Towner (Rotherham), Sammy Troughton (Glentoran) & Stewart Watkiss. Blair, Crainie, McGarvey and Rodger were born in Scotland, Bayly in Eire and Troughton in Ireland.

SUMMARY: Supporters at a second public meeting insisted that cash should be made available for new signings but the only purchase was Towner, whose experience had been restricted to other divisions. The new owners had spent approximately £220,000 on four players during their reign but when their plans for a £22m redevelopment scheme were blocked the doubts about Wolves long-term future increased. The team failed to win any of their first 16 games making a record 19 in all and they were heading back to D2 already. Gray was sold for £180,000 so while Barnwell had worked wonders in selling players the club had lost over £2m on three of his buys - Gray, Thomas and Gallagher. Apart from Dodd (46) nobody appeared in more than 37/47 matches as Hawkins tried various permutations before being sacked in an untidy manner at the end of 1983-84, with the effervescent ex-Scotland Manager Tommy Docherty being appointed in June.

LEAGUE: 22nd (29). Gray was floored and Palmer's penalty after 87 seconds was the season's first goal in England, but Liverpool's Ian Rush was equally quick off the mark in the second half to make it 1-1 before an audience of 26,249. A neat effort by Clarke gave Wolves expectations of a 15th home game without defeat only for the expensive Charlie Nicholas to respond with two for the Gunners. He also revealed that when he had a trial at Wolverhampton some youths chased him in the town centre and, already feeling homesick, he decided to leave to add to the household names Wolves had let slip away in the past couple of decades. The opening week was completed by an ominous drubbing at Norwich.

Wolves were only given respectability at Sunderland by two late replies, the initial win remaining elusive despite incessant attacking after the interval against Birmingham. There was a couple of disastrous 4-0 hidings which prompted Hawkins to make five alterations and he must have felt hard done by as Southampton snatched a late, dubious winner. Spurs were then coasting at 3-1 with 10 minutes to go before Wolves staged a grandstand finish, Gray treating the North Bankers to their first goal of 1983-84 as well as being involved in an ugly skirmish with Graham Roberts, while Towner was denied an equaliser by a somewhat harsh decision.Therefore, the joke continued about the difference between Wolves and a triangle, the latter having three points.

Although Wolves fans were probably considering prayers it was television that was responsible for bringing Sunday afternoon football to the town. It was the second in a series of live games, Wolves drawing with Villa thanks to a cheeky backheel by Clarke that relieved the monotony. The slump to 22nd had been delayed by Leicester's poor start but Wolves were duly propping up all the others following their visit to Old Trafford. Gray made a miserable farewell at Nottingham and even though he had managed only 28 D1 goals for Wolves his departure heralded an early surrender in the relegation fight. Wolves broke their 'duck' at the best possible venue - The Hawthorns. At the break they looked incapable of scoring but on-loan Crainie struck with a left-footer, then two minutes later made a surging run and hit an unstoppable shot from the edge of the penalty-area. Wolves followers sang deliriously in the rain as Mardenborough put Clarke clear for number three, Albion getting a late consolation. With three fixtures against fellow-strugglers imminent there was a strong belief that this could be the turning point. Watford's Maurice Johnston had other ideas as he blasted a quick hatrick on one of Molineux's bleakest days, Leicester then also hitting five past the sorry Wanderers. Fears of a first post-war League attendance of under 10,000 were justified, in fact 8,679 endured the goalless stalemate with a Stoke outfit who had not won on any of their last 13 trips to the ground. A fruitless journey to Ipswich left Wolves marooned on eight points, half the amount of the 21st team.

Even Gray's return in Everton colours could not attract a decent-sized Christmas crowd, Eves squeezing in a goal to make it 1-0 at half-time. Crainie's swirling free-kick plus a glancing Clarke header ended a nightmare eight months without a Molineux triumph for Wolves. There was a mere five-day wait for the next one, as Troughton and the now-permanent Crainie indicated the future was not totally black with Norwich failing to win in Wolverhampton for the 13th time, Wolves were pipped by two late goals at QPR but when they broke through in the ninth minute at Anfield they did not let the advantage slip. Burridge performed admirably to clinch Wolves first success there since 1950 despite 21 attempts. Liverpool were set for another title yet in their last seven meetings with Wolves they were 4-2 down on victories and 9-5 behind on goals, the Molineux men usually rising to the big occasion.

Notts County and Stoke were the main relegation candidates while Wolves had a chance to get within two points of Birmingham. They ruined their recent work by losing at home to bogey side Luton as Blues surprisingly won away, making the gap an intimidating eight points. There was an air of resignation about the Southampton defeat and a drab derby at St. Andrews against those perennial Birmingham strugglers. A well-taken Troughton goal provoked mixed reactions from the most recent example of a 20,000 + gate at Molineux and only the eighth in three seasons, Burridge then keeping the £4m Man Utd at bay until he was fooled by a wicked 80th — minute deflection. Slender escape plans emerged again as Wolves obtained useful results against top four Forest and West Ham. Wolves were now scrapping with Notts to avoid bottom spot while Stoke and Ipswich were nine points clear having both played one extra. As Wolves had to tackle that duo and Notts twice their fate was still in their hands. The dream died in the next three games as Wolves strikers had a lean time, ironically as on-loan Eves did well at Huddersfield. They went from bad to worse as the crowds dipped to 7,481 v. Notts and 6,611 v. Ipswich and it was poetic justice that Gray scored for much-improved Everton to send Wolves down officially.

An Albion man was sent off in a messy affair at Molineux before Wolves signed off at Molineux with their first win in 12 outings, Smith doing the damage to Leicester with a fine volley. Wolves woe of 1983-84 was completed at Stoke, where Paul Maguire rammed in four goals for the hosts while Wolves meagre total was six in 18 matches, underlining that the likes of Richards should not have been discarded. The worst season in Wolves history to date was summed up in statistical terms as they equalled their highest number of defeats (25) and their lowest number of victories (six). In fact there were many unwanted club records, Wolves also having a dreadful goal-difference as they had the worst attack in D1 (27) and the worst defence too (80), bottom five: Stoke 50, Coventry 50, Birmingham 48, Notts County 41 and Wolves 29.

MILK CUP: Wolves still could not get beyond the second round stage of the Milk Cup even when drawn against D3 Preston. They actually led 2-1 at the interval in the first leg seen by 7,790 fans yet lost both ties, Preston going down in all their four League fixtures in between to emphasise the depth of Wolves plight.

F.A. CUP: In-form Coventry took a quick lead but in the 15th minute their keeper could not hold an Eves shot and Clarke pushed it over the line, only to spoil his day by feebly shooting a late penalty at the Coventry 'goal-minder' as Wolves called the tune. There was a poor first half in the Molineux replay but Eves coolly netted after a decisive run, Coventry grabbing a late equaliser. Economics now ruled that a toss of the coin should determine the venue of a second replay although Birmingham would provide a perfect neutral location. In effect Wolves were drawn away twice and having let City off the hook in both ties there was a feeling they would be eliminated, Burridge letting them down for once as they crashed 3-0.

RESULTS: LIVERPOOL 1-1 (Palmer); ARSENAL 1-2 (Clarke); Norwich 0-3; Sunderland 2-3 (Towner, Eves); BIRMINGHAM 1-1 (Eves); Luton 0-4; QUEENS PARK 0-4; Southampton 0-1; MC PRESTON 2-3 (Clarke 2); SPURS 2-3 (Gray 2); VILLA 1-1 (Clarke); MC Preston 0-1; Man Utd 0-3; Forest 0-5; WEST HAM 0-3; COVENTRY 0-0; Albion 3-1 (Crainie 2, Clarke); WATFORD 0-5; Leicester 1-5 (Clarke); STOKE 0-0; Ipswich 1-3 (Clarke); EVERTON 3-0 (Eves, Crainie, Clarke); NORWICH 2-0 (Troughton, Towner); Queens Park 1-2 (OG); FAC Coventry 1-1 (Clarke); FAC COVENTRY 1-1 (Eves); Liverpool 1-0 (Mardenborough); FAC Coventry 0-3; LUTON 1-2 (Pender); SOUTHAMPTON 0-1; Birmingham 0-0; MAN UTD 1-1 (Troughton); Villa 0-4; FOREST 1-0 (OG); West

Ham 1-1 (McGarvey); SUNDERLAND 0-0; Arsenal 1-4 (McGarvey); Spurs 0-1; NOTTS CO 0-1; Coventry 1-2 (Livingstone); IPSWICH 0-3; Everton 0-2; ALBION 0-0; Notts Co 0-4; Watford 0-0; LEICESTER 1-0 (Smith) & Stoke 0-4.

RECORD: PLD 47 W 6 D 13 L 28 F 31 A 89 (4-9-10 & 2-4-18).

SCORERS: Clarke 9, Eves 4, Crainie 3, Gray 2, McGarvey 2, Towner 2, Troughton 2, Livingstone 1, Mardenborough 1, Palmer 1, Pender 1, Smith 1 & OG 2.

FAREWELLS: Bennett 8-0 (Cambridge), Blair 10-0, Bradshaw 243-0, Burridge 81-0 (Sheff Utd), Clarke 146-33 (Birmingham), Coy 45-0 (Chester), Daniel 194-16, Eves 212-53 (Sheff Utd), Gray 159-45(Everton), Hibbitt 553-114 (Coventry), Jackson 1-0, Kellock 12-3 (Southend), Livingstone 22-4 (Derby), Mardenborough 9-1 (Swansea), Matthews 79-7 (Scunthorpe), McGarvey 13-2, Rodger 1-0 (Coventry), Rudge 25-0 (Preston), Smith 39-3, Towner 28-2 (Charlton), Troughton 13-2 (Hull), Watkiss 2-0 (Crewe) & Wintersgill 3-0 (Wimbledon). PAUL BRADSHAW was born in Altrincham and like many of those who have worn the green jersey for Wolves in modern times he was capable of amazing saves but also made quite a few errors. At times he looked destined for a great career but did not dominate the area as well as a man of his stature should do and having good reflexes was not enough to prosper to the very highest level. Bradshaw was an ever-present in 1981-82 but missed the following season through injury. He was not satisfied with a couple of brief spells in the side in 1983-84 and moved all the way to Vancouver White Caps.

WAYNE CLARKE was a member of the famous Willenhall footballing family, one of the others being Derek who briefly made the grade at Molineux. Wayne scored five goals in as many games for England Schoolboys in 1975-76, including a hatrick as Ireland were swept aside 5-0, continuing to find the net for the national youth XI in 1978-79 and then being top reserve scorer in 1979-80. He lacked the steel of England striker Allan and he did not establish himself as a regular choice until 1982-83, his eighth season at Molineux, standing out in the Wolves forward-line during the former half of 1983-84. His full talent did not really surface at the club so he decided to seek pastures new at the beginning of the next term, an industrial tribunal deeming that his fee should be £80,000, though Wolves were supposed to get half of any profit should he be sold again.

PETER DANIEL was a full-back from Hull whose persistence and aggression meant opponents had to work hard to get any change from him. He was converted to a midfield berth by Wolves but often found it difficult to live up to his huge price-tag. In 1980-81 his leg was broken and he discovered that modern players are not always pampered as he had to carry on for a few agonising minutes, later having a cartilage removed that had been damaged on impact. Daniel then fell out with those running the club in 1983-84 and in somewhat controversial circumstances joined the American bandwagon, though he was soon back appearing for Sunderland.

MEL EVES was one of the more modern Wednesbury products, the tall striker topping the Central League list in 1977-78 and showing considerable promise. He had mixed fortunes for the next four years before proving he could score with great regularity in 1982-83. All that seemed forgotten as he did not get a fair crack of the whip in 1983-84 and his career at Wolverhampton, which had been plagued by injuries, simply petered out when they were not actually over-blessed with goalscorers.

ANDY GRAY arrived as the costliest footballer in Britain and though he did not always look the part in 1979-80 it was to be his best campaign for Wolves in terms of goals. The Glaswegian was a centre-forward of the old school renowned for putting his head in where it hurts, but as his style caused him to receive knocks he was occasionally asked to occupy deeper roles and even appeared on the wing a lot. When placed in his most effective position in the thick of the action Gray did not usually get the service required in the way of accurate centres, though his scoring was also limited by his apparent desire to burst the net when presented with an opportunity. However, his very presence kept Wolves in the news and the vast majority of their fans were unhappy at his autumn departure.

KEN HIBBITT cost Ronnie Allen a paltry £5,000 yet within 48 hours of the deal the manager reluctantly packed his bags leaving the Bradford youngster feeling a little homesick. Hibbitt's ability gradually shone through and he marked his debut at Chelsea almost two years later with a goal, this being in 1970 when his old club sadly lost their Football League status. The industrious midfielder could pass a ball neatly as well as being an outstanding striker of the round object, often scoring from a fair distance as he made a major contribution to a useful Wolves team in the early 1970's, then sharing the lead in their appearance chart of 1974-75. Hibbitt was still a vital member of the side when they came good again in 1979-80 and his testimonial prior to 1981-82 was richly-deserved. It was held on a Sunday morning as over 6,000 watched Wolves beat Derby 2-1, Peter Knowles showing his respect by making a 15-minute return to the ground as substitute. Hibbitt reached double-figures in both the League Cup (12) and F.A. Cup (10), only failing to score in 1983-84 when he made 21 appearances. He was just a few months past his 32nd birthday when he was given a free transfer to end an association with the club that lasted over 15 years during which he gained many admirers. Hibbitt had a genuine affection for Wolves, unlike some of their staff in the 1980's, and was prepared to re-join them as their decline accelerated but for reasons that are hard to comprehend he was not allowed to do so.

1983 - 84 ENDPIECE

West Bromwich Albion are the team Wolves have generally regarded as their major rivals over the years, the clashes this season being the most recent ones. Wolves full record against them is as follows: PLD 127 W 45 D 33 L 49 F 206 A 208 (30-14-20 & 15-19-29).

Wolves have not met any team as frequently as Albion and although the Baggies have a slight edge overall it is the Molineux men who lead 44-42 in League fixtures, the complete breakdown of wins being: Wolves 39

Albion 30 (In 98 D1 games), Wolves 5 Albion 12 (18 D2), Wolves 1 Albion 7 (10 FAC) and of course there was the drawn Charity Shield in 1954. The years listed in the Wolves v Albion records here are the ones in which the season started.

(Wolverhampton Wanderers results versus West Bromwich Albion)

SEASON	COMP.	HOME	AWAY	SEASON	COMP.	HOME	AWAY
1885	FAC		L	1937	D1	W	D
1887	FAC		L	1948	FAC	W	
1888	D1	W	W	1949	D1	D	D
1889	D1	D	W	1950	D1	W	L
1890	D1	W	W	1951	D1	L	L
1891	D1	W	L	1952	D1	W	D
1892	D1	D	L	1953	D1	W	W
1893	D1	L	D	1954	D1	W	L
1894	D1	W	L	1954	CS	D	
1894	FAC		L	1955	D1	W	D
1895	D1	L	L	1955	FAC	L	
1896	D1	W	L	1956	D1	W	D
1897	D1	D	D	1957	D1	D	W
1898	D1	W	W	1958	D1	W	L
1899	D1	W	L	1959	D1	W	W
1900	D1	D	W	1960	D1	W	L
1902	D1	L	D	1961	D1	L	D
1903	D1	W	W	1961	FAC	L	
1906	D2	L	D	1962	D1	W	D
1907	D2	L	L	1963	D1	D	L
1908	D2	L	W	1964	D1	W	L
1909	D2	W	W	1967	D1	D	L
1910	D2	L	L	1968	D1	L	D
1923	FAC	L	D	1969	D1	W	D
1927	D2	W	L	1970	D1	W	W
1928	D2	L	W	1971	D1	L	W
1929	D2	L	L	1972	D1	W	L
1930	D2	L	L	1977	D1	D	D
1930	FAC	L	D	1978	D1	L	D
1932	D1	D	L	1979	D1	D	D
1933	D1	D	L	1980	D1	W	D
1934	D1	W	L	1981	D1	L	L
1935	D1	W	L	1983	D1	D	W
1936	D1	W	L				

1984 - 85

DEBUTANTS: Alan Ainscow, David Barnes (Ipswich), Scott Barrett, Steve Biggins (Derby-loan), Campbell Chapman, Cavan Chapman, Mike Coady, Tony Evans (Palace), Tim Flowers, Ray Hankin (Peterborough),

Ricky Herbert, Dave Heywood, Andy King, Tommy Langley, Jim Melrose (Celtic-loan), Derek Ryan, Nicky Sinclair (Oldham-loan) & Peter Zelem (Chester). Herbert was born in New Zealand, Melrose in Scotland and Ryan in Eire.

SUMMARY: Docherty's brilliant wise-cracks could not prevent an even more depressing campaign resulting in further demotion, to end 55 years of Wolves being either in D1 or amongst the leaders in D2. The manager tried his best, bringing in a quartet of Englishmen who were playing abroad, but Wolves still went a record 21 games without victory as they mustered a pitiful seven goals. They also went 15 matches at Molineux without success, while some of their rejected players rubbed it in by doing well in 1984-85. Results apart the club received endless bad publicity with internal feuds leading to the January resignation of Dougan, who must have now realised he had done the club no favours by putting them in the hands of Allied Properties. Not content with spoiling our winter Wolves continued to worry us in the summer with increasingly disturbing reports about their financial situation, Docherty being sacked on July 8th though it was a mystery what he had done wrong in the two months since the season finished.

LEAGUE D2: 22nd (33). An unfamiliar Wolves XI rushed into a 2-0 lead over Sheff Utd, though by the whistle few would have begrudged the Blades their point. Neville Hamilton, a free signing from Rochdale, was unavailable due to suspension and he was never to make his proper debut because a heart attack in training curtailed his career. Wolves almost seemed to have a curse on them, losing their first away fixture at Leeds after being 2-1 up, while goalkeeper Burridge was at loggerheads with the club and refusing to play.

The visit of much-fancied Man City commenced well as Dougherty craftily dragged the ball inside with his left foot to beat his marker, then rifled it in with his right. An Ainscow cross was deflected past the City keeper though Wolves were worthy of their 2-0 win, Buckland shaking the woodwork with a powerful drive. Langley settled a poor encounter with Charlton in the 53rd minute, the Londoners being unfortunate to see their series of Molineux failures extended. Wolves in turn made their 14th joyless trip to Ayresome Park in terms of winning, though they made it four draws on the trot there. Defeat at Oxford left Wolves 11th with an even record (W 2 D 2 L 2 F 9 A 9) but a future hint was that top of their scoring list were own goals, which numbered three.

The Doc made his first unenforced changes against Birmingham who were to strike twice late in the game, some consolation being derived from the seasonal best attendance of 16,698 which increased the Molineux average to nearly 14,000 — a big improvement on the latter half of 1983-84. The defensive frailties of Wolves were revealed at Barnsley as they let in three in four minutes, cracking up again a week later after coasting at 2-0 versus Notts. Twice they left open spaces that an agoraphobic would not dare venture into, then skipper Pender tapped the ball over his own line when under no pressure whatsoever. Evans perserverance was rewarded with a brace of goals at Oldham but it was to no avail as Wolves slid down to a disgraceful 19th.

They worked hard to see off a Palace side who were beginning to regard Molineux as a jinx ground, then a Melrose header created a shock result at Portsmouth with Barrett making a fine debut in goal in place of the injured Flowers. Wolves rose to 13th by whipping Cardiff 3-0 but the day was marred by the news they could not raise the £40,000 required to buy Melrose, who had overcome early problems to transform the team since he had settled in. Docherty also received knocks of a physical nature in an accident as he drove to Grimsby and there was little therapy as Wolves crashed to the Mariners for the first time in their most recent 15 meetings, the £35,000 Barnes lobbing in an own goal to make the visiting fans regret the money had not gone on Melrose instead. Barnes made amends with a lovely free-kick as Wolves built up a 3-1 lead over Wimbledon which they promptly wasted, though a good effort at Fulham left them in a safe-looking mid-table position after 16 matches.

Wolves sank to seven consecutive defeats, being particularly awful at Christmas when 4,000 fans cheered them on at Shrewsbury and then had the further indignity of seeing Melrose lay-on all four goals for Man City against them, having already netted five since his move there. Wolves missed the guidance of Dodd, their most experienced defender going presumably because his wages were too high as the entire campaign degenerated into a shambles. A couple of draws stopped the rot before Wolves lost to Barnsley, fielding the unlikely striking duo of Cartwright and Buckland. Portsmouth were unable to win at Molineux for the first time in 13 tries but the 0-0 draw was no use to Wolves either, with the on-loan from Albion Eastoe unfortunate not to score as he returned to the club that had sold him for £80,000 over 11 years ago. There was no Grimsby protest as Langley fired in a sixth-minute goal that Molineux supporters had longed for since November, yet they were as demoralised as the team when it was disallowed and Grimsby got the one that counted. A miserable March was summed up by the collapse to an Oldham side who had never won in 15 visits to Wolverhampton, the gate being just 5,275. Wolves had now gone seven outings since their last goal while forwards Evans, Langley and Crainie had all been borrowed by other clubs and midfielder Troughton had not been given an opportunity all season.

The appalling record of 19 League matches without victory was ended at Carlisle to the delight of Wolves dedicated band of followers. Evans was recalled after missing a dozen games and in the 62nd minute side-footed home a cross from Ainscow. Middlesbrough, Notts County and Cardiff all fared badly and it seemed remarkable that Wolves were still in with a chance of avoiding the drop despite not scoring in 10 home matches — possibly a League record. They faced D2 leaders Oxford and for once Flowers was caught napping by a free-kick before Wolves crowned a fine display with a beautiful sweeping move that was completed by Chapman, only for Oxford to steal the points eight minutes from time. Crainie was back at Wimbledon after missing 16 matches, setting up the goal that earned Wolves a draw in front of a mere 3,277 crowd, though they slipped to 21st. Cardiff won in midweek to put Wolves bottom but it was far from a lost cause when they met Fulham on April 27th. The only printable thing that can be said about the 4-0 defeat is that it took Wolves a big step nearer D3.

Brighton caned Wolves 5-1 which meant they had won all their eight League contests with the Midlanders, and only 4,422 bothered to see if Huddersfield could win at Molineux for the first time in their last 18 visits. Wolves worst-ever sequence at the ground was ended thanks to a half-volley from Ainscow, their best outfield player of the term, and substitute Ryan. He and another lad endeavouring to make the grade at the club were being filmed in a documentary that would be screened early in 1985-86. The television cameras were also at Blackburn on the last day when Wolves appeared relieved to keep the promotion-hopefuls down to three goals. Wanderers had the worst D2 attack (37) and equal worst defence (79) yet there was another marvellous example of support at Ewood Park. People who only associated with Wolves during better days would doubtless question their sanity, but if nobody had loyally stood by them in the years either side of the first World War they would not have had their 1950's memories because the club would have died. There was a lot of sympathy in football at Wolves plight and the tragedy of seeing them in D3, though perhaps the fire at Bradford City's ground that day that claimed dozens of lives put Wolves worries into perspective, bottom four: Middlesbrough 40, Notts County 37, Cardiff 35 and Wolves 33.

MILK CUP: A year after Alistair Brown had been pictured wearing a Wolves shirt only for the deal to comically fall through he was scoring for D4 Port Vale against them. Wolves recovered to win 2-1 and their goal bore a charmed life in the second leg at Molineux as the 5,964 crowd anxiously synchronised their watches. Melrose was in sparkling form as Wolves came within seconds of glory at D1 Southampton, but he had gone by the time of the replay when victory would have been rewarded by a home tie with QPR that would have paid a huge slice of his fee. As it was Wolves were urged on by an enthusiastic gathering who were undaunted when they conceded a soft first half goal. Wolves really set about the Saints with the lively Cartwright twice hitting the woodwork while penalty appeals were rejected and Shilton was at his best. Southampton added a late breakaway to compound the travesty as a fairer result would have been 2-0 to Wolves, who have not tangled with D1 opposition since.

F.A. CUP: It was a shame to see that a match even in this great competition should attract so little interest, the 8,589 witnessing a Huddersfield opener that was cancelled out by Pender, then both Langley and Evans should have found the net in a frantic scramble. Wolves seldom looked like producing the goods in a snow-affected replay.

RESULTS: SHEFF UTD 2-2 (OG, Langley); Leeds 2-3 (Ainscow, Dougherty); MAN CITY 2-0 (Dougherty, OG); CHARLTON 1-0

(Langley); Middlesbrough 1-1 (Buckland); Oxford 1-3 (OG); BIRMINGHAM 0-2; MC Port Vale 2-1 (Evans, Dodd); Barnsley 1-5 (Dodd); NOTTS CO 2-3 (Buckland, Langley); MC PORT VALE 0-0; Oldham 2-3 (Evans 2); PALACE 2-1 (Evans, Melrose); Portsmouth 1-0 (Melrose); MC Southampton 2-2 (Melrose 2); CARDIFF 3-0 (Pender, Buckland, Evans); MC SOUTHAMPTON 0-2; Grimsby 1-5 (Langley); WIMBLEDON 3-3 (Barnes, Ainscow, Butler); Fulham 2-1 (Buckland, Cartwright); BRIGHTON 0-1; Huddersfield 1-3 (Buckland); BLACKBURN 0-3; LEEDS 0-2; Shrewsbury 1-2 (Ainscow); Man City 0-4; CARLISLE 0-2; FAC HUDDERSFIELD 1-1 (Pender); MIDDLESBROUGH 0-0; FAC Huddersfield 1-3 (Ainscow); Sheff Utd 2-2 (Chapman, Butler); BARNSLEY 0-1; Cardiff 0-0; PORTSMOUTH 0-0; GRIMSBY 0-1; Palace 0-0; Charlton 0-1; OLDHAM 0-3; Notts Co 1-4 (Hankin); Birmingham 0-1; SHREWSBURY 0-1; Carlisle 1-0 (Evans); OXFORD 1-2 (Chapman); Wimbledon 1-1 (Ainscow); FULHAM 0-4; Brighton 1-5 (OG); HUDDERSFIELD 2-1 (Ainscow, Ryan) & Blackburn 0-3.

RECORD: PLD 48 W 9 D 12 L 27 F 43 A 88 (5-6-13 & 4-6-14).

SCORERS: Ainscow 6, Evans 6, Buckland 5, Langley 4, Melrose 4, Butler 2, Chapman 2, Dodd 2, Dougherty 2, Pender 2, Barnes 1, Cartwright 1, Hankin 1, Ryan 1 & OG 4.

INTERNATIONALS: Englishman Pender proved it was all relative when he was chosen for the Eire Under 21 team to avoid another complete international blank for Wolves. Apps: Pender (ROI U21 - 1).

FAREWELLS: Bayly 10-0 (Coventry), Biggins 4-0, Buckland 50-5, Butler 21-2 (Hereford), Cavan Chapman 1-0, Dodd 98-5 (Stoke), Eastoe 8-0 Total 14-1, Evans 24-6 (Exeter), Hankin 9-1, Heywood 8-0, Humphrey 163-3 (Charlton), Langley 26-4 (Aldershot), Melrose 8-4, Palmer 466-15 (Burnley), Pender 127-4 (Charlton) & Sinclair 1-0. JOHN HUMPHREY formed a promising full-back partnership with Hollifield in his early Wolves days, a highlight being when they kept Liverpool in check during the 4-1 romp. Despite his obvious ability, Humphrey often suffered through lack of confidence as successive managers strived to get the best out of him. Humphrey was an ever-present in 1982-83 and 1984-85, Burridge sharing the distinction in the former season, and the speedy Londoner loved to attack down the wing knowing that his pace would get him back to his rightful position should there be a quick break. He finally became another victim of Wolves finances when sold for £60,000.

GEOFF PALMER was from Cannock and soon gained a reputation for somewhat wild tackling, being fortunate not to receive a few more dismissals in his career. However, he often marked top wingers out of the game by completely fair means and was one of the quartet of ever-presents in the 1976-77 promotion campaign. Palmer's loyalty to the club was unquestionable, Wolves beating Leicester 4-1 in his 1983 testimonial, and as well as being an uncompromising defender he got some spectacular goals, though most of his latter efforts were from the penalty-spot. When Palmer left for £5,000 he was the last of the 1980 Wembley dozen of whom nine had been given away including substitute Brazier, as it was considered savings in wages were of paramount importance which proved to be misguided economics.

JOHN PENDER was a rugged central defender from Luton who sometimes looked to have a brilliant future only to fail through lapses of concentration. He was an Eire Youth International in 1981-82 and 1982-83 while in 1984-85 he usually coped well with the responsibility of captaining a relegation-bound team. This was to be his final season at Molineux as the club fought to carry on trading into 1985-86, being forced to sell Pender for £40,000. They managed to satisfy their most pressing creditors who were owed around £100,000 with the summer sales of Humphrey and Pender, so both could be said to have made an important contribution to the football future of Wolverhampton.

1984 - 85 ENDPIECE

May witnessed another tragedy for the sport when 39 people were killed when all they wished to do was enjoy a game of football, this being in Brussels prior to the ECC Final between Liverpool and Juventus. The sickening difference to the Bradford nightmare was that the victims, mostly Italian, died because of the sheer stupidity of man. They were crushed as they attempted to escape from the English hooligans who had charged at them to blacken the name of our country further still. Murder may not have been the intent but it was the result, television graphically recording the scenes that will always haunt the more humane amongst us. English clubs were immediately banned from European competitions but that was little consolation to the folk who had lost their loved ones.

There had already been at least a dozen deaths in or around Football League grounds, and with battles in confined spaces happening all over the country each week it was amazing that such a catastrophe had not occurred before. Sadly, two Wolves fans have died following matches though neither tragedy was directly concerned with the games they had attended. One young man returning from Ipswich was struck on the head by a brick thrown when the coach stopped in Cambridge, while the other safely got back from Leeds only to be caught up in town centre gang-trouble.

The anti-football brigade called for the sport to be banned altogether which would only succeed in punishing many innocent people rather than the guilty minority, while if the same logic was applied then pubs, discotheques and even some shopping centres would have to be closed down. Football suffers from it's own popularity and merely reflects on how society has changed — youngsters now regard crowd segregation as normal whereas older people find it incomprehensible that fans are wary of displaying their team's colours or shouting encouragement in case they get assaulted by a complete stranger. It must be said that most hooligans confront their like-minded rivals but it is inevitable that passers-by get involved. Molineux is one of the safer places to visit thanks to an efficient local police force and the much-maligned Ring Road! The away contingent can be escorted along that route all the way back to the Railway Station with the coaches conveniently parked on the way too, making it easier to keep the warring factions apart.

There is a lot of talk about football hooligans, although that in itself is a deceptive phrase as they are hooligans generally who may go on the rampage at a fun-fair without attracting any publicity, as the event unlike a big match would not be nationally reported. We had the warning signs of violence and vandalism when the teddy boys went on wrecking-sprees at the dance halls then the mods and rockers fought on the beaches, before things really got out of hand in the mid-to-late 1960's. It has continued to get worse with the E & S and Radio Beacon telling us daily of crimes almost unheard of not so long ago — yet much of it is not reported. Wolverhampton had a year in the 1980's when there was an average of a murder-per-month and 1986 was not going to prove any more cheerful as there were 27,000 crimes in the town with £8m worth of property stolen. Several people were seriously hurt in attacks, many during the daytime, while one of the year's horror stories from Birmingham was the rape of an 86-year-old blind woman in her own home, so football can hardly be blamed for this sorry state of affairs. Another unfortunate aspect to it all is that these things overshadow the fact that much time and effort is put into worthy causes by this generation of youngsters, as they are by no means all bad.

The majority of law-abiding citizens have been complaining about lenient sentences for a couple of decades, though also more needs to be done to establish why there is more violence, especially against the elderly, with even babies and handicapped people often subjected to thuggery. It sometimes appears that the yobs, scroungers and wierdos are slowly taking over, which would mean the normal human beings would not be, if you understand. However, there have been even less-civillised times as these patterns of behaviour tend to come in cycles, so in the summer of 1985 we could only hope that both Wolves and society were going through a bad phase.

1985 - 86

DEBUTANTS: Nicky Clarke, Dean Edwards, Niel Edwards, Roger Eli (Leeds), Mick Holmes (Burnley), Keith Lockhart (Cambridge), Geoff Lomax (Man City - loan), John Morrissey (Everton), Andy Mutch, Stacey North (Luton - loan), Jon Purdie (Arsenal), Willie Raynes (Rotherham), Robert Rosario (Norwich - loan), Steve Stoutt (Huddersfield), Floyd Streete (Derby), Kim Wassell, Clive Whitehead (Albion - loan) & Darren Wright. Streete was born in Jamaica.

SUMMARY: On July 29th Allied Properties, who had recently pledged they would give Wolves a much-needed cash injection, were taken to court where the judge ordered the club to be wound-up and it was 1982 all over again as the news was written about in several countries, though Wolves were given a 10-day stay-of-execution. Mike Channon had frequently scored against them and was considered a strong candidate to be their first player-manager, but chief scout Sammy Chapman, whose sons had their debuts in 1984-85, became the boss. Wolves survived their pre-season crisis but Chapman was only given temporary control before McGarry was chosen as the first person to be re-appointed to the post, only to relinquish his duties after 61 days to enable Chapman to take the reigns again though he could not prevent yet another relegation. The instability of the team was underlined by the fact that Purdie topped the appearance chart although he had missed half-a-dozen of Wolves fixtures. The latest miserable chapter to Wolves history ended with rumours of them moving out of Wolverhampton to share a stadium with Walsall and Birmingham, something that even the most fanatical followers would not tolerate.

LEAGUE D3: 23rd (43). Wolves quartet of League debutants did well in the first half at Brentford, only to be stung as the Bees went ahead after the break. Their scorer was then sent off and in the 67th minute Neil Edwards, snapped up from Oldwinsford 48 hours earlier, took the ball half the length of the field before equalising. Nevertheless, the humiliations of 1985-86 began as 10-man Brentford stole a late decider. The opening home match saw unbelieveable chaos at the turnstiles with many of the small crowd missing at least 15 minutes play. Molineux had been a major victim of new safety regulations following the Bradford disaster with both the North Bank, famed for it's warmth and atmosphere, and Waterloo Road side of the ground closed indefinitely. Another bombshell came in the form of huge increases in admission to see Wolves most inept team as it now cost £3 on the South Bank and £4 in the John Ireland Stand with no reductions for juniors or pensioners, the visiting fans being situated closer to the pitch in both sections as Wolves home advantage diminished further. A poor Newport outfit who would have struggled against fairly recent Wolves Reserve teams defeated the hosts 2-1, then at Derby the Wanderers equalled their previous total of three D3 losses, the worry being that there were still 43 fixtures to negotiate.

Flowers was fit for the visit of York and ensured a welcome victory with a last-gasp reflex save, this on a day that Neil Edwards conjured up the sort of goal that gave us hope for the future with a dynamic run and shot. Wolves quickly had their backs against the wall once more at Bolton and were now bottom - 68th in the League. The pain went on as an average Swansea side raced into a 5-0 lead at Molineux within 55 minutes, their only problem being whether to kick the ball in or head it! That same afternoon key defender Zelem was reported to have achilles trouble that was to keep him on the sidelines for four months, and three days later Hazell fell with a similar injury that was to rule him out of the entire campaign. He had left Wolves seven seasons ago, returning on loan from Leicester with the likelihood of a permanent move and his comeback had been going reasonably well. A terrible night was completed as 3,244 fans witnessed a 4-3 win for out-of-form Bristol Rovers after Wolves had led 2-0 and been well in command.

On a day that Charlton lost their identity by moving into share the

Crystal Palace stadium the Wolves prospects took another knock at Plymouth, leaving them with 3/24 points. The variety of Molineux disappointments continued, where Lincoln drew having trailed for 77 minutes at a venue where they had lost on all 10 previous occasions. Wolves did carry on their own sequence of defeats at Bury, extending it to 11 before a Neil Edwards brace at Rotherham lifted them off the bottom and took his tally to seven in 11 games. There was still little joy at Molineux as Wolves led Doncaster 1-0 at the interval only to go down 2-1 and then had a drab derby with Walsall, during which Edwards twisted his knee and tragically failed to recover in 1985-86. Ryan looked a suitable replacement at Reading when he prevented a 14th successive win for the Berkshire boys who had made a record-breaking start, but Wolves were the same team in name only at Bristol City, where another good crowd made them the biggest away attraction in D3 though cynics might have disputed the reasons why.

Purdie's 70th-minute individual goal pipped Darlington and he soon notched another winner in a far more entertaining clash with Blackpool. Wolves were 20 places below a team they had led by three divisions just 18 months before but on a typical wet and windy November 5th night they were superior to them again, even though one wag claimed the Seasiders had brought their own weather with them! The storm clouds gathered again for Wolves in the resort of Bournemouth, while Gillingham soon broke the deadlock at Molineux. In the 79th minute a free-kick was pushed to King who levelled matters in style, only for the Kent men to restore their lead immediately as if they could score at will. Wolves drew at Cardiff and followed it up with a fortuitous point against Wigan, half of whose team sank to their knees in despair after a glaring miss in the last seconds. Defeat at Newport sent Wolves back to 24th for Christmas and even Palmer's return after a year at Burnley could not halt Notts from adding to their impressive run of results against Wolves. There were similar gifts for Derby at Molineux to the delight of their supporters who probably outnumbered ours.

A pitiful New Years Day gathering saw a thrilling climax as Wolves hung on to their slender advantage over Chesterfield in a dramatic period of injury-time to take them to 23rd position. New Coach Brian Little was not the only change as two more loan players were introduced at York to complete the club's seasonal quota of five. Brentford came to town in January to take on 11 men, none of whom had scored more than a single goal all term as King had gone, Edwards was injured and both Purdie and Ryan were dropped. It was Wolves rearguard who let them down as Brentford surged 4-0 ahead in 50 minutes, Dean Edwards pulling one back. Since being released by Telford he had turned out for Wolves on a non-contract basis and in between D3 appearances he was also lining-up in the town's Sunday League, prompting remarks that the amateurs were wary of letting him play for Wolves!

At least Wolves won by a two-goal margin at Swansea, which was something they had not achieved away in 1985. As usual hopes of a change in luck were dashed at home, by the League's other Wanderers on a bitterly cold afternoon. A snowy morning in Walsall saw Holmes silence the locals with a header in the 10th minute, but Wolves were still unable to beat their neighbours. There was a series of postponements with fans seemingly losing what bit of interest they had left as 2,838 watched Rotherham force a goalless draw, Palmer wasting a penalty. Only 2,367 witnessed the Plymouth debacle which meant Wolves were seven points adrift and even after a surprise win at Doncaster a mere 2,202 were present against Bury, the lowest gate at a Molineux League fixture since 1892.

A fighting win over Bristol City and a draw at Rovers gave Wolves hope of staying up, Streete being dismissed in the latter game in which Rovers scored from a harsh penalty award. Wolves flopped at Chesterfield with their most valuable asset, Flowers, briefly on loan to Southampton, the Easter period deteriorating after they had shared four first half goals with Notts. Although Wolves showed little adventure after the break there was still a golden opportunity for Holmes in the closing moments and two days later they led at Darlington with seven minutes to go, yet still came away empty-handed to bring the unthinkable prospect of D4 football nearer to reality.

Over 1,000 supporters cheered Wolves on at Blackpool and there were jubilant scenes as big-hearted Dean Edwards finished off a neat move to take his team off the bottom, the party atmosphere continuing for 70 minutes against leaders Reading. Wolves scored twice and Edwards hit the inside of the post only for the ball to almost defy the laws of gravity by not crossing the line, while an inswinging Lockhart corner appeared to have done precisely that. Wolves looked set to rise to 21st with the great escape well and truly on until they surrendered midfield which allowed Reading back into contention, then Palmer's back-pass was intercepted to start the visitors off on a three-goals-in-nine-minutes spell. The stunned crowd were left to rue the fact that the fixture had been originally called off at a few hours notice because Reading, who had just crashed 6-0 at Walsall, were hit by injuries and illnesses, a predicament Wolves had little sympathy for.

A deflated Wolves just appeared to go through the motions against Bournemouth yet victory would have kept their slim chances alive as their rivals stumbled. Barnes received his marching orders at Gillingham as Wolves went down 2-0 while the quartet they were most likely to catch all won. In the final home game Wolves led 2-0 at the interval and the dream lingered for one more moment as the announcer stated that other scores were going in their favour, but in fact neither Lincoln or Swansea were losing and Newport were on the way to the win that would seal Wolves fate. Cardiff, their opponents that day, were also doomed while the only target left for Wolves was to avoid a hatrick of finishing last in their respective divisions. They achieved that on goal-difference and were well supported at Wigan and Lincoln, with Mutch bringing his haul to seven in 11 games. The 98 goals conceded was the highest total in the entire League and explained why Wolves were heading for D4 only two years after playing in D1. Bristol City were the only team in the League to have previously been relegated three consecutive times but they had never propped up the table. The fast-falling Wolves had now gone down on eight occasions in their history, half of them being in the last five years, bottom five: Bury 49, Lincoln 46 Cardiff 45, Wolves 43 and Swansea 43.

MILK CUP: Wolves had to compete in the first round and somehow the pairing with Walsall came as no surprise. More than 11,000 fans watched the Saddlers get in front at Fellows Park, before the Wolves followers really got behind their team in a pulsating second half with Purdie's 81st-minute volley being just reward. The 11,310 attendance at Molineux was to be the largest in 1985-86, and they were given confirmation that Walsall finally had a better football team than Wolverhampton. Daley and Brazier returned to their old ground and were shocked at the changes on a night Wolves were relieved to lose only 1-0 and have four players booked — even the weather was foul.

F.A. CUP: Wolves also found themselves in the first round here but the greatest humiliation was the result itself. Although they had six players absent there was no excuse for a 6-0 slaughter from Rotherham, who had not won in 12 outings, or for the type of behaviour that led to four bookings and the dismissal of Clarke as Wolves youngsters lost their heads. It was Wolves heaviest defeat since 1968-69 as well as their worst result in more than 100 years of F.A. Cup involvement.

FREIGHT ROVER TROPHY: This tournament for teams from the lower two divisions was in it's third year, enabling them to have a realistic chance of appearing at Wembley as many NL clubs did. Wolves were drawn in the group containing D4 Exeter and Torquay in the Southern section — times really were changing at Wolverhampton! A paltry 1,278 saw them gain a fortunate draw at Exeter then 1,618 crammed into Molineux to watch the 92nd-placed team in the League toy with Wolves after going ahead, though a second half improvement led to an equaliser. Torquay shaded Exeter 1-0 to top the group with three points, Wolves going out with two as did Exeter with one.

RESULTS: Brentford 1-2 (N. Edwards); MC Walsall 1-1 (Purdie); NEWPORT 1-2 (Clarke); Derby 2-4 (N. Edwards, Purdie); YORK 3-2 (Coady, King, N. Edwards); MC WALSALL 0-1; Bolton 1-4 (Morrissey); SWANSEA 1-5 (King); BRISTOL R 3-4 (King 2, N. Edwards); Plymouth 1-3 (N. Edwards); LINCOLN 1-1 (King); Bury 1-3 (King); Rotherham 2-1 (N. Edwards 2); DONCASTER 1-2 (King); WALSALL 0-0; Reading 2-2 (Ryan 2); Bristol C 0-3; DARLINGTON 2-1 (Ryan, Purdie); BLACKPOOL 2-1 (Crainie, Purdie); Bournemouth 2-3 (King, Barnes); FAC Rotherham 0-6; GILLINGHAM 1-3 (King); Cardiff 1-1 (King); WIGAN 2-2 (Ryan, Holmes); Newport 1-3 (Purdie); Notts Co 0-4; DERBY 0-4; CHESTERFIELD 1-0 (Purdie); York 1-2 (Rosario); FRT Exeter 1-1 (D. Edwards); BRENTFORD 1-4 (D. Edwards); FRT TORQUAY 1-1 (Cartwright); Swansea 2-0 (Streete, Cartwright); BOLTON 0-2; Walsall 1-1 (Holmes); ROTHERHAM 0-0; PLYMOUTH 0-3; Doncaster 1-0 (Chapman); BURY 1-1 (Chapman); BRISTOL C 2-1 (Mutch, D. Edwards);

Bristol R 1-1 (Mutch); Chesterfield 0-3; NOTTS CO 2-2 (Mutch, D. Edwards); Darlington 1-2 (Mutch); Blackpool 1-0 (D. Edwards); READING 2-3 (D. Edwards, Lockhart); BOURNEMOUTH 0-3; Gillingham 0-2; CARDIFF 3-1 (Lockhart, Mutch, Holmes); Wigan 3-5 (Dougherty, Mutch, D. Edwards) & Lincoln 3-2 (Mutch, Purdie, D. Edwards).

RECORD: PLD 51 W 11 D 13 L 27 F 60 A 108 (6-7-12 & 5-6-15).

SCORERS: King 10, D. Edwards 8, N. Edwards 7, Mutch 7, Purdie 7, Ryan 4, Holmes 3, Cartwright 2, Chapman 2, Lockhart 2, Barnes 1, Clarke 1, Coady 1, Crainie 1, Dougherty 1, Morrissey 1, Rosario 1 & Streete 1.

INTERNATIONALS: Herbert played in the heart of the New Zealand defence in a World Cup Qualifyer with Australia to become Wolves 58th Full International. Apps: Herbert (NZ 1).

FAREWELLS: Ainscow 62-6 (Blackburn), Cartwright 66-4, Campbell Chapman 52-4 (Preston), Coady 14-1, Crainie 72-4 (Dundee), Flowers 72-0 (Southampton), Hazell 1-0 Total 35-1, Herbert 47-0, King 30-10 (Luton), Lomax 5-0, Morrissey 6-1 (Tranmere), North 3-0, Raynes 7-0, Rosario 4-1, Wassell 2-0, Whitehead 4-0 & Wright 1-0 (Wrexham).

1985 - 86 ENDPIECE

Attendances had been slumping everywhere for years but the numbers had dwindled to an exceptional extent at Wolverhampton. The average Molineux crowd in all matches to the nearest thousand had been as follows in the 40 post-war seasons: 43, 40, 45, 46, 41, 35, 37, 36, 38, 36, 35, 38, 40, 38, 32, 26, 25, 23, 24, 24, 26, 35, 30, 30, 26, 29, 25, 24, 23, 24, 23, 22, 22, 26, 23, 16, 16, 13, 8 and 4. These latter figures were bewildering to the fans who can remember frequent 50,000 gates although Wolves did manage to pull in that many more recently — unfortunately this latest 50,000 attendance was an aggregate of the last 15 home matches!

The cost of watching football is cheap compared to some other sports and forms of entertainment, but with refreshments and programmes getting dearer a lot of people stay away simply because they cannot afford it. Money is the root of the game's evil according to some who claim that certain leading players fail to justify their wages either in effort or ability. The working man and the many unemployed find it harder to relate to the modern footballer, and perhaps if pay was based on attendances we would see a more attractive spectacle. This would also apply to managers as currently there is plenty of incentive to win but little as to how it is achieved. Tactics is another dirty word as far as the old school are concerned — Jimmy Greaves still insists that a coaching manual is a Spanish bus-driver! However, Wolves undoing against Barcelona was their tactical naivety and it obviously helps to know your opponents strengths and weaknesses, not that the great stars need to fill their heads with information because they instinctively know what to do. Apart from fitness, only the negative aspects of the game seem to have improved and we see too much of the back-pass, offside-trap and generally unsporting acts.

Dominance by the big-money clubs is also a threat to football as the wealthy five of Liverpool, Man Utd, Arsenal, Everton and Spurs may soon have it all their own way which would decrease interest for the others. United were to disappoint in 1986-87 but only Coventry prevented the elite making a clean sweep of the main English trophies and there is a worry that the best players from the rest of the League will continually be signed up by the big five. This problem could be solved by using the same principles as Yorkshire Cricket Club with only men from a certain radius eligible, though in fairness to those from more remote areas two 'outsiders' could be allowed. That is all very unlikely to happen but if it did at least it would end so-called North v. South battles when only a minority of the 22 are actually representing their region, it would also give fans more pride in their genuinely local team and pinpoint where the real football strongholds were.

There needs to be a re-structuring of the football programme as well as the reduction that is now taking place in D1, as it is difficult to retain sharpness and enthusiasm over 60 matches especially if the public are not keen on a particular competition, the inevitable consequence being that there are some boring affairs and one such non-event could get a supporter permanently out of the habit of attending. There is a repetitive tone to the English season with too many League fixtures while the introduction of the ridiculous Full Members Cup (now Simod Cup) in 1985-86 means that eight D1 teams could appear at Wembley each season which devalues the achievement of getting there. More appropriate new tournaments would surely be a British Cup or Regional Cups, the former has long been overdue especially as the game in Scotland is enjoying a new lease of life and the latter would attract large crowds with little clubs having a welcome reduction in travelling expenses, after all it does seem astonishing that Wolves had gone 62 years without meeting their closest neighbours Walsall in anything other than wartime soccer. These could perhaps replace the originally-titled League Cup and be staged alternate years, because that is too similar to the F.A. Cup and copies rarely match the originals, in fact it is akin to holding two Leagues in a season. Even the F.A. Cup would benefit from an alteration as it is unfair that teams from D1 and D2 should join in as late as they do, almost a handicap system in reverse. If the 92 League clubs and the best 36 NL had a straightforward knock-out there would be considerably more romantic, lucrative and exciting ties with the winners needing to eliminate seven teams rather than six which would make their feat greater. Another curiosity is the traditional holiday derby fixtures which particularly affects London clubs. A game against a side from the capital will provide a good pay-day for them as would a game at Christmas, so by playing fellow-Londoners in the festive season they are reducing the number of potentially large attendances. In Europe both the ECC and ECWC are self-explanatory but the UEFA Cup seems utterly pointless and though it was a money-spinner for Wolves in 1971-72 such competitions have diminished people's interest in football as they seek quality rather than quantity.

Television can be a good advert for the sport though live games + recorded games + goals on the news + Saturday previews leaves only the dedicated wanting to attend matches as well. An increased variety in leisure pursuits available is a major factor of the attendance decline while treatment of the fans is still grim with poor facilities and organisation. All this is a shame as one of the greatest thrills in life is watching a good football match yet the ticket distribution for the F.A. Cup Final epitomises how the loyal supporter is hard done by, being the occasion he or she would want to enjoy above all others. Both participating clubs receive 25,000 tickets when even 49,000 would not be sufficient for many of them, as even if you have seen your local team just once all season you are more entitled to a Wembley ticket than someone who has no interest in the result, whatever they many have done for football. Every year fans who have followed their team all over the country for comparitively meaningless fixtures miss out on the one they have dreamed of seeing, painfully aware that thousands of neutrals will be there instead — when supporters really do come first a lot of them may actually come back.

Chapter 5

1986 - 87 to January 1988

1986 - 87

DEBUTANTS: Vince Bartram, Chris Brindley, Steve Bull (Albion), Brian Caswell (Leeds - loan), Robbie Dennison (Albion), Matt Forman (Villa), Ian Handysides (Birmingham - loan), Matt Hellin (Villa), Robert Kelly (Leicester), Mark Kendall (Newport), Eric Nixon (Man City - loan), Darren Oldroyd (Everton), Alistair Robertson (Albion) & Andy Thompson (Albion). Dennison was born in Ireland, Hellin and Kendall in Wales, Robertson in Scotland.

SUMMARY: The Receiver had been called in again in July and there was even talk of a swap with NL Enfield to guarantee the continued existence of Wolves, about whom a book could be written in the 1980's without actually mentioning football. It was the third summer in five they had looked set to go out of business before an unusual deal involving three separate parties saved the day. Wolverhampton Council purchased the ground along with surrounding land while Gallagher Estates Limited in conjunction with supermarkets Asda would pay off the debts — subject to building permission. The football club itself was to be run by a consortium containing Chairman Dick Homden and Director Jack Harris, the president being Wolverhampton millionaire Sir Jack Hayward O.B.E.. They put Coach Brian Little temporarily in charge instead of Chapman though he had not inherited much of a squad, the last three years producing a transfer profit of almost £470,000. Secretary Keith Pearson showed the true spirit of the club by volunteering to work without pay in the early days of this new era.

The opening four Molineux matches were lost but Little turned things around only to be sacked prior to a third successive win, Villa cast-off Graham Turner taking over. This determined man who had made his name at Shrewsbury shrugged off the initial hostility of the fans, and Homden's generosity enabled him to bring fresh faces to Molineux with Albion Reserves providing an unlikely supply line, notably £64,000 striker Bull. The arrivals of Thompson, Kendall, Kelly and Dennison cost a minimum of £85,000 and to the great credit of Turner they all justified their fees. On the field the agony had continued for Wolves with an even worse F.A. Cup humilation than in 1985-86 and they went into February fearing the prospect of finishing bottom to be the first club automatically relegated from the Football League, while their reserves were unable to impress even in the Midland Intermediate League.

Results changed dramatically after 12 wins and 16 defeats, with only one reverse during the next 12 successes which included eight in a row for the second time in Wolves history. They had done well on their travels all season, breaking their record 14 wins on opponents ground and winning more than they lost for the 14th time, so it was at Molineux where their fortunes were transformed. Wolves had looked certain to have more defeats than victories there for the fifth year out of six, something that had happened twice in the previous 82 campaigns, yet they won 9/10 at home having mustered 20/95 prior to this spell. Molineux crowds averaged well above 6,000 with over 10,000 for the last 10 games as the Wolverhampton public finally had reason to smile. Wolves appearance chart was topped by Stoutt (56) as they enjoyed a settled line-up during the latter three months when they were the outstanding D4 team, having used 86/268 post-war players in four seasons! The Wanderers unluckily missed promotion and two days later Coach Gary Pendrey became manager of Birmingham, who had played their part in an unsavoury saga that looked likely to deny Wolves any revenue from their transfer of Wayne Clarke to Everton. Turner deserved more for his efforts yet was never even chosen as manager-of-the-month, while the seasonal prizes predictably went to the bosses of the four divisional champions. Surely the manager of 1986-87 was Wimbledon's Dave Bassett who had guided a club of very limited resources to sixth in D1 four years after they had been in D4, a story to hearten Wolverhampton Wanderers.

LEAGUE D4: 4th (79). A cloud appeared to have lifted from over Molineux as exactly 6,000 turned up on the opening day hoping to witness the start of a new era as Wolves fielded four debutants, but the party was spoiled by a late Cambridge winner. However, Wolves struck twice in the closing minutes to win at Aldershot and the pattern of them doing better on their trips was maintained until they slipped to leaders Northampton, leaving them a depressing 18th. Wolves were sixth within a fortnight after three wins but even a Nixon penalty save could not bring them any reward from Swansea, and from then on the familiar rot set in as they quickly trailed 2-0 to a poor Halifax side in a candidate for the worst-ever 45 minutes at Molineux.

Wolves could normally be relied upon to beat Orient at home, duly doing so as Handysides converted a penalty and Nixon stopped one at the other end. Then came a couple of abysmal efforts before victory at Torquay was marred by the behaviour of their fans throughout the weekend, surpassing their antics at Blackpool earlier in the year. Wrexham won at Wolverhampton with ease to make it a sad farewell for loan players Nixon and Handysides who were possibly the best Wolves had, the misery continuing at Lincoln a week later. This was an unhappy return for Barry

Powell who had left the club for £70,000 some 12 seasons ago, the Kenilworth man ending a spell of foreign football in a bid to lift Wolves spirits. There was a hard-fought win at Hartlepool but a woeful Christmas ensued, Wolves only point coming after they had led Exeter 2-0, the Devon men equalising after being reduced to 10 men. New Years Day showed no indication that matters would improve in 1987 as Wolves slumped 3-0 to Peterborough, reaching the milestone of meeting all 91 other League members in competition. Goalkeeper Kendall was beginning to exert his influence on the defence as 0-0 draws at Wrexham and Cambridge halted the slide, though Wolves were a sorry 16th after 25 games with 29 points and only 22 goals to their name. The new play-off system meant the any of the top six could be promoted but that group looked well out of reach: Northampton 24-61, Southend 24-44, Preston 23-41, Swansea 24-40, Colchester 25-38 and Wrexham 22-36.

A fifth win in eight visits to Ninian Park cheered Wolves, especially as they had drawn the other three, but a second successive Thompson penalty could not prevent Crewe from winning at Molineux as Peter Bodak blasted a hatrick. Yet another home defeat seemed imminent against Stockport until three late strikes eased Wolves worries and gave them a rare double, just 3,238 attending. They then trailed 2-1 at the interval at Turf Moor where they were attempting to extend an unbeaten run to 11 League games, this being achieved by an incredible recovery as Wolves hit five for the first time since 1982, though a wreckless tackle left Neil Edwards with a broken leg at a critical point of his career as he was starting to put injury problems behind him. This was followed by their first three-goal margin success at home since 1984 as Mutch grabbed a brace to give Wolves confidence for the visit of Northampton. Some Wolves fans actually damaged the seats of their own teams ground as Holmes cancelled out Northampton's early breakthrough. Wolves attracted the best D4 gate so far in 1986-87 when they drew 2-2 on Preston's artificial surface and a win over Colchester shot them up to fifth. They had won four and drawn with the top duo but even after these six good results they would be down to 12th if their rivals took advantage of their games in hand. Holmes epitomised Wolves revival as he had not previously netted all term yet now equalled a post-war club record of scoring in seven consecutive League outings, though both his and Wolves run ended at Orient.

Wolves removed any doubts that they had truly turned the corner by reeling off eight League wins in a row for only the third time ever which left them fourth and all but mathematically sure of qualifying for the play-offs. This joyful period began with a 4-0 trouncing of Swansea and was rounded-off on Easter Monday as 10,730 saw Hereford become the sixth team running who had failed to pierce the Wolves defence. A similar crowd at third-placed Southend watched Wolves hopes of ensuring promotion thwarted by a first half goal, and though they pressed after the break they could not equalise and were missing top scorer Mutch who had been hurt against Torquay. Despite it being a Friday night the Wolves away support was brilliant in the sense that around 3,000 made the long journey, some of them creating more seaside disturbances that went on until well after midnight.

There were no celebrations when Wolves clinched their play-off place as Bull added two more to his personal tally, the fans realising that Wolves had wasted their opportunity not to be involved with them. Plenty of heart was displayed at Exeter where they conceded a couple of penalties and had Robertson harshly dismissed yet still recorded a handsome triumph. Robertson followed in the footsteps of Eli, Lockhart and Clarke who had all received their marching orders in 1986-87 away games but this decision was likely to have the most serious repercussions, as the experienced central defender would be suspended from the two legs of the play-off final should Wolves be contending. Southend finished the season with two fixtures against teams with nothing to play for thus the final day was something of an anti-climax, Bull livening up proceedings with the first Wolves hatrick for approximately a decade but invasions of the pitch led to the South Bank having a high and very expensive fence erected.

It was frustrating that Wolves required a solitary point to pip Southend and had to enter a play-off system with the likes of Aldershot and Colchester who required an extra 10 points to pip Wolves, the group being completed by D3 Bolton. Wolves had gained 27 points from their last 10 games with just that one vital setback at Southend, who still only mustered 15 from the same period. At Molineux they had gained 29/30 points yet their eight home defeats were as much as anyone had in D4 so it was Wolves away form that had made it possible for them to change division for the sixth year on the trot, top six: Northampton 99, Preston 88, Southend 80, Wolves 79, Colchester 70 and Aldershot 70.

PLAY-OFFS: It had been decided to reduce the number of D1 teams to 20 and increase the D2 total to 24, bringing it into line with the lower two sections. It might have been more sensible to have five divisions with 20 teams in each but it was agreed that only the top clubs needed to cut down on their fixtures, all this re-structuring somehow prompting the idea of play-offs. Instead of a straightforward relegation of four D1 teams being replaced by two from D2 the League decided to do it over two seasons as it would be slightly unfair to the D2 participants of 1986-87 otherwise, though a drawback to this was that it would leave a team in both divisions without a fixture every Saturday. It was typical of Wolves ill-luck that they became the first club to occupy fourth place in D4 and not automatically go up, and while there was some logic in a play-off with fourth-from-bottom of D3 Bolton the idea of having to overcome teams who had finished lower in the table meant that the seasons best sides would not always be the promoted ones.

The other chief sufferers of the new system were Oldham, Swindon and Lincoln, while those who benefited seemed oblivious to the unfairness of it all. Oldham came third in D2, well clear of Leeds (seven points) and Ipswich (11 points) yet they had to prove their supremacy over Leeds again in order to have a chance of returning to D1 after an absence exceeding 60 years, while Ipswich met D1 Charlton. Swindon were third in D3, ahead of Wigan (two points) and Gillingham (nine points) but would have to beat both of them again unless D2 Sunderland defeated Gillingham. Having proved themselves better over 46 matches fròm August to mid-May Swindon contemplated that it all now depended on who was best in the latter half of May, extending a season that already went on too long. Lincoln were victims of a ruling that the 24th team in D4 should leave the League altogether, their fate being greeted with relief in footballing circles as a club steeped in tradition, Burnley, had been in danger. Lincoln went out on goal-difference knowing one more win would have taken them out of the bottom six so they could hardly be proved to be the League's worst team. It was their first term in D4 for six seasons and unlike Aldershot and Colchester who had less to lose they were not allowed another chance. Victims may never fully recover from this setback and it would be more reasonable to evict a team who were wooden-spoonists twice in succession, or perhaps have play-offs in these circumstances.

League officials judged the whole idea a success as they claimed it had increased end-of-season interest and attendances. This was true in some cases but did not apply to Wolves, whose final home games were virtually meaningless as they had long been favourites to be fourth. Even if these arguments are accepted only a small amount of clubs can make small gains out of it all, which does not justify making a mockery of the entire League campaign which in effect would be settled by mini-Cup style games. If extra revenue was the sole criterion perhaps Coventry and Tottenham should have had another F.A. Cup Final, the fact that Coventry won 3-2 being no excuse for not staging a replay! If extra interest was the sole criterion perhaps there should be rules to ensure one-sided matches do not peter out and if a team leads 4-0 at half-time then the goals should be scrubbed off! If there has to be an end-of-season incentive to make games livelier a Divisional Cup which did not affect the tables would be more suitable, with the top eight competing in a knock-out which would not greatly add to the fixture list as half of them would only play once and the finalists three times. To cap everything Wolves were dealt a further blow by the ruling that the percentage of the receipts kept by the hosts would be reduced for the play-offs that commenced on May 14th.

There were no set guidelines regarding ticket allocation and Wolves travelled to Colchester with only a fraction of the supporters who wished to follow them, the Essex club having their highest gate of the season of only 4,829. Kendall denied Colchester in the opening forays before Kelly headed home in the 28th minute, the in-form Bull shortly making is 2-0 on a pitch covered in sand and water. Wolves remained in control and 16,330 gathered for the second leg despite the fact that some of the regulars had difficulty in getting to Molineux for noon on a Sunday. The 0-0 draw was regarded as poor but Colchester produced some neat approach work and Wolves could be pleased with the result for the 19th time in 21 games. At least they and Swindon were in their respective finals, the unfortunate Oldham losing to Leeds on the away goals law so for them victory in the League + a draw in the play-offs equalled defeat overall.

Aldershot had beaten Bolton 3-2 on aggregate which meant many Wolves fans would again miss out on seeing the away leg while the media announced that attendances for the first part of the play-offs confirmed the fans wanted them. This was not the reality as any local survey would have shown, but supporters were hardly likely to ignore matches with so much at stake even if they disapproved of the concept. Wolves had beaten Aldershot in 1986-87 by nine points and two positions, they had completed a 5-1 aggregate double and had a superior goal-difference yet all that became irrelevant as the teams started from scratch. Somehow it was not surprising that Wolves went down 2-0 on another disgraceful surface, with the capacity 5,000 present taking the number of D4 members to have had their seasonal best crowd against Wolves to six. The away goals rule was dropped for the final and though Wolves often threatened to snatch the goal that would make the tie wide open it was Aldershot who scored in the 83rd minute, after which some of the 19,962 audience went on the rampage with several policemen injured. Justice was done for Swindon who were promoted after 51 games while even Oldham had slight consolation as Charlton hung on to their D1 status so they did not lose out to a team below them in the table, only Wolves of all the 92 League clubs suffered that fate.

LITTLEWOODS CHALLENGE CUP: The programme for the first round tie was the same one Wolves had used for their League opener, such was the rush to get ready in time for 1986-87. Lincoln underlined that the Wolves team was not quite ready either, though Bartram should have saved their late decider in the first leg of a competition under new sponsorship. He atoned himself in the return as Wolves won 1-0 to force extra-time, only to fall to that cruel away goals business.

F.A. CUP: Wolves were drawn against Chorley from the lower reaches of the Multipart League, so even by NL standards they were not exceptional. Their Lancashire base was unsuitable and the tie was held at Bolton, with Mutch heading Wolves in front after an unsteady first half only for Chorley to quickly equalise. Another 1-1 draw at Molineux following extra-time was an even greater embarrassment, though there was more than a suspicion of offside about the Chorley goal. The minnows won the toss to stage the second replay, again electing to play at Burden Park where the score was an unbelievable 3-0 to Chorley as Wolves sunk to new depths. They had failed to come out on top in any of their last 10 F.A. Cup-ties and in all Cups had won just 3/30 — all against D4 opposition.

FREIGHT ROVER TROPHY: Wolves commenced their Southern group activities in Wales, with a 1-0 victory over Cardiff as Bull got off the mark for them. They next beat D3 high-flyers Bournemouth 4-3, little Dougherty sharing the goals with Bull before going to try his luck at the American indoor version with San Diego. Bournemouth beat Cardiff 1-0 as Wolves reflected on the irony of coming second in their group in 1985-86 when only one qualified and now being top when two went through to the next round. They did automatically receive home advantage which did not do them any good on a wet Monday night as they slipped to a 1-0 defeat to Hereford, their FRT home gates being 1,923 and now 2,892 this season.

RESULTS: CAMBRIDGE 1-2 (Zelem); LCC LINCOLN 1-2 (Mutch); Aldershot 2-1 (Mutch, Lockhart); LCC Lincoln 1-0 (Lockhart); CARDIFF 0-1; Crewe 1-1 (Stoutt); Stockport 2-0 (Lockhart, D. Edwards); BURNLEY 0-1; Northampton 1-2 (Mutch); PRESTON 1-0 (Mutch); Scunthorpe 2-0 (Forman, D. Edwards); TRANMERE 2-1 (Forman, Mutch); Swansea 0-1; HALIFAX 1-2 (Handysides); ORIENT 3-1 (Handysides, Stoutt, Mutch); Colchester 0-3; ROCHDALE 0-0; Torquay 2-1 (Forman, Purdie); FAC Chorley 1-1 (Mutch); FAC CHORLEY 1-1 (Forman); WREXHAM 0-3; FAC Chorley 0-3; Lincoln 0-3; FRT Cardiff 1-0 (Bull); Hartlepool 1-0 (Bull); FRT BOURNEMOUTH 4-3 (Bull 2, Dougherty 2); SOUTHEND 1-2 (Bull); Hereford 0-2; EXETER 2-2 (Bull, Thompson); PETERBOROUGH 0-3; Wrexham 0-0; Cambridge 0-0; Cardiff 2-0 (Thompson, Bull); FRT HEREFORD 0-1; CREWE 2-3 (Thompson, Holmes); STOCKPORT 3-1 (Thompson, Holmes, Bull); Burnley 5-2 (Holmes, Mutch, Thompson, Purdie, Barnes); ALDERSHOT 3-0 (Mutch 2, Holmes); NORTHAMPTON 1-1 (Holmes); Preston 2-2 (Stoutt, Holmes); COLCHESTER 2-0 (Holmes, Bull); Orient 1-3 (Bull); SWANSEA 4-0 (Holmes, Thompson, Purdie, Mutch); Halifax 4-3 (Mutch 2, Stoutt, Thompson); Tranmere 1-0 (Dennison); SCUNTHORPE 1-0 (Bull); TORQUAY 1-0 (Dennison); Rochdale 3-0 (Dennison, Purdie, Kelly); Peterborough 1-0 (Bull); HEREFORD 1-0 (Purdie); Southend 0-1; LINCOLN 3-0 (Bull 2, Barnes); Exeter 3-1 (Bull, Forman, Kelly); HARTLEPOOL 4-1 (Bull 3, Thompson); PLAY-OFFS Colchester 2-0 (Kelly, Bull); COLCHESTER 0-0; Aldershot 0-2 & ALDERSHOT 0-1.

RECORD: PLD 58 W 28 D 10 L 20 F 80 A 64 (13-5-11 & 15-5-9).

SCORERS: Bull 19, Mutch 13, Holmes 8, Thompson 8, Forman 5, Purdie 5, Stoutt 4, Dennison 3, Kelly 3, Lockhart 3, Barnes 2, Dougherty 2, D. Edwards 2, Handysides 2 & Zelem 1.

FAREWELLS: Barrett 35-0 (Stoke), Caswell 1-0, Dougherty 29-5, D. Edwards 30-10 (Exeter), Eli 18-0 (Crewe), Handysides 11-2, Hellin 1-0, Lockhart 29-5 (Hartlepool), Nixon 16-0, Oldroyd 13-0, Palmer 23-0 Total 489-15, Ryan 29-5 & Zelem 54-1 (Preston).

1986 - 87 ENDPIECE

The statistical summary of Wolves history is very interesting as they go into 1987-88, the 89th season of the Football League. Wolves have spent 59 of them in D1, 26 in D2, two in D3 and now sadly two in D4.

D1	1888-1906	(18)	D2	1965-1967	(2)	D1	1983-1984	(1)
D2	1906-1923	(13)	D1	1967-1976	(9)	D2	1984-1985	(1)
D3N	1923-1924	(1)	D2	1976-1977	(1)	D3	1985-1986	(1)
D2	1924-1932	(8)	D1	1977-1982	(5)	D4	1986-1988	(2)
D1	1932-1965	(26)	D2	1982-1983	(1)			

Wolves have met 76 teams on under 10 occasions, the total matches against them being 219, while 3,667 games have taken place against 65 other teams. This list shows the number of meetings with those 65, the number in brackets indicating how Wolves have fared in terms of victories and defeats: Albion 127 (-4), Derby 123 (-14), Everton 121 (-13), Stoke 120 (+20), Villa 110 (-11), Bolton 102 (+4), Forest 102 (+12), Arsenal 100 (-17), Burnley 100 (+16), Man City 97 (+1), Preston 96 (-5), Birmingham 95 (+20), Leeds 95 (-12), Chelsea 94 (+6), Sunderland 94 (-7), Blackpool 93 (+7), Liverpool 92 (-11), Man Utd 87 (-7), Sheff Wed 87 (+1), Spurs 83 (-16), Leicester 81 (+4), Blackburn 80 (+1), Sheff Utd 77 (+1), Newcastle 76 (+6), Middlesbrough 70 (-10), Notts Co 62 (+9), Fulham 61 (+6), Huddersfield 60 (+5), Portsmouth 57 (+8), Grimsby 55 (+7), Charlton 51 (+15), Southampton 51 (-3), Bury 50 (-3), Coventry 48 (-9), Barnsley 47 (-2), West Ham 47 (-8), Hull 46 (-2), Ipswich 45 (-8), Orient 45 (+3), Bristol C 37 (+8), Cardiff 36 (+12), Oldham 31 (+1), Palace 30 (+6), Stockport 30 (+9), Bradford PA 26 (+1), Lincoln 26 (+9), Norwich 25 (+13), Port Vale 24 (+13), Rotherham 24 (+3), Bradford C 23 (+5), Swansea 22 (+1), QPR 21 (-2), Glossop 20 (+7), Luton 19 (-2), Gateshead 16 (+9), Millwall 15 (+7), Plymouth 15 (+4), Reading 15 (+1), Accrington 14 (+5), Carlisle 14 (+5), Chesterfield 13 (+4), Brentford 12 (-2), Gainsborough 12 (+4), Brighton 10 (-6) and Darlington 10 (+5).

Wolves have played 2,270 matches in D1, a total of 1,056 in D2, 302 in the F. A. Cup, 88 in D3, 61 in what is now the Littlewoods Challenge Cup, 46 in D4, 20 in the UEFA Cup and 12 in the Texaco Cup. Their wins out-number their losses in all these events with somewhat more mixed fortunes in the ECC (eight games), Charity Shield (five), FRT (five), AIC (four), ECWC (four), Play-Offs (four) and Watney Cup (one). Wolves total record in all competitive fixtures is this: PLD 3,886 W 1,600 D 854 L 1,432 F 6,548 A 5,954 (1,099-409-430 & 501-445-1,002).

1987 - 88

Graham Turner was determined that if Wolves did miss out on promotion again it would not be due to the lack of strength-in-depth of the playing squad, making a quartet of useful summer signings. Peterborough received £8,000 for the services of Jackie Gallagher, and although the strong forward had spent a large proportion of his career in NL soccer he was seen as ideal cover for the Bull-Mutch combination. Gallagher was born in Wisbech, whereas Phil Robinson (Stafford) and Keith Downing (Oldbury) came from a bit closer to home, the former being a tigerish mid-fielder who was secured from Villa for £5,000 while the latter was a decent all-round player who was surprisingly given a free transfer by Notts County. The most expensive of the quartet was Gary Bellamy, a tall defender who hailed from Worksop and cost Wolves £17,000 though Chesterfield felt he was worth considerably more, a tribunal deciding the fee. Competition for places would be a healthy aspect to 1987-88 and with three reasonable goalkeepers Wolves were able to release Barrett for £10,000. They then lost the services of promising midfielder Kelly who had scored in D1 against

Man Utd in 1986-87 before joining Wolves, but a serious back injury looked like ruling him out of the new campaign. Barry Powell was to be appointed player-coach while the only significant pre-season match was the 2-2 draw away to Burton Albion, the scorers being Stoutt and Thompson, in the BSC Final that had been held over from the previous term.

Wolves reluctantly kicked-off another D4 flirtation at the venue of the club who had replaced Lincoln in the League — Vauxhall Conference Champions Scarborough. Barclays had succeeded Canon in sponsoring the League, making their announcement a few days before the opening day, the sting in the tail being that they would withdraw should hooliganism increase. Indeed the eyes of Europe were on England's notorious fans as a relatively trouble-free campaign would probably culminate in a return to European competition for their clubs, who had been sorely missed even if their followers had not. Sadly, the Wolves supporters caused thousands of pounds worth of damage and although the only serious injury was self-inflicted the circumstances meant that the incidents received intense media coverage for the next few days. The presence of television cameras were a major factor in this response too, because similar scenes besides the seaside had occurred when Wolves went to Blackpool, Torquay and Southend in the previous 16 months yet that was hardly mentioned except in the local newspapers. Wolves drew an entertaining match 2-2 (Bull, Stoutt) but that became almost irrelevant as retribution was demanded against their supporters, although there were nasty clashes all around the country during the ensuing weeks that attracted comparatively little publicity. When it came to apportioning blame for the events at Scarborough and general problems of this nature it was not only the yobs themselves who came in for criticism, with some people placing the responsibility for it all on the shoulders of parents or even teachers. The League had clearly blundered in making arrangements to hold what was always a potentially-explosive fixture on the first day, when there is traditionally larger-than-normal away exoduses while Scarborough were also in the wrong in not ordering it to be an all-ticket affair. Yet the punishment was handed out to two completely innocent parties, namely the football club and their more respectable supporters. Wolves were fined £5,000 and the genuine fans were banned from six away matches as well as having the inconvenience of buying a ticket in advance for their trips for the rest of the season. The annoying aspect of it all to these good folk was that they knew that many of those who ran amok in the holiday towns were not real supporters and a minority of them did not even attend home matches. Wolves themselves added to the misery by imposing their own two-game ban as there were a couple of rare Midlands trips before the official ban commenced, an unpopular decision but an unavoidable one in view of the possible consequences.

The Molineux programme began under something of a shadow as Wolves faced D3 Notts County in the first round of the LCC. A fine attacking display lifted the gloom with the striker that Chapman had snapped up from Southport for £5,000 looking a bargain as he netted twice in the last two minutes to create a more realistic 3-0 (Mutch 2, OG) scorline. Even this night was marred when Holmes broke his arm while Wolves were already resigned to losing Barnes, who had played in both matches to take his appearance total up to 105 (four goals). He was the 61st person to pass the 100 milestone for Wolves since the war having been signed by Docherty who had seen him perform in D1 and considered him a great prospect. However, Barnes did not exactly endear himself to the locals when he made a rude gesture to the North Bank, who had merely groaned with disappointment as he put a cross behind the goals when there was a clear opportunity for Wolves to score a much-needed goal. This was part of the problem for the chirpy Londoner who joined the club at a very bad time, in fact a stranger to the country would have thought their name began with S as they were constantly referred to as 'Struggling Wolves'. It said a lot for the character and ability of Barnes that he gradually won most of the fans over and towards the end of 1986-87 he showed in glimpses what he could really do in a winning team. Unfortunately he was never completely happy in the area and Turner, safe in the knowledge that midfielder Thompson looked even more efficient at left-back, sold him to Aldershot for £16,000.

The second Saturday of the season was another dismal one as Wolves again failed to cope with Halifax at Molineux, going down 1-0 on this occasion. Yet Wolves then completed a remarkable 5-1 aggregate over Notts when they won 2-1 (Bull 2) at Meadow Lane, the home goal being notched by Andy Gray who briefly joined forces with Barnwell again, Notts new manager loaning him from Villa. Despite the sending off of Downing the Wanderers also emerged as 2-1 (Bull, Mutch) victors at Hereford to open their League wins account. Two days later on the August Bank Holiday Monday Wolves finished in clinical fashion to thump Scunthorpe 4-1 (Bull 2, Mutch 2) in what was a fairly even contest on the balance of play. On the Wednesday a happy little spell was completed as Wolves secured the BSC for the first time since 1924. Goals by Purdie and Forman helped a virtual reserve side beat Burton 2-1 in the replay at Molineux watched by 1,125 fans, who cheered enthusiastically as the trophy was paraded before them which we hoped was an omen for the future.

Welshman Nigel Vaughan was transferred from Cardiff for £12,000 and though the midfielder was lacking in match-practice it seemed Wolves hardly had anyone who was fully-fit in this important department. Vaughan was soon forced to come on as substitute as he ironically made his debut at Ninian Park and he did not take long to silence the jeers of the crowd but Wolves lost 3-2 (Vaughan, Bull). A rare mistake by Kendall changed the course of the proceedings with Crewe, the keeper mis-kicking hopelessly to present the visitors with a gift goal. Two substitutes were allowed now and one of them salvaged a last-gasp equaliser for Wolves in a game they looked likely to win comfortably at one stage, the final outcome being 2-2 (Bull, Gallagher). Kendall was excellent at Peterborough as the honours were shared 1-1 (Bull) before Wolves improved further to win 2-0

(Robinson, Mutch) at Stockport. Robinson's previous goal had been in more salubrious D1 surroundings but he and his colleagues could now look forward to playing at the fine Maine Road Stadium. It was the first leg of the LCC second round and Wolves pulled off a magnificent victory which was well-deserved although the late decider was due to an error by Eric Nixon. Wolves beat D2 Man City 2-1 (Bull, Dennison) as their Tipton-born striker scored his 10th goal in 11 outings.

After that trio of good away results Wolves flopped 2-1 (Bull) to a well-organised Torquay who were also on a high after defeating Spurs 1-0. Wolves never looked convincing in beating Rochdale 2-0 (Bull, Mutch) and they lost a dull affair 1-0 at Bolton to a late penalty. Predictions Wolves would emulate Northampton were proving over-optimistic as they were 11th after 11 fixtures, ahead of three teams only on goal-difference and just a point clear of the 17th-placed side. Success had been confined to the LCC but Wolves somehow trailed 1-0 at half-time of the return with Man City. Spurred on by a 13,843 turnout they attacked incessantly and perhaps naively as a 1-0 defeat after extra-time would have put them through. Wolves had struck the woodwork three times when City broke to steal a decisive 88th-minute goal to win 2-0 on the night and 3-2 on aggregate. Following a reasonably promising start Wolves had lost 3/4 and were thankful that nobody was really setting D4 alight in 1987-88.

Wolves bounced back with a 1-0 (Bull) win at Carlisle but more significantly they put their mediocre Molineux form behind them with two easy wins in three days. Tranmere were trimmed 3-0 (Mutch, Vaughan, Bull) though Bull was dismissed when judged to have fouled the keeper and Cambridge also fell 3-0 (Bull, Mutch, Vaughan). There were other similarities as the goals were again all at the North Bank end of the ground in the first half. Everything was suddenly looking brighter and it was nice to have their vociferous supporters back for the long haul to Darlington, although small groups of them had thwarted the bans covering the previous eight trips. Wolves could not maintain their winning sequence but a splendid 2-2 (Mutch 2) draw meant they were fourth and apparently a good bet for promotion after all. A tremendous 81st-minute equaliser gave them a 1-1 (Bull) draw at Swansea in the FRT but their new goal-hungry star was suspended for the meeting with lowly Newport. For 70 minutes the clouds had produced what was not the only shower of the afternoon as Wolves were a goal in arrears with a drop to almost halfway down the table imminent. However, football situations can alter very quickly and Wolves scored twice in two minutes past Paul Bradshaw to win 2-1 (Vaughan, Mutch) and leap to the top of D4 as other results went in their favour, seven teams being a point behind them.

A second successive Tuesday journey to Swansea on November 3rd saw Wolves provided with another incentive regarding the Football League's Centenary celebrations. For the next 15 games the two teams gaining the most points in D4 would be able to play at Wembley against some of England's greatest clubs, Wolves themselves celebrating this good idea with a 2-1 (Bull, Gallagher) victory. The partnership of Bull and Mutch were featured in the popular Central Sport on Friday night, having accumulated 29/39 Wolves goals so far but that day ended with Colchester at the head of the table. Wolves were anxious to re-claim the position but but were kept at bay by a disciplined Burnley until 20 minutes from time when a beautiful 25-yard drive broke them down, sparking off an enjoyable spell for the 10,002 fans as Wolves won 3-0 (Downing, Gallagher, Vaughan) and it was refreshing to see them do it without having to rely on the predatory instincts of Bull and Mutch. It would have seemed laughable to enthuse over five-figure gates at Molineux a few years ago but when VCL Cheltenham were caned 5-1 (Bull 3, Vaughan, Downing) in the F.A. Cup there was almost as much pleasure derived from the 10,541 gathering as the result. Nightmares of Chorley had been revived when Cheltenham went into a shock lead but Wolves soon levelled and Bull's hatrick made it 20 goals in 23 appearances. It also saw the 100th Wolves competitive match for Stoutt who did not make much of an impression in his early Molineux days but improved to such an extent he was voted player-of-the-season in 1986-87.

Colchester were second to Wolves but a penalty separated the teams 1-0 (Thompson) at Layer Road to widen the overall gap, the visitors joy being tempered by the fact that Bull received his marching orders after an off-the-ball skirmish. Wolves record of behaviour in recent years was developing into something of a disgrace, although at least the over-aggressive nature of Bull was disuading teams from higher divisions from putting a bid in for him. He was shortly to be described by a Radio Two reporter as the sort of striker who gets his retaliation in first but he had outstanding qualities such as speed and a single-minded determination to hit goals, which he was very capable of doing with his head and both feet. The leading scorer in the country maintained his prolific form as Wolves beat D3 Bristol City 3-1 (Bull 2, Vaughan) in the FRT though they could have lost 1-0 and still qualified as City had pipped Swansea 1-0. It did seem unfair that Wolves could have to overcome the men from Ashton Gate again to win the trophy, especially as nobody had a better record in it.

Hopes of a record-breaking run were cruelly dashed as Wolves dominated matters against Wrexham yet incredibly lost 2-0, as Vaughan failed to score for the first time in seven Molineux outings though like many others he was often close. It was particularly bleak for Bull prior to his two-match suspension and he took it out on Peterborough in the MIL, scoring five as Wolves Reserves romped home 8-1 while the injured Kelly had to have two discs removed and was ordered to remain on his back for several weeks.

Wolves long-overdue F.A. Cup success continued at D3 Wigan, despite them trailing at the interval to an early goal. They roared back with three in seven minutes shortly into the second half, and it stayed 3-1 (Gallagher, Robinson, Dennison) so Wolves had won all their four meetings with above-average D3 opponents this season. The following Monday was a dismal one for the club as far as Cup activity was concerned, the senior team being drawn away to in-form D2 Bradford City when they desired either the glamour of a home tie with one of the big League or the chance of progress against any of the five representatives from NL soccer. In the Youth Cup that night Wolves, having already whipped Hednesford 6-0, visited holders Coventry and somehow lost after being 2-0 up with six minutes to go.

A 0-0 draw at Hartlepool meant Orient were presented with the opportunity to go top, with Wolves next on their fixture list. Two contrasting strikes after the break were the only real difference between the teams as Wolves gained a vital 2-0 (Bull 2) win before 12,051 spectators, with Beacon's Pat Foley winning an entertaining penalty competition during the break. The Boxing Day trip to Torquay had been switched to February which enabled Colchester to replace Wolves in first position, the Midlanders seeking their 36th victory of 1987 against Exeter on December 28th. This was duly done as a striker ended his barren spell, a midfielder scored an individual gem and a defender converted a spot-kick, the result being 3-0 (Mutch, Dennison, Thompson). Wolves ended the year with an unbeaten run of seven away matches under their belt and the knowledge that if they took advantage of their game in hand they would lead D4, their main rivals turning out to be Colchester, Orient and Cardiff to date. The Exeter visit brought in a marvellous 15,588 crowd to boost the Molineux average to well over 8,000 with another huge audience expected on January 1st, 1988, when Wolves would meet Hereford.

FINAL ENDPIECE *(The Author)*

My long-awaited first away match came at the unlikely venue of Southampton in 1968-69. As the teams lined-up for the kick-off I suddenly had a severe nose bleed, thus spending almost 30 minutes in the first-aid hut. Southampton were on their way to victory when I emerged, though a 'Tiswas-style' food fight and sing-song on the coach journey home cheered me up. There was no malicious behaviour that day, despite the drivers constant references to what he called 'hooligism'.

I had a more traumatic day out in 1971-72 when I arranged a morning's sight-seeing in London with a friend prior to the Crystal Palace match. He decided not to go at the last minute but I carried on regardless, arriving in the capital at nine am. After some hectic touring I absent-mindedly asked someone the time on Westminster Bridge, then had to dash to Waterloo Station as it was getting on a bit. I enquired if a train went to the appropriate station for Selhurst Park and was informed it did, the British Rail worker omitting to mention that it did not stop there!

Stranded at Epsom without even the consolation of a race meeting, it became evident that the next train direct to my destination would be too late. After devising a complicated series of short journeys I did manage to see the last 20 minutes of the match, including a well-worked Wolves goal. Altogether that day I had a dozen train or tube rides, passing the ground of Tooting & Mitcham F.C. twice from both sides!

Even the 1974 Wembley triumph did not go too smoothly, as the coach took until midnight to return home while stopping at the 'Man City service station' gave us little chance to let off steam. The first celebratory drinks were at a Wolverhampton night club where there was the odd appropriate song or dance, but I regretted not staying in London as many Wolves fans lived it up in the West End. As for the match itself I had difficulty in following what was going on being a fair distance from the pitch. This made me suspect that I needed glasses, a fear that was confirmed at work when asked for a casting vote as to what was the time shown by a clock outside — I did not know, in fact I had not even realised it was there.

In 1980 my allegedly gold-tinted spectacles had not returned from modifications at the Opticians, with me typically stuck at the very back of the vast arena unable to distinguish George Berry from Willie Carr once they got beyond the half-way line! Being the only season-ticket holder in my group I was in a different part of the stadium and afterwards got lost and mis-directed to the station used by the Forest fans. Surrounded by a sea of red I proceeded to hide five scarves, a rosette and a badge before eventually catching the last special train back to Wolverhampton. There was a brief pub sing-song in the town but again I ended up wishing I had spent the weekend in London.

I travelled by car to Middlesbrough the next year in the F.A. Cup QF and was cut off from my companions again, being in the corner reserved for visitors while they had stand tickets. Police kept Wolves supporters in Ayresome Park until well after the final whistle, the object being to clear the streets and reduce the risk of trouble. This tactic works well for those escorted back to their trains and coaches but only streets within a small radius of a ground can be adequately patrolled. The local 'baddies' know that anyone returning from the direction of the ground at around five pm is likely to be an away fan and there is no protection for those using their own transport, yours truly being forced to make a deviation to my route back. I must have toured every side street in the area before finally finding a familiar landmark that told me the car park was round the corner. My heart sank when there was no sign of the vehicle, an hour having passed since the match and it transpired I had missed my lift home by a matter of seconds.

Soaking wet, I trooped dejectedly to Middlesbrough Railway Station to be told that the next West Midlands-bound train was on Sunday, not that they would let me on as I had not got enough money. I contemplated sleeping rough in the town and hitching a ride back in the morning, not the most relishing of prospects. Then a group of around 30 Wolves fans arrived having been abandoned by their coach after rowdy behaviour, prompting hectic consultations between Police and British Rail staff. A train was delayed to make other connections possible and we finally made it to Wolverhampton at two am, when we queued to give our particulars. I had often walked the three-mile journey home from town alone and had some frightening experiences, so I decided to get a taxi which pushed the cost of my long trip home to almost £20.

Despite the stories mentioned here I have a lot of happy memories of following Wolves around the country and although I have travelled with dozens of friends over the years the best aspect is probably the cameraderie with complete strangers. Like the majority of supporters I now long for the day that being a Wolves fanatic means watching them performing once more at England's finest football stadiums.

1988 UPDATE

Wolves beat Hereford 2-0 (Bull 2) before 14,577 fans and the following morning won 2-0 (Mutch 2) at Crewe which put them in good heart for their F.A. Cup-tie. Despite a fortuitous early breakthrough they could have no complaints about a 2-1 (OG) exit, with Bradford often looking two divisions better than Wolves. A disappointing 1-1 (Vaughan) draw at home to Stockport ensued, though the swirling fog made it difficult to see exactly where Wolves had gone wrong. In the FRT D3 Brentford were crushed 4-0 (Bull 3, Dennison) and Wolves completed an eventful January with a fine 1-0 (Mutch) victory at Scunthorpe.

There was an opportunity for Wolves to take a commanding lead at the top of D4 when Cardiff came to town, but the Welshmen pulled off a 4-1 (Bull) shock while their national rugby team were beating England. Wolves responded well with a 4-0 (Bull 2, Dennison, Mutch) FRT pounding of Peterborough and a 4-2 (Bull 3, Purdie) success at Exeter. However, their problems were not over as they lost 2-1 (Bellamy) at Halifax then drew 0-0 at home to Scarborough when Bobby McDonald, the Scotsman on loan from Leeds, made an accomplished debut. Wolves were happier with the goalless draw at Torquay after which they thrashed challengers Bolton 4-0 (Bull 2, Dennison, Robinson) with all the goals coming in a tremendous first half.

March began with a 1-0 (Holmes) win in Rochdale only for a 3-0 slump at Tranmere to remind Wolves they still had plenty of work to do. They eliminated Torquay 1-0 (Bull) in what was now called the Sherpa Van Trophy and then trimmed Carlisle 3-1 (Bellamy, OG, Mutch), yet McDonald chose to return to Yorkshire after seven appearances. As Thompson was injured the number three shirt was given to Mark Venus, a £40,000 buy from Leicester, but the North-Easterner had an unhappy debut as Wolves slipped 1-0 to Peterborough on a wet Molineux night. Corby-born Phil Chard was signed from Northampton for £35,000 and slotted neatly into the midfield on his debut against Darlington, with Venus also showing up well as Wolves won 5-3 (Bull 3, Robinson, Chard). The ill-fated Neil Edwards moved on to NL Kettering having made just one of his 32 appearances this season and never adding to the seven goals scored in his early days at the club, while at the end of the month Wolves received more bad publicity when at least 60 of their hooligan element were arrested in dawn swoops at their homes.

A superb 3-0 (Holmes, Bull, Mutch) win at Burnley was followed by a 2-0 (Bull 2) victory over Colchester on Easter Monday, Bull setting a

Wolves seasonal record of 44 goals. A 1-1 (Mutch) draw at Cambridge came two days before the first leg of the Southern Area Final in the SVT, when a late Notts County equaliser meant another 1-1 (Bull) result. On April 16th it was 1-1 again as Wolves met League Champions Everton in a 40-minute centenary match at Wembley. Dennison scored a beauty from 30 yards to force a penalty shoot-out, which was level at 2-2 thanks to the efforts of Chard and Thompson. Everton then missed to cheers of the vociferous Wolves following but Bellamy also failed, the Toffees going ahead with a spot-kick that was not cleanly struck before Mutch had his penalty saved. Wolves benefited from the experience and quickly clinched a return visit by brilliantly beating Notts 3-0 (Bull 2, Downing) to spark off amazing celebrations. The only blemish was that thousands of their supporters could not obtain tickets for a game watched by 18,413 people due to worries of segregation and safety, prompting fresh appeals for the North Bank to be re-opened. Wolves were the first D4 team to reach the final but 30 minutes later Burnley joined them, having defeated Preston 3-1 after extra-time. Wolves overcame Swansea 2-0 (Robinson, Bull) though a late Scunthorpe penalty delayed their official promotion. Wolves achieved that 3-1 (Bull 2, Mutch) at doomed Newport which gave their star striker a remarkable 50 goals while Dennison made his debut for Northern Ireland 24 hours later, another exciting week ending with a 4-2 (Chard, Mutch) reverse at Wrexham.

On May 2nd Wolves beat Hartlepool 2-0 (Bull 2) in front of 17,895 fans at Molineux to complete an incredible 16 days for the club. Following five years without anything substantial to celebrate Wolves had really enjoyed this period in which they had played at Wembley, reached a Wembley final, gained promotion and now they were champions of their division for the seventh time in their history. They were the only team to have topped all four sections and their average attendance was almost 10,000 which they could probably improve by 50% if they have a successful D3 campaign in 1988-89. Goalkeeper Kendall created a Wolves seasonal record of 26 clean sheets and Bull's 52 goals (League 34 + SVT 12 + LCC 3 + FAC 3) was a mere two less than the highest post-war total by any Football League player. Both had the advantage of more fixtures than their counterparts but they were still two of several Wolves heroes of 1987-88, such as never-say-die defender Robertson and Mutch, whose vital 19 League strikes had been somewhat overshadowed.

Wolves triumphed 2-0 (Dennison, Robinson) at Orient to deny the Londoners a place in the play-offs on a day that third-in-D3 Walsall were left cursing the system. Wolves had now won 53/83 matches and lost just 16 while in what was hopefully their last D4 term they had easily the best goal-difference of + 39, top six: Wolves 90, Cardiff 85, Bolton 78, Scunthorpe 77, Torquay 77 and Swansea 70.

The season was far from over as the play-offs continued to provide more controversy with a Middlesbrough defender being ruled out of the European Championships because of his club's involvement; serious crowd trouble at Chelsea and another example of injustice as Swansea went up instead of Torquay. On the credit side there was excitement, high attendances and promotion for Walsall, though had they drawn their 51st 'League' match of 1987-88 their fate would have been decided on penalties.

Wolves participated in an infinitely more pleasant occasion on the last Sunday of May, when a staggering 80,841 audience enjoyed the Sherpa Van Trophy Final at Wembley. Bellamy clipped the bar early on and then in the 23rd minute Bull flicked the ball on for MUTCH to head Wolves in front, sparking off joyful scenes amongst their amazing following of approximately 45,000 supporters. DENNISON, who by now had also appeared for Ireland in a World Cup Qualifier, beautifully curled a free-kick into the top corner of the net to make it 2-0 after 51 minutes. However, Wolves had lost two players while others had received treatment for injuries so it was hardly surprising that Burnley dominated for a long period in which they did everything but score. Yet it was Wolves who finished back in control with Mutch hitting the post as they proved worthy victors on a wonderful afternoon for football. Team: Kendall, Bellamy, Thompson, Streete, Robertson (Gallagher), Robinson, Dennison, Downing, Bull, Mutch & Holmes (Vaughan).

RECORD: PLD 61 W 38 D 11 L 12 F 117 A 54 (22-3-6 & 16-8-6).

SCORERS: Bull 52, Mutch 23, Dennison 8, Vaughan 8, Robinson 6, Gallagher 4, Downing 3, Bellamy 2, Chard 2, Holmes 2, Thompson 2, Purdie 1, Stoutt 1 & OG 3.

At the end of the month Wolves had 23 players on their books with first team experience, their total appearances and goals being as follows: Mutch 126-43, Streete 126-1, Stoutt 114-5, Bull 95-71, Purdie 94-13, Robertson 91-0, Thompson 90-10, Holmes 89-13, Kendall 89-0, Powell 13-0 Total 84-7, Dennison 70-11, Clarke 64-1, Robinson 53-6, Vaughan 43-8, Downing 38-3, Bellamy 32-2, Forman 28-5, Kelly 16-3, Brindley 9-0, Gallagher 9-4, Chard 8-2, Bartram 6-0 and Venus 4-0.

1988 UPDATE (Continued) Second Edition

In the summer Stoutt (Grimsby), Purdie (Oxford), Holmes (Huddersfield) and Forman all departed, before Wolves began their 1988-89 D3 campaign with a 3-1 (Streete) slump at Bury. However, they promptly overcame D2 Birmingham 3-2 (Bull 2, Dennison) in the LCC and Reading 2-1 (Dennison, Chard) in the League, watched by two good Molineux attendances considering the admission increases. A 1-0 defeat after extra-time in Birmingham meant Wolves slipped out of the LCC on away goals but they then won 3-0 (Dennison, Robinson, Chard) at Chesterfield. Back in Wolverhampton the Wanderers drew 0-0 with Notts County and pipped Aldershot 1-0 (Bull), Northerner Mick Gooding making his debut in the latter, the midfielder being Turner's most expensive signing as Wolves paid Peterborough £85,000.

A 5-2 (Bull 2, Dennison, Robinson, Chard) romp at Swansea began a lively period with 14,108 fans at Molineux seeing Wolves score two late goals to obtain a thrilling 3-3 (Bull 2, Thompson) draw against Port Vale. The excitement continued at Fulham where it was 2-2 (Mutch, Gooding) though Wolves then struggled at Sheff Utd and could have lost by more than 2-0. Individually, Dennison made a third appearance for Ireland.

Wolves won 2-1 (Gallagher, Bull) v. Wigan, 2-1 (Dennison, Bull) at Bolton and also 2-1 (Mutch 2) v. Blackpool, before moving into second position after a 3-1 (Mutch, Robinson, Bull) triumph in Gillingham. They beat Southend 3-0 (Streete, Downing, Bull) to go top but Sheff Utd could overtake them by winning their game in hand. That situation did not apply after a fine 1-0 (Mutch) victory at Bristol City left Wolves five points clear. Huddersfield were trimmed 4-1 (Bull 2, Streete, Mutch) only for D4 Grimsby to stop the march with a 1-0 F.A.Cup shock. The Wolves response was to score six for the first time since 1976 while one of their players hit four for the first time since 1974, unlucky Preston being the 6-0 (Bull 4, Mutch, Vaughan) victims. It was the fourth occasion in their history that they had won eight consecutive League matches and with the Asda deal now granted things were going very well. Wolves drew 2-2 (Thompson, Bull) at D4 Hereford in the SVT but flopped 3-1 (Dennison) on a miserable Sunday morning in Northampton, with Robertson sent off as they failed to create a new club record.

Unbeaten in 15 games at Molineux, Wolves extended the run in a glorious week as they clinched their SVT group by thrashing Port Vale 5-1 (Bull 4, Mutch) and then whacked Mansfield 6-2 (Bull 3, Mutch, Gooding, Thompson). Steve Bull had now netted 25 goals in Wolves 24 fixtures and was showing remarkable restraint on the field and proving a splendid representative of the club off it. Altogether he had notched eight hatricks for Wolves and the three goals he got for Albion before his transfer made his career total 99. There was a 0-0 draw at Bath on Boxing Day against Bristol Rovers and the last day of a fantastic year saw Wolves manage a 2-2 (Mutch, Bull) draw at Brentford. The latest amendment to those dreaded play-offs meant a team could now gain promotion at the expense of rivals who finished three places higher, the leading two definitely going up and the next quartet fighting for that D2 spot. Despite several injuries the Molineux men were going into 1989 with plenty to smile about, top three: Wolves 21-44, Port Vale 20-40 and Sheff Utd 20-38.

THE END

As for the story of the book itself, I completed another revised version by January while Mr Witherington found an interested publisher. We decided it would be more professional to have the work put on a Word Processor but staffing problems meant the job took far longer than anticipated, and hopes of getting the book ready for the eventful month of May faded. After all that the publisher rejected it - as did two companies I wrote to requesting sponsorship - so hopes of having the book out for the new season were also dashed. I then set about publishing it myself though 1988 continued to produce more setbacks and complications than all the other years put together! However, I made Christmas my latest target date when I hoped Wolves would be further along the road back to the top of English football.

ACKNOWLEDGEMENTS

Wolverhampton Wanderers, Wolverhampton Express and Star, Wolverhampton Public Library (Leisure Services Dept.) + Eric Woodward, Albert Bates, Richard Binns, David Instone and Joe Witherington.

PHOTOGRAPHS

ISBN 0 9513991 0 1